A Place in Time

A Place in Time

CARE GIVERS FOR THEIR ELDERLY

TOM KOCH

PRAEGER

Westport, Connecticut
London

Library of Congress Cataloging-in-Publication Data

Koch, Tom.
    A place in time : care givers for their elderly / Tom Koch.
      p.   cm.
    Includes bibliographical references.
    ISBN 0–275–94483–2 (alk. paper)
    1. Aged—Care—United States—Case studies. 2. Frail elderly—
Home care—United States—Case studies. 3. Caregivers—United
States—Case studies. I. Title.
    HV1461.K63 1993
    362.6—dc20   92–1754

British Library Cataloguing in Publication Data is available.

Library of Congress Catalog Card Number: 92–1754
ISBN: 0–275–94483–2

First published in 1993

Praeger Publishers, 88 Post Road West, Westport, Connecticut 06881
An imprint of Greenwood Publishing Group, Inc.

Printed in the United States of America

∞™

The paper used in this book complies with the
Permanent Paper Standard issued by the National
Information Standards Organization (Z39.48–1984).

10 9 8 7 6 5 4 3 2 1

For
Heather MacNeil
and
Margaret E. Taylor,
who
showed me how

The spectator's judgement is sure to miss the root of the matter, and to possess no truth. The subject judged knows a part of the world of reality which the judging spectator fails to see, knows more while the spectator knows less; and wherever there is conflict of opinion and difference of vision, we are bound to believe that the truer side is the side that feels the more, and not the side that feels the less.

William James

Contents

Themes

This book is the second in a series that seeks first to present and then explore the experiences of both family care givers and the fragile, typically elderly individuals who are their charges. It is offered with the expectation that publication of this chorus of multigenerational experience will serve two separate but ultimately related purposes. First, it is hoped these volumes will provide support and education for care givers of elderly relatives who find themselves isolated, confused, angered, and perhaps exhausted by their role. To the extent that individuals can see their own dilemmas, frustrations, and doubts in the experiences of others, they may find not only comfort but also perhaps assistance and guidance in fulfilling the role they have undertaken. To the degree that one can understand the actions of self and others, sometimes the agony of different choices can be diminished. Second, the personal records of care givers and care receivers, when taken together, provide a platform from which social and social scientific assumptions concerning caring for others, and especially those who are both fragile and aged, can be examined in the light of individual experience.

This exploration follows and builds upon the first book in the series, *Mirrored Lives: Aging Children and Elderly Parents,* which described my five years as the primary care giver for a fragile and ailing parent. While generally praised by reviewers and health care professionals, the most gratifying response the book brought forth was from others who are now or have been care givers of elderly relatives. Several readers who are themselves senior citizens wrote, for example, to explain how my experiences reminded them of their own, years before, when they were young and their own parents were frail and old. More important, many said they saw themselves, today, in the book's portrait of my father's world.

For their part, younger care givers of elderly relations expressed relief at the voice they thought I had given their own experiential worlds. "I thought I was the only one," a woman from Pennsylvania wrote. "But now I know others have gone through the same things as me." A middle-aged correspondent who, with her sister, first cared for an ailing father and now assists a frail and emphysemic mother, brought the point home to me in a letter. "So often while reading your book," she wrote, "I was struck with the similarities between your situation and what I have experienced, especially your emotional reactions and feelings. So often articles are written dealing with the physical stress, financial problems, and other issues involved in being a care giver. But you have addressed what I feel is the most difficult aspect, the emotional."

I had assumed that, while the broad issues of care giving described in my story would have general relevance, the specifics of what my father and I shared were unique. But readers insisted that both the emotional and the practical details chronicled in *Mirrored Lives* were, in fact, quite common parts of a larger fabric. The question then became how best to uncover that larger pattern. If my own story had mapped the boundaries of a shared experiential world, I wondered if its terrain could be more thoroughly described through a collection of the stories of other care givers. Would a series of such narratives address the issues my own tale left unanswered?

Perhaps the most crucial question left unanswered was why anyone would accept responsibility for a fragile and failing other. Both academic and popular literatures agree that elder care is a burdensome, unrewarding, personally costly, and physically hazardous task. Two researchers, Elizabeth A. Binney and Carroll L. Estes, summarized the accepted view when they painted this rather grim portrait of what it means to be responsible for an elderly relative, neighbor, or friend:

The costs of caregiving are considerable; there are social costs, such as social intolerance, relegation of the caregiver to the private sphere, especially when only limited respite programs exist, and loss of outside production. Personal and psychological costs include depression and other affective disorders, separation and loss of personal control and independence, often for long periods of time. Finally, opportunity costs include vast financial burdens, including loss of outside employment (often a necessity to a family's survival), lost Social Security earnings, increase in the "years out" penalty, increased early retirement, and a special discrimination placed on unmarried women, who frequently are expected to become caregivers when necessary.

Even worse, these clearly adverse effects apparently increase the longer one person cares for another. Studies of care givers for the elderly report that health problems accumulate for the care giver over the months and years of responsibility for the other. Individuals progress along a trajectory beginning with a desire to help in a medical crisis, through periods in which tranquilizers or alcohol are used to control anxiety and stress, to a state in which medical and emotional problems are an expected side effect of the care-giving experience. Care giving, it would seem, is itself a debilitating disease.

Were it indeed so damaging an experience, a willingness to put oneself at such risk might serve, in a rational world, to disqualify as care giver any person who knowingly took up the support of another who was simultaneously elderly and frail. Can someone willing to suffer medical, financial, and social collapse be trusted to make appropriate decisions for another? And yet, time and again, individuals of apparently sound mind freely assume responsibility for their elders. In North America, over 80 percent of today's fragile elderly are maintained at home through the assistance of a family member or friend. That is not to say these seniors are maintained by their families—by a unit of people bound to that aged person through love and relations over time. As these stories make clear, it is only one out of every five or seven relatives who choose to work with those individuals who once stood strong before them but now sit beneath an old comforter or blanket, weak, confused, and frail. Indeed, it is the lack of active assistance or understanding from other family members, friends, or medical personnel that is often the most heartrending fact care receivers and givers must learn to accept.

Why do some take on the responsibility for fragile seniors while the majority of friends and relations do not? The professional literature says we act out of a sense of obligation to those who once cared for us; we feel as if we somehow owe those who, when we were children, held responsibility for our lives. Caring is supposed to be a social if not biological obligation, a primordial commitment to care for those who once cared for us. Again and again, social science researchers, policymakers, gerontologists, and psychologists have assumed that a type of reciprocal law is at work whenever a younger person decides to assist an elderly relative. This principle of reciprocity says we are compelled to balance the scales of former care, to "pay back" those who were mature and strong when we were young and weak. It is as if there was an emotional balance sheet, a double-entry bookkeeping of the soul that said: "You changed my diapers when I was a child. Now I must change yours in old age."

The problem is that despite our penchant for the cost-effective, efficient phrase, nobody has yet defined an accountancy of the heart. There is no way to balance the care of children with the needs of the elderly. Children of alcoholic and abusive parents, people like "The Only Child's" Katie O'Connor who, as adults, have little reason to remember with gratitude their childhood lives, still persist in caring for those adults who formerly neglected them. In other cases, those whose earliest years were idyllic believe the now ailing parent, grandparent, or spouse should fend for him- or herself. Even those who say they "owe" a senior for past gifts of kindness, "The Mattress Heiress's" Margaret Neilson, for example, are unable to say how that debt might be repaid and what they would do were it discharged in full.

The act of caring for an aging relative, these stories insist, is one begun not out of a sense of indebtedness, in hopes of remuneration, or in response to an ironclad, cultural (or biological) imperative. It is instead an apparently altruistic choice whose rationale, even to the care giver, is difficult to explain. Adult children of aging parents are driven to personally care for their seniors neither by legal requirement nor social stricture. Each of us is free to move away, to plead the press of other responsibilities, to deny the act of care because of professional obligations, a career's all-consuming demands, or the needs of our own, growing families and family lives. The motive force for caring, my own story said, must lie in the history of relations between two people and the lessons they have learned from it.

SPEAKERS, NOT SUBJECTS

To better understand both my own experience and the lessons I believed care giving might teach, five years ago I began interviewing other care givers, asking each person to describe his or her experiences and experiential world. Finding others willing to assist me in this work was not difficult. Those who have been or are currently caring for fragile elders were, almost without exception, eager to talk with me. Some of those interviewed for this book agreed to speak only because of my own tenure as a care giver. "I've never told anyone else this," one woman said to me, "but you've been there. You'll understand." Thus, if it was my experience as a care giver that led to the writing of *Mirrored Lives,* it was a continuation of that role— and a willingness to discuss with others my own history—that made many of these interviews possible.

Although this book is ostensibly the work of a single individual, those whose stories are reported in this volume are in fact its coauthors. Their names have been changed but the individual narratives, edited for clarity, are in their own words. Without the generous gift of their time and the courage to open their lives and actions for the examination of others, this book could not have been written. For this reason, I have avoided referring to those whose edited statements appear in this book as "subjects," the word almost universally preferred by social scientists to describe those whose experiences they choose to detail. Like the physician's insistence that an individual is "his [or her] patient" and the teacher's appropriation of people in a class as "my students," there is implicit in the social scientist's designation of "subjects" an assumption of superiority and possession. Those who agreed to speak before the audience of my tape recorder deserved, I thought, a better classification than that.

In a similar vein, I have diverged from the normal practice of using the familiar form of address—the first name—when referring to either the speaker or the elder. Most published case histories use only first names as if, by becoming a "subject," an individual loses the formal dignity and social rank North American culture typically accords an adult. This is the same false familiarity one finds in the offices of North American dentists and physicians, where a receptionist assumes we are all on first-name basis, except of course the doctor, who is accorded official rank. In the case of individuals younger than I—Ms. Neilson, for example—the familiar seemed to somehow devalue the experiences she described, to reduce her record to the story of a child rather than present it as the work of an adult deserving attention and respect. For those care givers who are themselves elderly—Mrs. Kumamoto and Mrs. Harding, for example— such familiarity, which I would not dare use in person, seemed false

when attempted on the written page. In addition, using first names
seemed to diminish the weight of the speakers' perceptions, to reduce
their vision from that of an adult to those of studied, objectified
nonpersons. So all speakers are referred to with formal designa-
tions—Mr., Mrs., and Ms.—or by first and last name together.

I began each interview—and the work as a whole—with the single
assumption that elder care by younger relatives is a natural and not
a heroic role, a reflexive and healthy choice made intuitively and
without consideration of its potential personal consequences. Care
giving, I assumed, might begin as a response to some specific medical
crisis, but that caring would continue long after the original and
critical danger was past. A first decision to help is affirmed again
and again over months and perhaps years of continuing care. By
focusing on this affirmation over time, by assuming that the strengths
of a personal relation were stronger than the debilitating effects of a
role, I hoped a new perspective on caring for the fragile might
emerge.

What results is not simply a catalogue of specific diseases, a recitation of geriatric ailments, or a list of care givers' woes. Rather,
these narratives describe an etiology of wellness, a portrait of personal
and interpersonal behavior that affirms and strengthens rather than
denies and enfeebles care receiver and care giver alike. This is especially important because the dilemmas shared by care givers and
their fragile seniors are an isobar across a more broadly scaled map
of potential fragilities. Families of developmentally challenged children; middle-aged adults who, with their partners, live with degenerative conditions like Parkinson's disease or multiple sclerosis;
people facing AIDS—all in their own way confront similar problems.
Individuals of both sexes and every age define themselves not simply
by a calendar or through reference to a personal yardstick of hopes,
values, and deeds but, more importantly, through their relations with
others and the perspective of society as a whole.

What is more generally at stake is the place we accord the fragile
individual as a member of society. Issues of home versus institutional
care, dependence and independence, the rights of the individual
weighed against the requirements of other family members, the needs
of the fragile person balanced against the resources of the community
at large—these same questions are argued by many who, like the
fragile elder and his or her care giver, live on the thin gray line
between medical knowledge and social choice.

All care givers live a life of intense relation, wondering sometimes how they will complete another day. Their focus is the fragile other each has chosen to maintain. Social science and social policy, on the other hand, are largely formed through a study of the anonymous whole in which the individual experience has little place. Officials manning the vast apparatus of social care are not interested in "The Teenage Bride" Tina Harding's life, history, or love for her husband. They are not informed by the insights of "The Anniversary Girl," Mitsue Kumamoto. For them, she is a number on a case file. Those charged with the "big picture" worry about the cost-control framework, the organizational requirements presumably needed to maintain a class of people defined as both fragile and old. This book attempts to bridge the gap between these two disparate views—one broadly institutional and the other intensely personal—by first providing a record of the experiences of care givers and then applying the sum of that experiential knowledge to the broad assumptions of the policymakers, medical professionals, and social scientists who supposedly serve us.

CARE-GIVER ASSUMPTIONS

The central assumption of those who act for elderly relatives is that their seniors have a right to live in the community with—and if necessary through—the assistance of friends, family, and society as a whole. If the narrators of these stories did not believe their elders' place was with them at home and in the familiar world, they would have early on abdicated personal responsibility for their loved ones, either to another or to an institution. But it is the specter of institutionalization that the narrators of these stories fight against again and again. Entry into a nursing home and the categorical regime of supervised care removes a person from the greater, shared world, marking an end to that individual's life as an active person in society. There are times and cases where that may be necessary, where disabilities are so extreme that constant and skilled professional care is an absolute requirement for continuance. But that continuance costs the patient autonomy and individuality, diminishing where it does not sever the relation between care giver and receiver. Those are prices the speakers in this book were uniformly loath to ask their elders to pay.

To be in society and not in an institution means to be among people as a member of family, church, community, and social group. It means to have rights and obligations, needs and entitlements that are rarely expressed or clearly stated. But when a person is institutionalized—or in the case of the fragile elderly, placed in a "home"— he or she by definition becomes objectified. Once placed in the category of patient (or resident), that person—like all those institutionalized or incarcerated for whatever reason—loses a measure of individuality along with the freedom to interact as a free and sentient adult. He or she cannot travel freely, eat at leisure, change residence or, typically, handle his or her own personal affairs. To be in an institution is to be outside the reach of one's community of history and to have finally relinquished the personal choices that, for most of us, are a large part of what makes us human beings.

A theme tying all these stories together is that the frail elderly are first and foremost members of our community and our lives, that they both need and deserve to be cared for at home and in society by those who have been a part of their lives. Each care giver begins with the conviction that the elderly relative is not simply a burden with a disease but, more importantly, a person whom they love and have loved being with over years. The literatures of gerontology and geriatric medicine may analyze the "Parkinson's patient," the "Alzheimer's victim," or care givers in the "sandwich generation," they may assign measurements to levels of care-giver stress and perhaps describe the need for additional nursing home capacity. But the subjects of these studies and assignments are, to their care givers, first and foremost people with whom each has lived in time and in relation. The elderly, in short, are neither an "It," a disease or faceless demographic group, nor a solitary "I," isolates who can be studied outside the context of community and communal history. Those who are aged and infirm are first and foremost individuals with a shared history, one part of a larger "We" that includes two or more individuals together over time. The official language may be mechanistic, but the daily language between care givers and receivers is of necessity both personal and social.

It is in this context that the stories of this volume take on meaning. By focusing on the experiences of relatives who have chosen to assist an aging relation, one sees precisely the strengths and tensions that result in and from a shared life. The decision to care for an infirm relative in need of help is the end point of a whole series of developmental choices and mutually experienced historical events, just as the acceptance or rejection of help by an elderly citizen is the result of personality patterns, individual attitudes, and shared experiences that, in a real way, stretch across a lifetime lived in dense association. In a similar vein, what is learned and affirmed by the care giver will affect his or her future, one the fragile elder will not see but may still affect through the history of shared relations.

Individuals in relation and over time are not discrete data. Rather, they are active elements in complex human equations composed of family and community members interacting over time. It is therefore impossible to understand care givers and their elderly—or any other relational complex—without first assigning attention to the specific, subjective case. To examine a painting as if it were reality is to ignore the thousands of subjective decisions the artist made in creating an impression of a moment in time. Similarly, the issues of multigenerational care, the relations between individual care givers and receivers, and the decisions made from within that relation when weighing past histories against some immediate need are all off-limits to the clinical, quantitative researcher. It is this view from the inside, a perspective closed to clinician and policymaker, that can be gained from these stories of care givers reflecting on their experiences with elderly relations.

CARE RECEIVERS

There is an almost irresistible tendency to make of old age a pathology requiring isolation, to see the elderly as separate and therefore separable. It is sometimes only through an act of conscious will that when encountering a person with wrinkled skin, bent back, and quavery voice, one can see in that individual not only sickness or degeneration but also the fact of health and physical strength. After all the fragile elderly are, first and foremost, survivors who have endured beyond the sickness and accidents, the wars and calamities that dispatched the majority of their childhood friends, relations, and early colleagues. To familial care givers, the elderly relative—that survivor—is a critical and once powerful parent, grandparent, or spouse whom each has lived with across the shifting plane of familial relations. The elderly are not, or at least are not supposed to be, something totally other. It is not only that younger relatives may see their future in an infirm senior's plight but that, simultaneously, the aged parent, grandparent, or spouse is an essential gateway and link to the care giver's past. How we treat them therefore says as much about us as it does about the elderly individuals and their historical roles in relation to our younger selves.

Care givers, their fragile relations, and the shared worlds both inhabit are not divisible units that can be taken apart like Lego-style interlocking blocks. The meaning of a younger care giver's actions is defined in relation to the frail elder, and individual care givers thus can only be understood in the context of an association reaching through shared histories to the present. It is a long and complex experiential trail of which only the immediate moment, the personal actions by care givers for their seniors, can be easily seen. But it is in this long history that these care givers describe, in the slowly changing relations that transform the once all-powerful adult to the petitioner lying in a hospital bed, that the current acts take place.

The result, I hope, is that in these records the lives of care receiver and giver will be seen to have meaning and dignity in equal and perhaps reciprocal measure. To the extent that this occurs, perhaps we will learn to see the world at large in a more generous way. After all, we all define ourselves by a few significant relations and live our lives with those interpersonal histories as the core set of our values. One would expect the greater body of experiences to be in accord with those central relations and not stand in opposition to them.

Voices

1

The Drifter

Craig Williams has had three careers. The first was in the U.S. Air Force, the second was as an employee for the state of Washington, and his third career has been as both full-time care giver and, simultaneously, volunteer counselor and facilitator for the Alzheimer's and Related Disorders Association. He became involved with the association in 1981, soon after his wife was diagnosed as having Alzheimer's disease. In the early 1980s when Mrs. Williams was first diagnosed, public awareness of Alzheimer's disease was minimal. In addition, concern for care givers of fragile elderly—whatever the disease—was in its infancy. Community support, respite care, and information about specific diseases were all largely unavailable to family members. Now, seniors and their relatives are generally aware of the potential problems of Alzheimer's, and any cognitive deficit is seen by some as symptomatic of an Alzheimer's decline. A huge literature—popular and technical— has grown up about Alzheimer's disease, its sufferers, and their families.

Like many individuals interviewed, Mr. Williams switches from past to present tense during his discussion, a signal of the importance of the memories which, during their recitation, are immediate and compelling. When this happens he is, I think, reliving in our present this temporally "past" moment. Graham Rowles calls this the "plethora of 'incident places' spanning the space/time trajectory."

During the 1960s, while still in the U.S. Air Force, Mr. Williams had been stationed in Hawaii, a period he and his wife looked back on fondly. As his wife's illness progressed, they returned to the Greater Honolulu area. Choosing to move during a progressive and debilitating disease is unusual, and in this story the decision was tied, as the interview makes clear, to elements of the family's history, Mr. Williams's disaffection with the Washington State community, and a genuine love for the island environment.

At the time of the diagnosis in 1981, I hadn't heard of Alzheimer's disease. Prior to her diagnosis she exhibited very odd behavior. It probably took two and a half to three years of testing, waiting for results, comparing one CAT scan to the next one. So it wasn't a snap decision by any of the medical people. You're probably aware that there isn't any one specific way of diagnosing Alzheimer's disease except for running the course of neurologists and psychologists and medical doctors—all giving their tests. It took some time. So she was diagnosed in 1981 and at that time it was called organic brain disorder. The doctor explained it in the terms we know today that describe a deteriorating person, and brain, but I wanted some written material. Very little written material was available.

Her primary doctor—he knew of the Alzheimer's care unit at the Veterans Hospital in Tacoma, and he contacted the doctor in charge, because I had requested to volunteer. Well, they had never had a volunteer on that ward, so he rather interceded for me and set the stage. I interviewed with the doctor at the V.A. hospital and he agreed to let me become a volunteer. Of course, at that time I thought I was going to learn a lot, that I could give something back to the veterans there. I would take them out for walks and so on and do things that the staff just didn't have time to do. And in the course of that I would read various articles that they had on the ward. Very little information was available. So I asked if I could take on a project compiling all of this information. And, I would read it so it would help me understand the disease. As well, I thought I was making a contribution to them because I could compile this in one place. And at the end of a few months I had accumulated enough information to fill a three-ring binder. And that was all the information available to the staff there.

I could relate some of those things that were happening at the hospital to what my wife was doing, what she was going through. At one time when she was still driving, she'd get lost. Going to a store three blocks away, which she'd probably done hundreds of times, even to get one item—a quart of milk, a loaf of bread, or some one missing ingredient . . . maybe she was cooking something and she needed that spice—something that would take you or me maybe fifteen minutes, would take her an hour. When she came back I would ask her, "Where have you been?" "I got lost," she would say. That was one very apparent thing that you could see because anyone who had their full mental capacity wouldn't get lost. She stopped writing. She used to correspond a lot with her relatives, her friends who were away from her (we met a lot of people all over in the service). I would try and dictate some of the letters and she would write, at that time. Really I should say she stopped thinking. She was able to write, and then she came to the point where she could not write anymore.

The last time I saw her sign her name was in April of 1982 when we were in an attorney's office and she gave me a power of attorney for her. Doing other things, even her medical care at the hospital, since she couldn't communicate, I was responsible for it by bringing the power of attorney into play. That's one of the most important documents that a person can give and in this case it enabled us, it enabled me, to handle the business affairs of selling property and buying property over here.

She stopped talking rather early in this disease. Some people don't. They're able to communicate quite a long time into the disease. She seemed to understand right up to maybe last year, but as far as communicating, talking, she could make noises and sometimes words, but you couldn't discuss anything with her. At least not a two-way discussion. It was, well, devastating at first to see a person at the hospital in such a bad condition and then come home and see her still able to get around but by that time knowing that the disease was irreversible and thinking, well, how long will it be until she's in that condition? That takes a toll on a person.

I retired January 1, 1981, and that was really because of her disease. I worked for Washington State and I could have stayed on, but it just became apparent that if we were going to do anything together that I'd have to retire. We were able to take short trips, weekends or short trips. I bought a pickup with a camper and we could go for a few days in Canada or down the coast of Oregon and different places where we hadn't been and do things that we wanted to, fun things. It wasn't like the normal aging couple where they can just be practically teenagers in their actions in doing whatever they want to do, wherever they want to do it. Our church friends would come, stop by or call me in advance and say, "Okay, I can come over

Thursday, spend some time. Do you want me to do that, Carl?"
"Sure, do that." The church itself, the church is a group of people,
a large group of people. A small group of people did that. No, I
wasn't disappointed in the church-group involvement. But I was
very thankful that I did have my friends, especially my wife's brother
and his wife. Throughout this whole course of time, my wife's
brother and his wife, they were very supportive.

I had an operation in 1982 and up to that time my wife was still
able to take care of herself. When I went into the hospital, I made
arrangements for my wife's sister-in-law to stay with her. During
that period it became very evident, just like turning on a light, that
she could not take care of herself. So when I came back out of the
hospital, I had a convalescent period at home for a couple of weeks,
and I hired somebody to come in to take care of her: fix the meals,
do the laundry and so on, because I was bedridden except to take
trips to the doctor. And that's a burden. This was the first time I'd
employed someone in the house. And ever since 1982 I've had some
care. It was part-time, but it was an aid for me because at that time,
when that lady was there, I could go volunteer at the Veterans Hospital, do my thing there, and, ah, I know that my wife was being
taken care of. I would come home and there would be dinner ready.
I did the shopping but I didn't have the details of home care.

I really don't know. I wish that I had kept a journal from the time
that she was diagnosed, or even before, from when her behavior
changed that brought about the diagnosis. But I didn't and therefore
I can't remember a lot of details. Some dates I can recall. Certain
events, certain things come to mind. I would presume that this affected her as it did me. But I can't say for sure. I just wish I could
look back and say now that we discussed this in detail and I knew
more of her feelings. But she began withdrawing at that time and I
can't really fix a point in time where she stopped talking. But I would
feel that this is the most devastating time for a patient who was
capable of doing so much—to find that they can't do big things,
major things, and they can't even do little things. They can't take
care of themselves in the bathroom. They can't undress and go to
bed. If they want to go to bed, they just go to bed with whatever
they have on. And things like that.

We had our neighbors and church people, children and friends.
Yes, we still communicate, through Christmas cards. A few of the
people are in touch throughout the year, but I'd say the great majority

of people have dropped us completely, and that was a little devastating. Right from the start they stopped coming by. They stopped telephoning. They knew that my wife had Alzheimer's disease but their interest in her care dropped completely. And this was very surprising and devastating because some people—a couple I can think of immediately—were really close to us. We had helped them through some of their difficulties. They had helped my wife when I was not at home, when I was away in the service. They had helped her take care of her mother. In fact, their families called my wife's mother "Grandma." I mean, it was that "close" an arrangement. As my wife's disease began progressing through the normal Alzheimer's course, these people apparently could not understand or accommodate themselves to seeing her deteriorate, and they just stopped communicating, except through Christmas cards.

I had a number of releases. I have a policy that the TV doesn't go on until the evening. I don't watch anything during the day— I hardly even listen to the radio. But in the evening, you might say that's my relaxation time. My wife, all through the course of this disease, she seemed to require a lot of sleep, so roughly [she would be] awake twelve hours and sleep three to twelve hours. So I'd put her to bed at seven-thirty or eight o'clock at night and do what I wanted to. If it was watching TV or working on a hobby-type thing.

I did picture framing. We lived right near an air force base that had an excellent hobby shop, and as a retired air force person I could use those facilities, and that taxes your brain a little bit in figuring out different ways of framing, cutting mats, and doing things like that. And it's something that takes a few hours to do, it's not . . . you can't just pick it up and do it in fifteen minutes. So that was one of my relaxations. We had a very large yard, we lived on three acres, and I always had yard work to do. It used to be a pleasure when my wife and I could do things together, landscape the place ourselves. But when it comes to one person, well, then it becomes a drudgery. In fact, that's why we moved over here. But I was able to do most of the yard work and kept the place up. Clear a lot of brush and that type of material. At least it was a way of keeping your mind occupied constructively. I wasn't a drinker so I didn't have to hit the bars. The thought never occurred to me. In fact, there's a little tavern two blocks away and in all the time we lived there I never went in. I knew it was there.

SON AND DAUGHTER

It means making all the decisions, for one thing. I was involved in making decisions for three people: my wife, the lady who took care of her, and myself. Here's a person who could take care of herself, and now she can't. The way you solve that problem is you diaper rather than not diaper. I think it was worse for my daughter than for me. A child diapering her mother.

Our son lived three hundred miles away in Washington State and our daughter lived in the same city. As it progressed, and I had procured written material from the Alzheimer's Association, the ADRD, the Alzheimer's Disease and Related Disorders Association, they understood about the disease. That it was incurable. That there was no specific treatment for it. They would give me some respite. At least my daughter would, because she was in the same city. My son was very cooperative and understanding. I can't recall the year, but one year he came home at Christmas and she didn't recognize him. That was devastating for him. And for me too, but primarily for him. When a mother doesn't recognize you . . . I can't recall specifically, but throughout the course of everything, there was an acceptance, because she couldn't think. We realized that. I say he was devastated. He just couldn't realize at first that the disease was that bad.

MOVING

In 1983 my daughter, my wife, and I came over here [to Hawaii] as tourists. Seventeen years earlier we had left here. I thought it possible that, while I knew there had been changes, we'd see a number of places she could possibly remember. Diamond Head, the Pali, the sunset south of the Waianae coast, things like this that you wouldn't expect to change. I wanted to see if any of these would trigger her mind and kind of, well, bring her back to reality. I can't say that they did—I can't say that they didn't, but I can't say that they did. During that time . . . we originally figured we'd be here a week, but it went so well, we stayed two weeks. We did rent a car, and we rented a wheelchair because my wife's feet were swelling up with all the walking we were doing as tourists. The following year, 1984,

I came over here by myself. My wife's sister-in-law stayed with her so I knew everything was okay at home, and I just bummed around on my own. It gave me the full-time respite I thought I needed. That's when the bug hit me that maybe we ought to move over here. In 1985, early in '85, I contacted a few realtors over here and told them what I was basically interested in and that I'd decided to come.

In March, my wife's sister-in-law stayed with her and her brother came with me. He'd never been here before, so while some of the times he was doing the touristy things, I would meet with the realtors. We'd get the basic look of an area: the North Shore, the Windward side, over here [central Honolulu], Waikiki, and so on. That enabled me to rule out living in a house because of the maintenance required and lack of security—if I ever left for an extended period when my wife was away [ie. in the hospital] or in a nursing home. Townhouses, every one that I saw had steps to it, which would make it difficult, very difficult for the wheelchair. Even those that had elevators had steps to get to the elevator. So that didn't work. So I settled on condominium types. When I was home [in Tacoma] I thought about the items that we needed. I wrote a whole column of our requirements, and another column of what it would be nice to have, and sent those to the realtors and told them, "Don't waste your or my time by taking me to places that don't have these, and if they have these, other nice-to-have features would be fine."

People at the Alzheimer's Association here gave me the names of people who could help and, since we attended the church over here in the fifties, I went to that church and even found several people who did this type of work. So I didn't figure we would have a problem getting a care-type person. And we didn't. Once we moved over here in 1986, we put a note on our bulletin board in the condo and someone who lived in the same building wanted that type of work, and that's who I employed.

HOSPITALIZATION

Last September I hired a full-time person, a live-in nursing assistant. Throughout the course of this disease, I figured that it would come to this. I procured a three-bedroom place so that person would have that third bedroom as her own. And a bath. Our place has two bathrooms. In September we were having difficulty in feeding her. She stopped feeding herself two years ago. We would feed her but she wouldn't chew. By massaging the neck and doing different things, trying different substances like baby food—puree—we were able to get food into her. But after a while she stopped eating, and then she got pneumonia and we took her to the hospital, and at that time they prepared me for her not coming out of the hospital alive. She was treated for the pneumonia and she was given a nasal gastric tube, which is an extra measure. We had her listed as "Do Not Resuscitate," but it's just that she didn't progress to the point where she needed resuscitation. I don't know where that point is.

But they did treat her and were able to get her back in a stabilized condition. Three weeks later, they told me this was the time for a nursing home, something I had dreaded all along. I felt we could do everything that needed doing at home, but because she was tube fed and she needs other injections and other care we didn't feel we could do at home, we were able to put her in a nursing home. I felt that through the course of this that I could—with help—take care of her. And then I found that I couldn't. And that's when she went to the nursing home. I have asked people here and elsewhere, "How do you know when it's time to go to the nursing home?" And the usual answer is, "You just know." And that's exactly what happened. When she was in the hospital and doctors suggested that we look for a nursing home, we did. And I accepted it right off the bat. Not that I accept what doctors say right down the line, but I could see that I couldn't take care of her at home with the type of care she needed, and decided that the nursing home was acceptable.

FINAL THOUGHTS

My first [media] interview as a care giver was probably right after her diagnosis at the University of Washington, and at that time they did ask me why I was taking care of my wife and so on. And I said, "Because I love her." And I still feel that way. This is essentially what? Nine years later and she can't respond back, but I have a feeling she knows that I visit her. Maybe she doesn't, but I have a feeling she does, and that's why I'm there every day. Oh, every day. That probably does me more good than my wife, because she doesn't know me. She sees, but I don't think her brain processes what she

sees. That's the difficult part. I know I can adapt to it—I have adapted
to it—but it's difficult to go there and see that she's drifting further
every day. It's like being on a life raft or something, and she's getting
further out to sea. She's on the raft and I'm the one watching. I reach
out and she can't reach me.

I look at her now, realizing everything that she's lost, but I still
see her as she was, too. When I think about it, certainly I'd like to
dwell on the times, well, when we lived here in the fifties; it was a
much slower life over here. I feel sorry for her in that she didn't
have a retirement. She took care of her mother for a long time and
when her mother passed away, then there were just the two of us.
Her children had already left home for college and were starting their
lives. And it would have been the ideal time for me to stop working
completely, even though we'd have had less dollars, but to stop
working and then do things together. And I do kick myself for not
doing that. But I know I can't change it.

I can't say my wife could go out and fly a plane, and there were
many, many things I didn't expect her to be able to do, but she was
very capable. When I was in the service, probably a third of the time
when we were married—when I was in the air force—I was away
from the family, and she not only raised the kids, she took care of
the bills, had the car fixed, bought another car, all of these things
which I guess you'd say a "liberated woman" would do nowadays,
but this was twenty, thirty years ago. She just picked up and was
able to do those things. She was a dependent wife, I guess you'd
say. Took her role as homemaker . . . that was her job. She didn't
work outside the home. She did a wonderful job raising our kids;
they couldn't be better. Couldn't ask for any more.

One thing does irritate me, and I feel I should bring this out. It
irritates me very much to see a married couple who quibble and are
attacking each other for such petty little things as what type of clothing they're wearing, or if they go to a restaurant, one wants to have
a beer and the other doesn't. They're quibbling about insignificant
things that don't matter a hill of beans. And they're at each other's
throats. They're not enjoying themselves or each other. And my
wife and I have been robbed of that ability to enjoy each other. And
it does irritate me very much to see a couple who have no reason to
argue or fight and do it. I have spoken to my brother-in-law and his
wife. I prefaced it by introducing the subject, the reason why I
mentioned it to them—I don't want to antagonize them, I just want

them to enjoy each other while they have that time. To see people getting so involved in arguments when the outcome is insignificant and the cause of the argument is insignificant . . . it doesn't matter one way or the other.

We can't change the situation. We can't stop getting older. Drastically, yes. You die, but that's a hard way to stop getting older. Throughout all of this, this whole episode, that's been, I guess, my strength. Believing in the Lord and loving her are the two things that have kept me going. I just accepted it. I wanted to find out as much information as I could about it, the disease, and do what I could about it. And take care of my wife. I joined a support group in Washington State, became the facilitator of that group. I did the same here. That's my outlet. I try not to talk too much at these meetings because everyone has so much to say. It's difficult to keep from offering advice when the person at that moment doesn't really need it. They're unloading, and if there's anything I've learned from our instruction here, our program for facilitators, [it] is that you do the person a much better service as a listener than as a talker.

Postscript

In many ways, Mr. Williams is a fulfilled man. Believing absolutely in what he does, care giving has also given him a place within the Alzheimer's Association community and a purpose that extends far beyond his own family context or his wife's disease. Unlike other care givers whose tales are described here, he is not isolated; throughout the course of his wife's disease, he has been able to find outlets in volunteer work and through family-supported respite. We met in Honolulu at a seminar for care givers where he regaled participants, some of whom were already caring for elderly relatives, with practical details of caring for incapacitated, elderly members.

With an almost unbelievable enthusiasm, he discussed varying types of adult diapers and showed a series of childproof locks to prevent confused elderly individuals from gaining access to kitchen drawers and bathroom cabinets. Like a clown at a children's party, he kept pulling things from a large kit bag: a specially designed spoon and partitioned plates to help with feeding, catalogues where child-proofed drawers could be ordered cheaply. His message was carried as much by demeanor as by words: "I did it," his whole presence said, "and so can you. It was worth it to me and will be rewarding to you."

Looked at in the context of literature about care giving, he seems to have intuitively done everything right. Mr. Williams refused from the start to be hampered by ignorance and used his time at the Veterans Administration Hospital to become something of a lay expert in the field. His volunteer work assured that he would not become isolated in the role of care giver. In 1980, the need for support groups for the family of infirm elderly was slowly being recognized, but the issue of care giver support had only just begun to gain attention in the gerontologic literature.

Further, throughout this long history of his wife's decline, he did not isolate her and, in fact, appears to have done everything possible to involve and include her in activities. As Barbara Silverstone and Sarah Miller have pointed out, the isolation of the disabled is often more disorienting and more damaging than the disability itself: "Brain disorders are not the sole cause of functional mental disorders, but rather, result in isolation which exacerbates the functional disorder." Although the Williamses accepted the diagnosis, they fought the isolation and attendant symptoms of the disease. Mr. Williams lived with his wife, ate with her, cared for her and, especially in the early stages of the disease, traveled with her on the Oregon and Washington coasts. One suspects that these activities not only made the early stages of degeneration bearable for his wife but that they also made the current adjustment possible for him. Although he had, by his own admission, been absent on business for a third of their married life, during this period he chose to be present and active in his wife's support.

While accepting the diagnosis and its prognosis, he did everything within his power to assure that his wife's last sentient years would be as full and as active as possible. His decision to return to Hawaii, where he and his wife had once lived, struck me as peculiar and unusual. The explanation given here is certainly incomplete and perhaps disingenuous. During the vacation of 1983, he may have wanted to see if past associations would spark his wife's memories but, as he admits, she was by then disoriented, unable to walk great distances, and mute. I suspect that trip was as much for his own benefit, to revisit a romantic location where they had been happy together, as it was for his wife's enjoyment. Further, that trip was made in the company of a daughter who had assisted in the care giving and may have been a means to reward her—and later his in-laws—for their efforts on his and his wife's behalf.

2

The Teenage Bride

Tina and Tim Harding live in a pleasant suburban townhouse about fifteen miles from downtown Honolulu. Tim Harding is seventy-seven, a retired civil servant whose primary career was as a high-level, civilian employee of the U.S. military. Mr. Harding had a benign brain tumor removed several years ago and suffers from a series of disorders, the most troubling of which is slowly progressive Parkinson's disease. Mrs. Harding is his care giver, an almost compulsive defender of her husband's abilities and, clearly, she is torn between the husband she knows in history—"he's still the same to me"—and the man others see as an invalid.

Mr. Harding demonstrates many of the symptoms of moderately advanced Parkinson's disease. Patients typically suffer confusion, cognitive degeneration, and emotional depression, symptoms that make them "grumpy" at times. Progressive muscular rigidity, a characteristic of the disease, leads to a stiffened, expressionless appearance, often called the "Parkinson's mask." Walking becomes difficult and has a marked tiptoe appearance, resulting from both a stooped posture and a step that relies on the ball of the foot rather than heel-and-toe movement.

I never wanted to go. I don't want the hereafter. I want it right now. I want to see real people and real things. I sort of feel, well, I've always been afraid of death. Recently I lost a friend who I'd had for thirty-some years. She played tennis and just dropped on the tennis court. She was seventy-six. Tim just asked me—I just had a little dizzy spell—and he said: "You haven't told me what you want done if you black out." And I said, "Just let me lay there." I was joking, of course. But right now I've sort of given up, because it's hard to watch someone you love very much deteriorate. Also, someone who was so independent to become dependent. And who cries, you know?

I've been married for fifty-six years and I would not hurt my husband and start an argument with him and stand up for my so-called rights at this time. At this time it is very important that he still knows he is the man of the house. People usually treat him like, "Oh, that senile old invalid," and my husband is not like that. He's seventy-seven, he looks . . . he has a better figure than most men at forty, and his mind is—you've spoken to him, so you know—his mind is excellent. He remembers everything. If I need a telephone number, I don't go looking up my records. It's "Tim, what is that number we had, when, in 1963?" And he'll still know it by heart.

We grew up in the times when women did not expect to be the equal of a man. They didn't want to be. They realized the man had a hard time. He had to work, and his lot in life in the end would be he had to support his wife. At that time, you didn't think of a career for yourself. So we gave him his due, at least I did. I loved him very much. Also, he's five years older than I am. He was in college and I was in high school. If he told me the moon was black . . . I thought he was so bright! I was the only girl who had a fellow going to St. John's University. And I was a kid in high school. I never had a high school boyfriend. I knew he was smart. I always told him he was smart, and he said that he wasn't smart until he met me.

People treat him different. Yes, they do, because he walks with a cane. Sometimes his voice breaks when he talks, which is part of Parkinson's . . . ah, the voice goes. He's not crying, but it sounds like he's crying. If he gets excited and wants to tell you something, his voice breaks. People usually treat him like, "Oh, that senile old invalid," and my husband is not. He's just sick and not feeling well, and he knows it. And he's upset about it. He gets cranky because of that. With Parkinson's, you have to be patient. There really isn't too much you can do. It isn't death immediately, so you can't do too much for it. Also, he's introverted by nature. He's not an "up" man, never was. I am the only one who really gives him . . . I'm his slave. I'm his mother. I'm his girlfriend. I'm his wife. I'm his, ah, nurse. Not really. He has a nurse. He doesn't want me to be his nurse. He doesn't want me to help him with a bath. He doesn't want me to help him dress. He barely likes me to even touch him. He wants to be The Husband, which he has always been. But he is very satisfied with his life up to now, and I think even now he keeps saying how lucky we are that we live in Hawaii and that we retired to a nice place and we have enough income to live comfortably and that we are together.

Before the Parkinson's, seven years ago, the doctor found he had a tumor on his brain. My oldest son came over and we did it [surgery] right away. We were lucky, and it wasn't malignant. But then there are these other things. And right now he worries he might get another tumor. Yesterday, he went for a CAT scan. I did not want him to go for a CAT scan, because if it was another tumor, I would not want him to have another operation. He's seventy-seven. If he doesn't know about it, fine. I will not go for a mammogram. My friend had one and she dropped dead anyway. She had a mastectomy at the age of seventy-five. I thought it was wrong to do that. No way, I don't want it.

The main thing is not to have the doctor brush it [a problem] off. He's had so many problems with the doctors, you wouldn't believe! The reason he found out he had a brain tumor was he went to the internist and they told him to get a GI series [gastrointestinal examination]. They treated him as if he was a hypochondriac. He had the brain tumor all the time and nobody ever even suggested a CAT scan! So he went for this test for a GI series or something like that and they did not send his chart down to say what he was allergic to. He was on medication of different kinds, for high blood pressure, for other things, and he had no idea they hadn't sent his chart down. They gave him this drug or something and Timmy had a stroke! At least, they thought it was a stroke. But it didn't look like a stroke, he knew where he was and everything. They decided they wanted to keep him in the hospital overnight. As they were taking him upstairs, I said, "He just came in for that GI series; I can't understand it." Then I found out they had given him some sort of drug he was allergic to because they didn't even have his chart. So Dr. K. said, "Gee, Tim. I didn't know."

STRESS

The stress. The stress is not being able to do what I want. It isn't Tim's fault, either. He has to have someone to tell, "I don't feel well.

I feel dizzy." At the same time, he needs to be motivated. He needs
to have people to talk to, the same type of people. He's tired of
seeing me around all the time. I don't think he's tired of seeing me,
but he wants to do what he wants to do. He takes over the whole
house. That's stressful for me! I'm not the best housekeeper in the
world, but I like my things in order. I want papers to be put away,
and Tim says I put them away and we never find them. Which is
true. He puts them away, he finds them, but they're all over the
house. And you dare not touch one of those papers. It's not my
house anymore. It used to be the opposite. "Oh no, you're not doing
that to my new table. Take it up to your den or your room, or I'm
going to throw it out." Well, I do not say that anymore.

I get so mad that I'll go up and . . . I have to cry quietly. He's
angry if I cry. He cries all the time, but I'm not supposed to. And
he gets very upset if I'm upset. If I get angry, he feels like I'm letting
him down. That I'm being . . . that I just don't want to talk. It's not
like me to not want to talk. So I feel like I can't get angry too often.
But what I do is sing a little song and he knows [I'm mad] if I'm
humming a little tune when he tells me something. Because it's part
of Parkinson's, that's part of the disease. They're, ahem, grumpy.
They do not smile. Well, I don't remember Timmy smiling too
much anyway. He's not that type of person. But he has a very good
sense of humor, and if we have people over, in the house, he interacts.
And he loves it. He has a subtle sense of humor. So I always have
to explain, "He doesn't mean that." But I've done that all my life,
so people don't get insulted.

[After my heart attack] he was a little more careful of me. They
told me it was stress. But I really was overweight. And I had cho-
lesterol, which I never knew because I swam two hours a day. I'm
a swimmer and, well, it's only the last two years, since I had the
heart attack, that I don't swim. I walk six miles a day, but I don't
swim very much anymore because the pool we have in our townhouse complex is not heated. And our—my—cardiologist asked me
was the pool heated and he said, "I'd prefer you walk. You can
swim, but be sure, you know, that it isn't a shock." I must say my
walking has helped me a great deal. Since the heart attack I've learned
to live alone. I've learned to take a walk myself. I'd rather have
girlfriends do it, or Tim with me, but I do it myself. And I feel
lonely. I feel like no one cares for him but me.

Actually, I'm glad when five o'clock comes. I do what I did with my children. After five o'clock, I'm nobody's mother. Tim's used to it, and he seems relieved. He gets to sit downstairs on the couch with his television. He likes different programs than ladies do—I like talk shows, he likes war pictures. So I go upstairs. I have a television upstairs in my bedroom. And I'll take my show, maybe write a postcard or something if I want to, and just relax. I can look at my television. I call down, "Are you all right?" He's had everything I can possibly give him. And I just stay up there.

I think he feels angry. I think he feels angry at me because . . . I think he's angry because I had a heart attack. I'm not supposed to be sick, I never was sick. I'm supposed to be there for him. Otherwise I am "Tina!" [He calls] and I hop. It's not scary because I know Tim. I know he loves me very much. And I know if he talks to anybody he can't stop bragging about me. He can't say, "I love you. You look beautiful." He has said it as we were growing up. But this is hard for him. Or to say, "I'm sorry." I never put him in a position to say, "I'm sorry." He cannot say it. I can say, "I'm sorry," even when I'm not sorry, just to make him feel good. I say, "I'm sorry. I was wrong." It doesn't bother me to say I was wrong even when I know I was right.

CHILDREN

Our oldest son, who is now fifty, is a California councilman and a vice-mayor. He was born in 1939. Our second son was born in 1944. Our third son was born in 1950, and our daughter was born in 1956. You can see I had an active life. Every time I sent one off to school, I had another baby! So each baby was like an only child. There was no birth control [pill] at that time. We used our own birth control. Nobody told us what to do. We didn't have children for five years. We said we wouldn't. I worked as a saleslady in a department store. Tim worked for the government and went to school at night. We transferred to Washington, D.C., lived there. Lived in Virginia. Lived almost every place in the country. And we had our children spaced apart. Nobody told us how to do that.

My oldest son is very concerned about his father. He's fifty, he's our firstborn, and he's very, very much attached to his dad and to me. He'll call, and he's very much involved, and wants him—Tim— to get the right pills. You know. Our oldest son calls at least two or three times a week, and he's been wonderful. And that's all Tim really wants. All he wants is to be respected, as he was before. He's a proud man.

Craig, the second son, was here about two years ago. He's a "yuppie," vice-president of a hospital, and now he is almost angry at me. He says, "You do not have to do this. He [Tim] needs supervised care. And you should give it to him." And he says, "I see people who give up the rest of their life and they're dead and the Parkinson's patient is still alive." And he said not to do it.

My third son is angry at his dad. Donald was here last year and it wasn't a successful visit. He has a little boy that he adopted and Donald just thinks no one else has had a baby. It's *his* boy! He's compensating, I think. Because his son, Loren, has been adopted, our son wants to know that we love him as much as the other grandchildren. Timmy wasn't feeling well and he wanted Glen to take care of his little boy by himself because it was right after my heart attack and Tim thought I was overworking for them but didn't realize I was doing the same for him.

Well, Donald visited and he watched me—and this was after a heart attack that I had about two years ago—he watched me, and he thought I was doing too much. Tim said, "Did the paper arrive today?" and I said, "Oh my god, I forgot to take it in." And Donald, who is a professor at the University of California, said, "Do you mean you fetch his paper every morning? Why doesn't he take a walk out there and get it?" Well, I said, "Donald, it isn't because he's ill. I've fetched his paper since before you were even dreamed of. About fifty-six years ago I fetched the paper! I don't resent doing that."

I get angry with them. In California, they're busy taking me out places, but they're never interested in going out with their dad. I feel that he's extra, even though he takes nothing from anybody, but I feel they would be so happy if it was over. Even when they call, they're speaking with me. They seem to be angry that he's sick. Otherwise, it's "Is Mom coming to visit?" or they're coming to visit *me*. And Mom has other things to do. Like Dad. I feel the less they see of us, the better. Now it's not fun anymore when they come. It isn't as easy. Now they're married and have a job—you don't just pick up and go. If mother sends the ticket you can. But I don't think they want to come. I think they're hurt, they're mad because he's sick. It's not that they don't love him, I'm sure that they do. How could you not love a father? He was good to them and, you know, took them every place and did everything a father should do for them. He was a strict father, though.

With May, we feel differently. She's the baby. She's just 34 years old. We're happy she's married and seems to have a good marriage. She has two little children, one is four and one is three. She lives over on the North Shore, and it's two and a half hours' drive from here. My daughter does not come too often. She's not very sympathetic. Her husband is a doctor, and she thinks Tim could do a lot of things more for himself. Actually, I love it that she's married. When you have three sons, you want them to be good citizens— and they are—and they're happy. But with a daughter, even though she has a husband who can care for her and she seems happy and she has two children, you still feel very connected, very much connected. You feel responsible, regardless. She's not sympathetic at all.

It seems awful, but you think you know your children and you really don't. I didn't raise them that way. We feel like there's no soul, there's no, ah, feeling of responsibility in them. Responsibility isn't the word I mean. Compassion. It's compassion. That's what they don't have. It makes me angry at the children because I feel they should give him more attention and sympathy for being a father who has been a good dad and a loyal dad. I feel that we've gotten to be, that we're old people now. We're a burden. We're not a burden financially, and we live far away. But we're a burden because they feel guilty.

I think Tim likes it better when we're alone, and they [the children] resent this for me. The first thing my third boy said [about Tim's illness] was, "Oh, Mother. Now you can come back to Long Beach and live. All your friends are there. You can come back and buy an apartment, a condominium here and you'll come back." And I said no, Tim does not want to live in Long Beach anymore. He likes Hawaii. And my son said, "Well, that's too bad. But you certainly can." And I said, "But what will I do with Tim?" And he said, "That's his problem." This is the third boy, and these are very bright children. And they were brought up with a loving father who was Cub Master and started Boy Scout groups for them and everything. They seem to resent the fact that I am going away from them.

They're kids. I feel that they are immature. You must remember each one was brought up at a different time period. If you think of a son who was brought up in 1939, you know why he is so attached and why he is so caring. Then think of a son who was born in 1944, who was brought up in the 1950s and '60s. And then think of another who was born in 1950. And so, they are the generation that is immature. Also, they're selfish. They've had everything. They've had cars, education. . . . Tim sent—our four children together have twelve [academic] degrees, so you know he must have done something right!

I don't want their help. I really wouldn't put it on them. Neither would Tim. He wouldn't want that. We don't want anyone to help us. As long as I'm alive, Timmy is going to be fine. I always handled the finances. He was an accountant. He couldn't count anything under a million dollars so he never worried about the money. If I gave him a dollar for lunch, fine. In fact, he can't even believe what I've done. If I'm not around, I have told my daughter and I put it in writing, she will be the guardian. She will get the complete estate—whatever we have. Tim's income goes on as long as he lives. He has three pensions. He worked for the government for thirty-six years, and then he has a company pension, and he has Social Security. And if anything happens to me, my daughter knows that all you have to do with Tim is get him a nice young girl to drive the car, prepare the food, and he can pay her as much—or more—to take good care of him. And he'll be fine.

"Go to California," they tell me. "Why can't you get up and go? You're able to travel if you want to, anytime." But it's no longer that much of a pleasure to travel alone. And when I did travel alone before, I never worried what Tim was doing at home, because I knew he could take care of himself.

FRIENDS

The friends we had here were in the travel business with us. We took our travel agent certificates together after Tim retired from the military. Pan Am sent us to London. I was the mouth, the salesperson, and he was the brain. We went to school in London, all paid for by the airlines. At one time they did that. We went to Caribbean Cruise, we did so many things and we've done them all together. When you said Tim, it was Tim and Tina.

My friends are angry for me. They feel I should be getting out more, doing things more. These aren't bosom buddies. They're people we met here. We'd take them to the Officers Club, which they loved us taking them to. These were business associates; they weren't personal friends like we had in California. Mostly my friends there were lady friends. In California, the friends I made were with the children. My children were growing up most of my life, so I had one in high school, one in college, one in junior high, and the baby. And with each child as they grew up, I had a different set of friends. I had friends in preschool [mothers of children her daughter's age] who had dated my oldest son. And I did all my socializing—I was PTA president, and I would belong to garden clubs. We never had close friends together because we were mostly friends with each other. Tim was never much of a person to have many friends. I am the one who had the friends. Tim never did. We never had friends we couldn't live without. We had each other.

I feel this is hard. I feel I need to find something else to do. And I can. I can get a job, I can do a million things. But who will take care of him? Now, it's like leaving a child at home. You'd have a guilty feeling. What is he doing? Did he fall down? Can he get up? Is he eating? And he does not take a glass of water unless I give it to him. As I was leaving this afternoon to meet you, he said, "You know, I feel so thirsty, I could die. Do you suppose I could have a drink of something?" Well, I went to the refrigerator and got him a Coke.

It's hard for people to understand how you feel, how badly you feel for someone who is deteriorating. It's a very difficult thing to watch. I think he's afraid to be alone. Even when I go away for only three or four days, he's so happy when I return. He's never stood in my way for going out, he won't say "You can't." But I think he's scared. I'm scared, too. I'm afraid he might fall, that something might happen to him. I don't want that. I want him to live to be 150. I'll be 145.

Now it's just the two of us. I don't have that kind of girlfriends here. My friends were mostly in Long Beach, so they would come here to visit. They would come over, but I no longer invite them because the house is taken over by Tim. He's sitting in his pajamas, his papers are in a heap in the living room. It's a small townhouse. We have three bedrooms but they're all taken. It's hard.

SCHEDULES

Each day is another day. There are days when Tim will get up in the morning and say, "Let's go." He loves to go for the ride around the Windward Mall. He loves the little island near Sea Life Park, the island in the middle of the bay. He thinks that's the most beautiful spot in the whole world. He loves the ridged mountains, and I do too. Usually, we'll get into the car about ten o'clock. He uses a cane because he can't walk too far. Maybe he's lucky if he does a half a block. He doesn't seem to want to do walking. He says he can't. He does have trouble with rheumatism and other things.

I don't like to drive at night anymore since I'm on the medication for heart and blood pressure and, though I don't wear glasses when I drive, my eyesight isn't too good. I don't know if it's on account of my age. Tim won't sit in the car when I drive, even though I've never had a citation and have driven for a long time. It makes him very nervous when I drive. He drives. So we go to the Kahala Hilton [an expensive Honolulu hotel restaurant]. We had an account there for years. And to Hickham [Air Force Base] Officers Club. And now, lately, we haven't been doing even that. I'll dash over to the local movie if there is something I want to see.

A bad day is a day he feels everything is gone. He's lost everything. He eats, thank goodness, if I give him the food. He has to have the same thing, all the same. And he will not take even a glass of water himself. If I leave, I guess he'll have to. My daughter says, "Mother, he'll eat. If he's hungry, he'll eat." But he likes me to do the feeding. So a bad day is sitting around. I give him his breakfast; I'll dash out to the store and I'll buy some things; then I'll come in and he's sleeping. He sleeps most of the time. If he's not happy, he sleeps. But then he stays up at night. He'll look at his programs and he'll go to sleep later. So that when he wakes up in the morning, he isn't really rested, so he'll eat his breakfast and have to go to sleep again.

I have two people helping, one a nurse's aide, and I was happy to get her because you can't let just anyone take care of Tim. He prefers a nice young girl, and we have one now. She comes at seven-thirty. I leave to take my walk. Sometimes he'll walk with her, just about ten minutes of walking with him. Then she gives him his shower and they have a cup of coffee, and he's happy. He would be happy, I think, if I could have her come every day for a couple of hours. Would I be, too? Yes. There's never been jealousy in our marriage. I don't know what that means because I've never had another boyfriend—he's never given me any reason. And if he tells me he's been out with someone, I say, "Great, as long as you had a good time. As long as it doesn't cost me anything."

Even just the two days that this young lady comes to visit, they have helped me so much. She gives him a bath, and he tells her stories. She's really interested because this is all new to her. He knows all about Asia. He knows all about Europe. And, ah, he knows stories that are all new, and people who have never heard them are just fascinated by them. Most everyone likes him, most of the ladies like him because he tells them tales. And they are good, they're very good stories. And they've helped me so much. I feel relieved that he's up. He feels good. He'll dress and he'll talk, and he's happy when he's stimulated.

EARLY YEARS

I was about thirteen years old when I met Tim, but I started to go with him when I was fourteen and I was married when I was not quite seventeen. I never had another boyfriend. To me he was like a father figure. He was like a brother. In fact, he looked a lot like my older brother, whom I adore. And he was everything. He was so bright! He would tell me about stars, and things that I didn't know because I had just started high school and he was going to college. We went with each other for two years and we were married, and we've been married fifty-six years. I thought everybody did that. It never occurred to me. I always said, "If Timmy didn't marry me, I don't know who would."

Timmy, I think, still sees me as sixteen. If I'm in a department store with him at any time, even when he was well, and if he didn't like what I was saying to him, or anything, he'd say "Tina!" and everyone would turn around and say, "Who is Tina? A little baby?" I am seventy-two! He still thinks of me as sixteen. If I tell him to do something, most of the time, now, I'm right. I feel sorry for him. I think of him as a young man. I see him the same. He doesn't look any older to me. I think he looks the same. I feel sorry that he can't walk. I can't believe it, because he would always be walking ahead of me as if we were from another culture, he walked so fast. I feel badly. I would rather it had happened to me. To me, he's always the same. He knows that I've grown a lot. He really raised me. There was a time I wouldn't talk about that [death]. Now, I don't think I'm afraid anymore. I don't want to go, I don't want to leave. I like it here. I like it here with Tim, no matter what.

Postscript _____

Several weeks after this interview, I met Mr. Harding and found him both more and less than his wife had described. Able to walk, carefully, within the house, his voice sounded as if he were crying whenever he became excited. This is a result of Parkinson's disease, and he warned me about it at our first meeting. When it was clear that I was not bothered by this problem, he became quite garrulous. As proud of him as his wife was, Mr. Harding was equally lavish in praise of his wife. He proudly told me tales of his wife's business acumen, praised her ability to meet people and develop friends, acknowledged her role in caring for him. The interview was complicated by her presence and their tendency to either speak one for the other, or for one to pause and ask the spouse to complete an idea or supply a name. After fifty-six years of marriage, each has become an indivisible part of the other.

3

The Miracle Pill

Ruth Pfeiffer works at a library near her home in central Ohio. It is the town where she was born and raised and where she and her husband, Denis, a native of New York State, have lived throughout their more than thirty years of marriage. For years, she cared for both her parents and, with her husband, was involved in the care of her mother-in-law.

The case of Parkinson's disease described here is greatly advanced from that described by Mrs. Harding. In some cases, Parkinson's patients may suffer a full dementia, but this disorientation can vanish, almost miraculously, if the right drug and dosage are found. So far, however, no medication has been discovered that can permanently arrest the disease's symptoms. See "Suggestions for further Reading" for more information on this disease.

The legal problems that resulted from the hiring of independent home aides and the questions of responsibility under Mrs. Pfeiffer's power of attorney are complex. Laws governing such issues vary state by state and province by province. As a general rule, however, it is fair to say that a person acting under power of attorney for another is, in broad principle, legally responsible for all contracts, debts, and obligations assigned under the power of attorney in the patient's name.

It is a common practice, and a good one where several individuals care for one patient, to keep a "nurse's log" in which each care giver daily notes the patient's condition, medications administered, and general thoughts on the care receiver's behavior and moods. This makes it easier to see patterns in complex cases, like this one, where medications are used. In addition, it provides substantiation of care and documents procedures followed should issues of legal responsibility arise.

Do I want to get old? Only if my mind stays intact. Tomorrow is Mother's Day, and my mother would love to go with us to my daughter Cheryl's. But oh no, I couldn't take my mother. My mother is too bad. She can't walk and she's totally disoriented and confused. All the time. I mean, she may be all right for five, ten minutes. But I could never take her on a trip like that. Never. I brought her here last year from the nursing home. But my father was living then. I brought them here for a cookout, and she was fine. But now she's worse. Last Christmas it was disastrous. She just wanted to go home, to her house. And she would just repeat, "I want to go home. Take me home. Take me home. Take me home." I think she means her house, not even necessarily the house she lived in when she was married. Her house may be where she grew up.

I just advised my best friend, Mary, to put her mother in a care center. I have a very good friend who is an only child, and we grew up together. Her mother had a stroke, but her mind is still good, and she's getting very frail. You see, my parents, one would not leave the other. But Mary's mother lives with her, her father lives in the family house that they had. But her mother is getting so bad, now, that I had to take her my mother's bedside commode and a wheelchair. And Mary works all day. And I said to her, "You told me one hundred times to do what you're not doing. And I'm telling you, you better do it." She knows. She knows, but I think as long as her mother isn't failing, she won't do it. And she has two children, one in California and one in Texas, that she wants to go visit. Now her father, he gets around fine, but he's eighty-two. He comes every day to visit his wife. She tells her father, "You have to come and take care of her." So she has her 82-year-old father coming to take care of her mother.

And I told Mary, "You know it's time, because she has to get around in a wheelchair and she can't take care of herself hardly at all." She has to bathe her mother, wash her hair . . . it's getting to her. And so Mary is on tranquilizers, see? She works during the week and she's gone full-time. It's just so stressful that when she is off on weekends and home with her mother all day, then she takes tranquilizers. I think she should get aides in to at least give her mother a bath and do her hair. But she won't do it, and she told me to do it! And we have another friend, Dorothy, whose mother had Alzheimer's. And she has only one sister, and she took her mother in, but her mother left the house [wandered off], and they couldn't find her, and things like that. And Mary said that Dorothy should put *her* mother in a nursing home, or get aides in at least to bathe her. And all the advice Mary gave us, she's not taking herself. So it's easy to give advice when it's someone else's mother. But when it's *your* mother, then it's not so easy.

Then, you just know when you can't do it any longer, and that's it. I knew the time, I knew that I could no longer put up with everything. It was in May a year ago. Mother just got so bad. She had kidney stones, and ended up in the hospital. And she couldn't walk, she was too disoriented to know how to walk or where she was. The nurse's aides couldn't even take care of her. They [the doctors] recommended the home a long time ago. I fought it for years. She would get disoriented, she'd get dementia from Parkinson's—she has Parkinson's that fluctuates just constantly, then you can't control it with medication. They recommended it years ago. I fought with one doctor after another. I felt she could be taken care of at home with nurse's aides and me. But it didn't work. Well, she went to a rehab hospital for six weeks, and she did well. Then came home. I think we tried, I don't know, almost a year.

My father made things worse. He thought she could do it. He would sit in the living room and give her orders, even if she walked with the walker. My father would sit and watch television all day. He was easy to take care of. All he needed was a television, a cheese sandwich for lunch, and he was happy. He really never caused me a problem. He never complained. He never wanted taking care of. My father had leukemia for fifteen years. He walked with a cane, I would say he could get by. He would be happy living here. He would be happy living there [at his house] totally alone. They wouldn't leave their home. They wanted me to go down there and take care of them.

They were living together, and he didn't want nurse's aides. He didn't want meals coming in. He didn't want anyone bothering him. He didn't want to be told anything. He couldn't deal with it. He wanted *her* in a nursing home! He had leukemia, you know. He thought he could handle himself, but he was getting bad. Then he broke his hip, and he ended up in the hospital, and he ended up in the rehab hospital. And they recommended I put him in a nursing home. And I said, "I have to give him a chance at home. Everyone deserves a chance." So I brought him home. Then I had two nurse's aides to take care of.

I was resentful because he didn't think about how I worked all day. And I came there on my lunch hour and after work, and I never came home to *my* house. All I did was sleep here. He never thought about it. He just took everything for granted. I was supposed to take care of him! His mother was put into a nursing home. And she had what would probably be Alzheimer's today. My mother and father both felt that they couldn't take care of her, because she was confused and disoriented. My mother and I would go up to visit, but my father was too busy. He worked. But I work eight hours a day, and he never thought I was too busy to come down to his place.

And when I put him in a nursing home, he never forgave me, I don't think. Did I visit him in the nursing home? Every day. Every day. They, my father and mother, were in the same nursing home, but not in the same room. Being in the same room never would have worked. He would have been hauling at my mother all day [laughs]. So every day after work, I would then go to the nursing home instead of to their house. And I would take my mother [from her room], and take her down to visit him. He couldn't handle her confusion. He couldn't handle it. He couldn't handle it at home either.

I always knew I would take care of them if they needed taking care of. In fact, when we bought this house, we knew where we would make a bedroom for them downstairs, so they would not have to climb stairs. I figured one of my parents would die, and I'd take the other one to live with me. I just thought if they couldn't live alone, they'd come and live with me. It didn't work out that way. Now, with my father dead, if my mother wasn't confused she would have moved in here and been fine. Or, I think if my mother had died and my father was left alone, he would have moved in here.

THE MIRACLE DRUG

One thing that I did have for my mother was a very good neurologist who was more like a friend. He would spend a lot of time. I could call him. He was very reasonable. He trusted me with the medicine. He knew I understood it, and he trusted me when I changed it. He said, "You know better than I do because you're with her all the time." And he is the one who told me when my mother had a stroke and he took care of her in hospital. And when you have a stroke and Parkinson's, well, you know you have a lot against you. And he said—this was like a couple of years ago—and he said, "Ruth, I really think now you should put her in a care center." And I said, "Well, let's try a rehab hospital before we do that." She did well there, and they agreed that she could come home as long as I had nurse's aides, and with all this help, and never be left alone. And I did that. But if I had listened to Dr. Anthony, the neurologist who wanted to save me all this grief . . . I don't know. I wouldn't be happy if I hadn't gone all the way. After I did that with my mother, when my father broke his hip and they said, "Well, he can't walk well enough to come home," I said, "Let's try the rehab hospital." The doctor that was head of that said, "You know, it's time for him to leave and he should go to a nursing home. You should not take this man home." I said, "Let me see him walk first with the walker." The occupational therapist said that my father was really doing well, and I said, "Okay, everyone deserves a chance," and I brought him home.

ROUTINES

I work, and I get an hour for lunch. When they both needed constant care, well, so I would go to work, and on my lunch hour I would go to their house and get them their lunch and see that everything was fine. Then I would go back to work. Then after work I would go back to their house and stay until I put my mother . . . helped my mother to bed, which was around eight o'clock or nine. And then I finally got to come home, and I wouldn't be home until about ten, ten-thirty, and then I would go back to see if she had to get up and go to the bathroom. And then the nurse's aide would come at eleven. I would never leave her alone at night. It got to be where I had aides day and night, and my husband and I took the three-to-eleven shift after work, so we had no home.

I just did it, I didn't think about it. It's taken years off my life. I missed just being in my own house, just enjoying my home. My husband and I just enjoy being together, and traveling, and we like to go to antique shows. The stress, it's awful. Working helped. I guess I didn't handle it too well because they ended up in the nursing home. It's still stressful. It's just a tremendous amount of work. They were both in the hospital. They were both in the rehab hospital. They both had Medicare and Blue Cross supplements. I had to pay all their bills, take care of all their household bills, do all their grocery shopping, do their taxes—everything. Get a secretary! [Laughs.] You have to keep everything, that's for sure. And of course if you're using their money, you better have a checking account. You better go to an attorney. I went to an attorney, and the one I went to didn't tell me I had to have workmen's compensation for these nurse's aides. And he knew what I was doing. He probably didn't know [that I had to] either, my attorney.

Were they grateful? If my mother had known what was going on, yes. But my mother was too confused, and my father was too resentful. He just wanted to take care of himself. I mean, he felt he could take care of himself. He could not take care of himself. But he resented me coming down there. He didn't want me to tell him anything. You know, God forbid I mentioned anything to tell him. You know, then he'd tell me to go home, that he didn't need anyone taking care of him. And that wasn't true. No one ever told him what to do. He worked in the steel mill. You never spoke back to him, and so there I come, telling him what to do. And no.

I guess I am bitter and resentful because, first of all, I tried so hard. I cared for them for five years without nurse's aides, and it didn't work, even with the nurse's aides and trying to keep them at home. If I'd listened to the doctor to begin with a year ago, the doctor who said, "Ruth, you know, she should be in a care center. You can't do this," I would have saved myself all this grief. My mother would get so bad that I would call Dr. Anthony, and I would say, "I'm bringing her in. You have to see her now! You have to see how she gets." She would fall, for example, but she wouldn't really fall. She would look at a chair, walk up to it, and sit on the floor next to it. You lose that depth vision: where she thought the chair was where it was, but it really wasn't. And if I wanted to go somewhere out of town, my daughter Hannah would come in for the weekend, or someone. And I'd take the wheelchair, and take her, and wheel her in and say, "You know, you're seeing her now. Now don't tell me you can't do something. Well, try something." I would increase pills and decrease pills and change . . . it's amazing, if you have Parkinson's and you get the right pill, you'll be perfectly fine. You need that one pill. For ten years, we played with pills. I took her to Cleveland, to Dr. Nadine. You see, I never gave up until now. I just wanted to find that one miracle drug, and it's not there.

DO NOT RESUSCITATE

When my father got really bad . . . right before he died, he got pneumonia. Several times. My father said he didn't want to get treated. I told the doctor this when she went to the nursing home to check him, and she called me from the nursing home. She called me at work and said, "Your father is too sick to make this decision. You'll have to make it." So I said, "Well, take him to the hospital." When I left work and went to the hospital where my father was in Emergency I thought, "I'm going to find this man who can't even talk." But there my father said, "Where is this doctor? She said if I came up here she was going to check me out of the hospital." Well, this is not a person whose mind is delirious. She just wouldn't accept his decision to not be treated. So the next time when he went to the hospital, I signed papers not to resuscitate him. And the young nurse looked at me and said, "Are you sure you know what you're doing?" I said, "I know perfectly well what I'm doing. My father is eighty-five years old and he has leukemia. There's only so much you can do. I'm sure he doesn't want to be all hooked up if he stops breathing." And then, the next time he got pneumonia, I told the doctor, and she said, you know, "I accept, I understand." So that's what we did. We didn't treat him.

It got me mad when I went to the hospital and saw he could speak for himself. He's not confused. I knew he didn't want it. My father's mind was fine. I know what they wanted. I know my mother would never want to be the way she is, if she knew. No way. It would be my decision, too, if it were myself. I mean, if I had leukemia, and I had it for years, and it's really gotten to the point where there's no hope or no help, and my life is at an end, I don't want to be saved with drugs constantly. At first, it would go into remission and he would get chemo, but he was still in good enough health that he got around. But once he got really bad and leukemia took over completely, you're not going to send someone with pneumonia to the hospital to be treated! They would have, but I had to sign papers that said not to.

BUREAUCRACIES

Like I say, the nurse's aides were a problem. The nurse's aides can cause as many problems as the patient: they don't want to work this day, they don't want to work that day. They're switching days. This one's complaining because she has to take her day off, and on and on. Or they'll call off—nine, ten o'clock at night they'll call and say, "I can't come tonight," and then I had to go and stay all night, then go to my work in the morning! And my mother was up all night. If I had it to do over again, I would definitely get an agency, because if someone calls off, they'll send someone else. I should have looked into that, into an agency, But I wanted the same person coming out, and I thought then that if you got an agency, they would send someone different all the time. [Ed. note: Switching home aides is a policy at some agencies designed to prevent excessive dependence on one employee.]

I had what would probably be your independent, full-time nurse's aide. The only person I hired directly was Judy. I interviewed her, and I hired her. She only wanted to work four or five days a week, so I had to get someone else, and Judy would usually know someone who wanted to work two days. She was in charge of scheduling hours. She handled the other nurse's aides for me so that when I needed a nurse's aide, she usually would come up with someone. She got me this one nurse's aide, Helen, who I was never really happy with. My mother didn't like her, and when my father was in the hospital—I think it was the night he had surgery and she knew I was really tired—she called me at two o'clock in the morning to tell me my mother fell out of bed. "But," she said, "everything's fine. She's back in bed. You don't need to come down. I just wanted you to know." And I remember this distinctly because when I hung up, I told my husband this, and he said, "Well, why did Helen call? Why didn't she just tell you in the morning?"

I was never happy with her. And she kept calling off, and I finally got an agency to send someone else out. And I was happy with who they sent. So I decided to go through the agency. And I told Helen—especially when she called off Easter Sunday after we went through this whole thing about, "Yes, she would work. Yes, she would work"—that I no longer needed her. This was probably four weeks after she said my mother fell out of bed, and she never ever had complained about hurting her back or anything before. But after I fired her, workmen's compensation sent me this letter that she'd hurt her back taking care of my mother, and I was responsible for paying into workmen's comp.

But I didn't pay into workmen's comp because I felt she was just working on her own. I didn't take taxes out of the paycheck. I'm familiar with workmen's compensation because I do my husband's workmen's comp and payroll. But I just felt she was working on her own and should have her own. She was independent, and they'd never mentioned it to me. If this is the story, then when they take these jobs, they should tell the people they're working for, "You have to carry workmen's comp on me. This is the law." And I would have gotten it. So the charge is I didn't pay into workmen's comp.

Of course, Helen said she was working for me, but she wasn't working for me. She was getting paid from my father's checkbook, and working at my father's house. She really worked for my father. That's the way I feel. But regardless, I still think if they're going to have the law, the people should be responsible for telling whoever they're working for: "The law is that you have to carry workmen's comp on me." And how would I have known this? So I showed up for the hearing and she didn't show up. And they told my attorney they had a note there that Helen didn't show up because she had to go for a test for cancer. So they said they'd schedule it again. They never scheduled it again. The next thing I got in the mail was a note that they had to decide who the aides were working for—my father or me. Of course, I've got an attorney.

What I want them to tell me is that if the nurse's aides know— and this one certainly does because it's the third case I know of where she collected workmen's comp (she worked at two nursing homes where she collected workmen's comp on both nursing homes)—if this is their law, it's also the aide's responsibility to tell the people that they are working for so that they will know. If this lady told me, "You have to have workmen's comp on me" and I didn't get it, then I'm responsible. I had no idea that someone . . . I considered her someone in her own business. She has a business of her own, you know?

NEGLECT

And then when I had them at home: It was Easter, it was Holy Saturday, and I told the day nurse's aide, "I'm not working tomorrow [at the library], you just stay home and enjoy your family, and I'll come down here." Well, then I left my parents alone for maybe fifteen minutes and my mother fell. With Parkinson's you can fall straight back, lose your balance. And she hit her head on the register in the kitchen. And of course, there was a lot of blood. And I had told my father, "If anything happens, call me on the telephone." I live three minutes from their house. Noooo. It was a nice day, sunny, there were kids playing ball on the street. He has to go on the front porch and yell for help. They came in and picked my mother up, and they called me. One of the neighbors. So I did take her to Emergency—she didn't even need stitches. Then I brought them here. But someone called Human Services and reported that I was not taking care of my parents because my mother fell! I was neglecting them and leaving them alone! I told them [the Human Services investigators], "There's a nurse's aide there. Go and check if you want to." The nurses kept a log, the nurse's aides. And they did go. But then shortly after that, they ended up in the hospital and in the nursing home. So I don't know what they ever did in terms of clearing my name down there. And I don't care.

Whoever reported me to Human Services did not know me, did not know all I went through to keep them home. It had to be a neighbor. There are some new, young people across the street. The old neighbors next door that have lived there for forty-five years would never have called. It has to be the ones that don't know me. They had no idea, and then Human Services just steps in, like, "My God, you're letting these two old people alone in this house starve to death." They called me on the phone to say I was reported for neglecting my parents. Aaagh. Right. If he [the investigator] came in person . . . I don't like speaking to people on the phone. I don't even know who I'm talking to.

And so Human Services was acting like I was not taking care of my parents when I was killing myself to take care of them. The doctor was begging me to put my mother in a nursing home. And this doctor was a very caring doctor. He spent a lot of time with me, and he was being honest. He really was, I could tell he was being honest. Now workmen's comp—I've had it. Plus my mother's Social Security check was stolen, and the thief is happy, and I have nothing but problems and paper-work and more paperwork.

HUSBAND'S FAMILY

My husband comes from a family of ten children. I'm an only child. He has six sisters, and my mother-in-law is just the most wonderful person you would ever want to meet. Four sisters live there, near her [a three-hour drive from the Pfeiffer home]. She is a joy to be with. When my father-in-law passed away, my mother-in-law was perfectly fine, but her daughters [who lived in the home-town] just didn't want her to be alone. They don't even have to take care of her. If you stay with my mother-in-law for a weekend, you don't have to get up at night with her. She's perfectly fine. She's not a fussy person. She never complains about a thing. She's just so nice.

The only thing is that after two years they got tired of not wanting her to be alone. Now, they're resentful. They insist, now, that their brothers go down and take care of her. There's three boys and a girl out of town. They sent a letter stating exactly what weekends each was to go. And they also said, "If you cannot make this weekend, don't call us. Trade with someone. We don't want to hear it." Then there is one other sister who is not helping them but lives back there. She got a letter, too. But she works full-time. All the people who got letters work full-time jobs. Four sent the letter to five. The four sisters back in New York State don't work.

Who they complain about the most is their brother Bobby. Bobby has Down's syndrome. They're just... every minute of the day, they want to know what he's doing, what he's into. "Don't let him touch this. Don't let him touch that." I said, "It's his house. He lives here. We don't live here! We're visiting!" Bobby'd run the sweeper all the time. They'd say he wore the sweeper out sweeping the rugs. So now they keep that locked up. They've caused half of their own problems, really. Because they would just go there to visit and they never stayed there. We'd go and spend weekends. For thirty-five years I've been going there, spending weekends. Bobby hasn't changed one bit. Bobby was always like that.

Well, they keep telling my husband they have to do something with Bobby. They want to put Bobby in a home now. And we all said, "You cannot do that while Mother is living. She didn't live eighty-six years to see this." She knows that it's going to be done when she dies. She knows that. She's very reasonable. She says, "You'll have to deal with that when I'm not here." They did tell my husband they want to do it now. But we said no. I think Bobby might do well in a halfway house where they will treat him like a person. I think he would do better than at home with someone constantly harassing him all day long. I think that's probably what they're looking into. Taking care of Bobby gave her a purpose. They took care of each other, really. Company for each other. To her, Bobby's company was a blessing.

My husband's sisters have created their own problems going down there, because they are meticulous housekeepers. All of them. My mother-in-law always had a nice home, but she's not meticulous. Now Bobby has to listen to everything they say. They are the boss. "Don't touch this! Don't do that! What's he doing? What's he doing in the kitchen?" Of course, then he doesn't listen. But see, they're driving themselves crazy with this being clean. They don't have a cup in the sink, every dish washed immediately. See, I'm not like that so it doesn't bother me. They would drive me crazy. But I've always liked them and I've always gotten along with them, and now I'm mad at all of them. I'm not telling them I'm mad at them, but I am. They know I'm mad. I'm not having a knockdown battle with them, but they know that I'm not happy. There's no sense in having this big argument. But the next time I go back there, if I see one of them I'll just tell 'em that no way does my husband deserve this letter, because he offered to help! We went back New Year's Eve so they could all go out!

I don't really want to be mad. I'll just tell them what I feel. Oh, it's all gonna come out. We have a big family wedding coming up [laughs]. Denis told them he wasn't happy. Of course, they're at the point they don't care if we never talk to them, just so we go back and take care of my mother-in-law. Well, each one of them spends two nights. But my sister-in-law Peggy lives close enough that she'll stay there at night. She'll come, like nine o'clock at night, stay all night, give her mother her insulin shot in the morning and go home. They each spend only two nights at a time. And then one of them takes care of Medicare, one of them takes care of the prescriptions, one of them takes their mother to the hospital. I think I was angry about it because I had to deal with everything myself. And there's so many of them. What are they complaining about? I had it all to do! What if they each had it all to do? And while we're doing all this here, they expect Denis—it's his mother—but we did go back when we could. I feel they should have called. I didn't like getting the letter. I think they should have called and talked to my husband, Denis. He's understanding. And he does understand.

We would go and stay weekends, when we could go. We go all the time, except that my father passed away in February. We were there New Year's Eve, and that weekend. Then we didn't go in the month of January, because my father was really bad. And he passed away February 2, and I just had too much to do. I have a whole house of [my parents'] furniture here to take care of, and their belongings. And now all this Social Security stuff from my father's death, and transferring it to my mother. Someone stole her Social Security check, I had to deal with that. I had to go to Social Security, I had to go to the bank. Had to prove that no way, could that be her signature. I thought it was all over, and now I have more papers to fill out. And the thief has spent the money a long time ago, and is happy and with no problems.

I wrote my mother-in-law a letter at Easter and I said, "Starting in June, I will not work on Saturday, so we will be coming back." And his sisters, I'm sure they read the letter. And I just don't think we should have gotten this typewritten subpoena. I've always been really good to my mother-in-law, and always went back to help. And my husband did, and I don't think he deserved it. I think his sisters should have called and said, "We really can't stand this, and something has to be done, and we're getting this letter together, and you're going to get it." I don't think we should have got it in the mail without a phone call. He was angry. They don't care if he's angry, just so he goes. They were all angry. Everyone who got the letter was a little angry.

That's another thing, they could have invited us down to talk about it. But they didn't. My father-in-law had a stroke. We of course went back. He was in hospital for probably a month. The day he died . . . the next day they were going to put him in a nursing home. They never called back to tell us. We'd never have known until it was done. So they didn't make us a part of that, did they? They didn't feel we should know that.

FINAL THOUGHTS

You just have to do some things. You have to go the limit. Probably, I would say if you have a good doctor that you really like—

like I had one, Dr. Anthony, and I knew he was reasonable—I probably should have listened to him more. I know I did everything that I could. But I know that Parkinson's cure is just that one drug. I just felt that there was hope. I still think when I go to the nursing home every day [to visit my mother] that if I could just find that one pill, if you can just find that one drug—if they would find that one miracle pill—my mother would be fine. It's not that she has a bad heart, it's that one drug. And it's not there. If you have Parkinson's and you're institutionalized, you're going to get one hundred times worse.

My mother is disoriented and confused, so I go there every day. Every day, every day there are people at the nursing home who I look at and think, "They could be home! They could be home living with someone!" My mother has a very good friend across the hall from her that she doesn't know [recognize] anymore, and that very good friend is perfectly fine. She can't cook, her hands have arthritis. Her mind is perfectly fine, and she can walk. And she likes it there. She says she won't be a burden on her children. And she's happy. They take her home every now and then, and she's perfectly happy. But the ones who are fine, they have a card club, they play cards, they socialize. They also take them out to the malls and things. And I think if only my mother could just be a little better, she has a friend across the hall. A woman she's known for years.

I'm still looking for that miracle drug. I have seen my mother be totally disoriented and confused, but give her a new Parkinson's drug and the next day she is totally normal. And it happened so many times that I kept looking for it to happen again. But it's not going to happen. There's a point where the Parkinson's just takes over. There's also a point where, if you're on the Parkinson's drug, that the medication will cause the same symptoms as the disease. We've tried every Parkinson's drug that has been out. All of them. One at a time, but when that no longer worked, we would switch. And when that one no longer worked, we would switch. The newest one . . . I could hardly wait for the new one to come out that they had in Canada [in 1990]. I offered to go to Canada to get it. And when it finally got here and we took it, it didn't work at all. It only made it worse. I badgered Dr. Anthony to death for it. Of course, he always said, "If I get Parkinson's, Ruth, I want you to take care of me."

I don't really want to be that disabled and cause all this hardship.

And I hope medical science doesn't keep me alive unless my life is worth something. Of course, medical science isn't keeping my mother alive, because Parkinson's medicine doesn't, you know, really keep you live. Medical science kept my father alive. He had leukemia, and if it wasn't for chemo, he would never have lasted. But then he did do well, and he never complained until he got real bad. And when he got really bad, he wouldn't accept the fact that he was bad. Even in the nursing home, they didn't tell him what to do. He told them. Medical science keeps us around so long that you have old people taking care of old people. And the old people taking care of the old people want to live their life a little bit because they might become disabled, and they get resentful because they think they don't have too many more years. And that's the way it is.

I told my daughter exactly what to do when I'm an old woman, but Hannah will have a very hard time doing what I say. "Don't put up with it," I said. "Don't keep me home. Put me in a nursing home. Just be sure I get good care." You know, check, but don't give up your life. I think when they're sitting in their own home and saying, "Take me home," it's time to give up because they don't even know they are at home! I have my name in already for a nursing home. I would understand, I wouldn't want Hannah giving up her life to take care of me. Or Cheryl. No, no, no one should do this. It's just too hard. I'm not so sure I should have gone even this far, no one should do it. You need care, and one person can't do it all. It's one thing . . . like my mother-in-law, she's fine. Her mind's fine. She needs an insulin shot, but that's no big deal. She sleeps all night. She's no problem. See, but if you're confused, if you have dementia, if you don't know where you are, it will help to keep you in your surroundings, but the other person just isn't going to make it that's taking care of you. Sometimes you get so bad that even the aides can't take care of you. It got to Judy, who took care of her for a year. It just got to her, she was up every ten minutes all night long.

I can't say I gave up that much. But if the person is totally disoriented and confused, then I think they would be the same [in a nursing home], as long as they get good care. If you're not disoriented, as long as the care giver doesn't have to be under constant stress, as long as you can be reasonable enough to be left alone, like my mother-in-law, then it's okay. Hannah understands it, but she'd have a very hard time doing what I've asked her to do. Hannah would have a very hard time selling this house. Cheryl probably wouldn't. But Hannah will also go the lengths I went, and Cheryl will give her a hard time [laughs]. So Cheryl can be in charge of what happens to me.

If I had to do it over again? I'd probably do the same thing [laughs].

Postscript

Perhaps nothing is more poignant than the hope and belief that a drug exists or will be developed that can reverse or retard, if not cure, a debilitating disease affecting both mind and body. Nor is this such an unreasonable hope. In the postwar era almost every class of disease has received the boon of modern technologies. The advances of the last forty years in understanding the brain's chemistry, the body's functioning, and the nature of viruses has been accompanied by a series of virtually miraculous vaccinations, procedures, and treatments. Out of this new knowledge has emerged a powerful pharmacology which sometimes seems capable of miracles, especially for those who remember polio epidemics, rampant tuberculosis, and the days before even minimally effective tranquilizers were available.

Parkinsonism was the first disease causing degeneration of the central nervous system to be treated by drugs that replace deficient neurotransmitters, the chemicals that facilitate electrical transmission between nerve cells. For parkinsonion patients, L-dopa, or levodopa, which was introduced in the 1960s, seemed indeed to be a miracle drug, and since then a slew of refinements have come to market. Even better, new technologies and new drugs have resulted from a host of insights into a variety of diseases, including Parkinson's, and each technique or drug holds the promise of a potential cure. Everyone hopes, but, as Mrs. Pfeiffer notes so sadly, miracle drugs and miraculous cures have remained just beyond her and her mother's reach. None worked for long and some did not work at all.

The appropriate medication at the correct dosage can remarkably transform—"awaken," in the language of Oliver Sacks—a previously disoriented and demented patient suffering from Parkinson's. It is this that is perhaps most trying for Mrs. Pfeiffer, who lives in hope that the next drug will work and in fear that if it does, the results again will be impermanent. Even in more general cases of broad impairment, this sense of hope and frustration with the limits of contemporary medicine is familiar to anyone who has cared for another through a serious illness. Virtually all care givers of progressively fragile elders suffering from cognitive disorder know the daily reversals, the feeling that if only a minute could be captured (or the complex of circumstances that caused it), that their charge would be, somehow, magically returned.

The discussion of institutionalizing Mrs. Pfeiffer's brother-in-law in many ways parallels the decisions and dilemmas regarding her own parents. In a later conversation, Mr. Pfeiffer told me that this middle-aged man could speak, although not clearly, and that while he needed help, it was clear to Denis that his sisters' plans were for their convenience and not necessarily in their disabled brother's best interests. Mr. Pfeiffer also agreed with his wife that Bobby and his mother afforded each other companionship and mutual assistance long after the other children had moved away. The degree to which institutionalization is often not a medical necessity but rather a matter of familial convenience is underlined in this story, both by the physician's encouraging Mrs. Pfeiffer to commit her mother before other options had been explored, and by her sisters-in-laws' desire to solve the problem of their brother's future without undue inconvenience to themselves.

4

The Toronto Boy

Bill Lypchuk has spent the last twenty years as a parental care giver. Now in his early forties, Bill Lypchuk first took charge during his mother's long illness and eventual hospitalization in the 1970s. Currently, Mr. Lypchuk is the primary care giver for his father who, while living alone in the old family house, is under his son's daily supervision. His narrative jumps back and forth between these two very different levels of caring and maintenance, the extensive medical demands of his mother's illness and the less clinically critical but still personally taxing necessities of his father's case.

I'm really going to miss my Dad when he goes. Sure, sure I will. Probably much more so than my mum, although I always thought I was closer to my mum than my dad. I've gone through so much with him, especially in terms of looking after her. But you see, with my mum, the concern was... I was one of those kids who was always afraid of his parents dying. When my mum died a few years ago, even though you're now an adult, I always thought it was going to traumatize me. And I grieved, and so on and so forth. But I guess I was always intimidated by the whole funereal process, of seeing someone who was vital to you now so immobile. Dead. But what I found was that the whole thing was not as difficult or traumatizing as I thought. In part, I think, the fact is, my mother died in bits and pieces over the years. So she was already dead as a personality long, long before that. That won't be the case with my dad, right now.

And he has had a couple of seizures; it is always a possibility that it could happen very quickly. There are one or two of these incidents which have happened, you know? Yes, I will miss my dad, I will miss my dad. In fact, I sort of have to address my life on the other side of my dad.

I keep a close eye on him. He's well enough that he can sort of . . . he does not require nursing. He can sort of put together his own sandwich type of a thing and he's not so ill that he needs anything approximating nursing care. He still has his own money, writes his own checks. He still pays his utilities and so forth. He has more than enough [awareness] with him to be able to do that. He watches the hockey games, the baseball games. He has never really watched any kind of dramatic TV shows. I can never remember him watching a drama on TV, ever, in all the thirty-eight-some years that we've been here. And he was never really that much into hockey. But now that he doesn't get out as much, that is his prime social activity, to watch hockey in the winter and baseball in the summer.

It's sort of—being around—it's creating more of what I call an "ambiance of living," of life going on as opposed to, to isolation. It is taking him to the doctors when he has to be taken to the doctors. It is trying to get him out at least once a week to the grocery store because he can still sort of do a little shopping. It's taking him out to my brother's house once a week or once every two weeks, taking him out for Christmas. Dropping in, being around. It's what I call "creating an ambiance of living" so that you're not dead, you're not isolated. There is some kind of a life although it is limited because his interests, his will is in some ways small. But if it weren't for my doing what I do, it would probably be smaller still.

Until just a couple of years ago, my father was quite robust. Even when he was in his early eighties he would periodically sort of—to my great lament—he'd be up on the roof trying to look at things that were wrong with the roof. He shouldn't have been on the roof when he was in his eighties. But periodically he would go up there and then you'd start figuratively yelling and screaming, "What are you doing up on the roof?" But there was kind of no stopping him. He was always proud of his vitality. Now he's gone to the other extreme as he sort of began to feel the aches and pains and things going apart. It's kind of funny, because he was always quite boastful about his vitality and how robust he was for his age, and how strong he was and how vital he was. Now, I'd say 85 to 90 percent of his conversation revolves around his various ailments.

He talks about dying. He talks about death a lot: "Oh, I'm going to die." Or, "Oh, I've got maybe another year or so." But never about killing himself because he's basically, by comparison, in pretty good health. He complains about ills, and he has them, but to look at him many days . . . although there are now occasional days when he does not look well, but for the most part and most of the time he looks like a very vital eighty-nine-year-old. It does become a little irritating sometimes. Do I ever feel like telling him, "Stop your bitching?" Oh yeah, oh yeah. You say, "Don't talk about dying all the time," because that's all he wants to talk about. I try to tell him, but when you're talking old-world ethnicity, it's not like talking to an equal where you can talk about a relationship and hash it all out, because those are terms with which he has no familiarity. Like, you cannot say, "Father, you are obsessed with negativity."

He is fundamentally a very negative person, but that's not a context in which he would relate—"What's this negative stuff you're talking about?" But, in fact, it's always "no, no, no" and always the bad side of things and always, "Oh, the prices of houses are going down." If he sees anything in the newspaper, on the news, there's a natural gravitation to the negative. But you try and talk to him about that, it's not something he will relate to or understand. He also talks an awful lot about death and dying and his immanent death. Meanwhile, all these people are popping off around him and he's still, you know, carrying on, you know? And yet, somehow, there's no real appreciation, if appreciation is the word, that he's in much better health than the majority of people his age and that in fact the majority of people around him are less well, and in some cases younger men are dying. Some of my brothers' friends are dying, and here my father's outlived them all!

On balance, that is his primary activity now, complaining about his ailments. To me it's kind of strange, but the bitching is like a joy. It is his life, kind of thing. There is not a depression about it. In terms of being around, it's sort of like this game, you just don't take it seriously. You know, just know, that's okay. He's bitching. He's been bitching like this for three, four, five years now. But is it debilitating? It's annoying, a little bit. But is it debilitating or particularly depressing? It is not. It's the other side of the coin of his boastfulness of before. But now, instead of boasting about his vitality, he bitches about his ills. So you just sort of take it with a grain of salt because for the most part my father's life is not a bad lot.

That's why you cut through, look for what's really, really . . . anything that really might be off. That's part of my job, now. To sort through when he complains, to differentiate real ills and real complaints from the bitching. Part of my task right now is actually to sort through what is real and what is kind of preoccupation because that is now his life. His life is his ailments, in many ways. So there is, I think, a deterioration of the eyesight. My brother, who is an ophthalmologist, says there is a cataract there. Um, but he can still sort of watch the baseball game on TV, kind of thing. But I do believe there is a deterioration of the eyesight. I don't think that's completely imagined. He's been for many years complaining of a kind of, like a dizziness. So I took him to the doctors for CAT scans and all like that and there doesn't appear to be anything there. He had an infected foot, which I took [him] to a plastic surgeon [for].

There is a certain kind of psychology I have to use with him—whether it works or not, I don't know. At a certain point you do develop techniques that might work—or that might not. For instance, next Tuesday I've got to take him to the outpatient [clinic] for an ingrown toenail because it is quite infected. The doctor wanted him to soak the foot before he came. There are some things you've got to do. So here I had to get a pan. And you've got to put it there, and if you go away he'll complain and he'll bitch about it—which he has done—but he'll do it. But if I stay beside him the whole time, he'll balk. There is a psychology, and especially dealing with my dad. I suppose many old people have their own personalities and you've got to deal with their particular idiosyncrasies.

MOTHER'S ILLNESS

There has always been a need to do some psychological maneuvering of some sort or another, because he'd had his opinions. For instance, my mother was in the chronic care hospital for many, many years, probably five, six, seven years. I had her into The Provincial, a very good [extended care] hospital. They really, really looked after my mother well, and given my mother's state, that was at least some comfort. When you hear some of these horror stories I can say, without equivocation, that she got superb care. But it cost, and the longer she stayed there—inflation—it grew. While he's in many ways a generous man to me and my brothers, another side of my dad has always been very frugal, an old world type of frugality. It therefore required a certain amount of duplicity on my part for him not to know that we were in fact paying for my mother's stay in the hospital.

I had to structure it in different ways. Because I had sort of control to some extent of the family assets—like rentals from houses and so on and so forth—I'd channel part of that toward my mother's care and also arrange it with my brothers, who had a more regular income than I did; I got money from them, type of thing, so we were able to keep it together. But even to this day my dad does not know that we were paying for my mother's upkeep there. And the concern there, especially in the early stages—in the later stages when his own care began to fail somewhat he much more appreciated the care that my mother got there—but in the early stages I had this fear that had he known how much I was actually paying, he would have just carted her back home and tried to look after her himself to save money.

She had a very, very extended degenerative period, I'd say twenty years. She took her illness with such gentility. She took it all and even while she was going downhill, and still had her faculties, she was always cheerful and smiling. She just took it with such great nobility that I admire her in hindsight and admired her at the time. Exactly what she had, I don't know. It started with a bad back and degenerated over twenty years so that first she had the cane, then you go to the walker, then the wheelchair, then there was a bedridden kind of existence. Then into the hospital, and then her mind started to go. It was a very long, slow kind of degeneration on her part so that by the end there was nothing of her mind left and, really, there wasn't for the last several years of her life. What exactly the name for it is, I don't know.

The first couple of indications of things going awry are just such a shock. I think the very, very first tweak with my mother was, she was at a hospital in Hamilton, and we were talking, talking, talking normally. She made reference to her [deceased] mother having just been there. That first sort of twinge of something not being all there is always such a shock. Then there was something about I was going to go off to war. The radio was on and there was something on about a war. Then she would be lucid. Then in bits and pieces it went. The first couple of incidents were shocking, and somewhat traumatic and difficult. And every little step down was always a bit of a shock, a bit of a shock, another stage down, another stage down. At a certain point, there was, I suppose, a kind of acceptance which kicks in. You know where you're going and this is just another stage of it all.

This was still my mother who was sick. This was *always* my mother. In many ways, while my mother's slow demise was a sad thing for her, a sad thing to watch, in some ways it was a godsend to my father. I'm not sure, but if she had died while she was still vital and while he still had some relationship with her, I think he would have been totally devastated to the extent that he would have had trouble tolerating it. I saw how he was when she was just sort of sick. He would not have taken it well. But since she died in bits and pieces over years she was, even for him, effectively dead even before she died. Consequently, when she did actually die, she'd died already in bits and pieces and there was not the trauma I knew there would have been if she'd been still vital.

In some ways, when he was still vital he was very, very devoted. He looked after her as well as he could. He fed her, he looked after her in the traditional sense one envisions in an ideal situation: a spouse doing for his mate. He looked after her well. Not necessarily well, but with a great deal of loyalty. Reasonably well. Hygiene was never his strong point because he comes from an old world kind of . . . you cut a rag and that suffices as a bandage. That's the kind of thinking that prevailed with him. But as she got worse. . . .

It all happened in increments, right? It reached the point where she had to go into hospital and we made it so that while there was still some brain faculty left, she would be coming home on weekends. He would look after her on weekends and she'd go back into the hospital for the week. That meant they could keep her together, clean her up type of thing. She'd come home for the weekend and that suited my dad fine. The care was not as good at home, but it was only for a couple of days. And all that had to be arranged, too, with a certain amount of duplicity, with arranging for the ambulance and the expense. So it went through stages varying with the degree of my mother's illness.

The later stages of my involvement in looking after her was primarily facilitating my father's access to her. His requirement for access to her also degenerated as she got sicker and sicker and became less of a personality, even for him. In the initial stages of his visiting her he would take the bus and he would make a special point of, you know, feeding her supper and so on and so forth. Toward the end he himself did not feel well enough and relegated the feeding to the nurses. In the end, we would just visit for five minutes. The act of caring for my mother was really with the hospital, for the latter part of her life, as opposed to myself or my father.

DRUG ABUSE

There was a period where it was just getting very, very, very difficult. The nursing home became a necessity because caring for her just became more and more difficult and it was sort of made more so by my dad's own eccentricities, because of the pills that he was taking. There was a period while my Mom was still sick that there was an incident. That was probably the worst period. When my mother still had some vitality but was getting worse, my father himself . . . his behavior was somewhat bizarre. There was a moodiness, just a depression, just a tremendous negativity. And, increasingly, there were some symptoms that made you think that he himself was going senile. There was specific incidents. There was a time when I came home and my father was just all doped out. I didn't know what it was but he was all doped out and I found a whole slew of pills strewn all over the floor. I'm not sure if that was the first time I suspected that pills were a problem. But he was just doped out, and he must have been doped out for a couple of days. Meanwhile, this was on a weekend when he was supposed to be looking after my mother.

He was taking some stuff on his own. The pills were in some ways an extension of his conceit that, "I can look after myself." So he would find these old pills, so he was looking after himself. And he wasn't looking after himself, but there was this kind of old-world arrogance kind of thing, which has now gone and been replaced by this other facet. Bitching. There was one pill he took that really was a knockout job. Doped him up entirely. And in that doped-up state, the eccentricities were accentuated. That's the thing, there were all these eccentricities that you attributed to the brain going, type of thing. In fact, of course, in hindsight, it was the drugs, the pills he was taking.

There was an incident whereby he was again really out of it. And so I thought [before knowing about the pills] that well, he's really gone. And I remember very, very vividly he was barely moving and sitting at a chair and trying to eat soup or something like that. And he just all of a sudden stopped. He had the spoon halfway up to his mouth and he just stopped in midmovement, type of thing. He's had a couple of seizures, too.

So there was something that was off, and you had to determine that something had to be done. He was probably in his eighties by then. I think I talked to my brothers, but I was the one who was there. My brothers weren't really around. I knew something was wrong and called my brother and he said, "We've got to get him to a hospital." I think he was going to come a little later, and I was walking by my father's bedroom door, and I looked in, and he had these burns all over his body.

What it was, as I was able to piece it all together in hindsight, as part of his frugality, to save money, he somehow found this old charcoal lighter type of thing, a heating element. You know, it's a raw element? My father is modestly wealthy and he didn't have to live the way he was living. It's just save, save, save: "Don't spend money." So he sort of plugged it into the kitchen and just sort of had it sitting there, bare, to heat up the house! Meanwhile, he's semi-doped-up anyway because of the pills. And what he told me subsequently happened is that his shirt was kind of hanging loose, hits the element, catches fire. And he burned himself. So he somehow managed to put it out. He maintained second-probably third-degree burns and then maintained that silence about what happened for two, three days until I saw the burns.

That was the incident that in fact got him into the hospital, to have the burns attended to. And it was, like, after two or three days in the hospital, it was like night and day. There was this vital man there again. Clear-eyed, good spirits, good humor kind of thing. And I thought, "Well, you see. He just needs to be looked after," because it was like night and day. These were kind of old prescriptions and he arranged it for himself. It was unbeknownst to anybody—at least to me—that my father was doing what he was doing. He was, in effect, psychologically addicted to these things.

CURRENT RELATIONS

What I've related to you is history. Once my mother passed away [two years ago], there was this gradual debilitation for him. Once my mother died, there was this gradual liberty which set in [for me] because one area of concern was eliminated. So these stories I've related about my father were primarily of a somewhat different epoch. And his state now—given the fact that he complains of aches and pains and his joy in life is talking about aches and pains—but he is not now fundamentally drugged up. And when he's feeling good, he talks. But he does not require total supervision. It's not like I have to make him breakfast, make him lunch, make him supper, seven days a week. You make something, you bring it over. If I'm there and I make a sandwich and say, "You want a sandwich?" I make him a sandwich. But he basically eats what he wants.

I'm there an awful lot. I'm a mile away. Yeah, I'm living with him but I'm living apart. I find that it's not difficult being with him, but it's nice having a refuge. It's not too bad a situation. I'm there a lot, because I don't mind it and it's okay and I can sort of keep an eye on him. But I also have my own place, and if I need some room, I'm a mile away. So I'll spend time there. If it gets a little too much, I just pop off to my place, cool off as necessary. And he's okay. And that's how I handle it.

Our family is fortunate. We're modestly wealthy. We're not rich by any means. But we're not poor. For most of my life, there's always been enough money around. It's not in our family been a major, major cause of trouble—although it has a potential to be— but during the years we're talking about my father was reasonably well off and retired. My father made some investments and he's got about four of these bungalows. I do the taxes. I collect the rents. My father is probably a millionaire, although he certainly doesn't live like one. Certainly a million dollars is not what it once was. It doesn't go as far as it used to. But my father, not withstanding, is a millionaire, and that's something most people of retirement age cannot say.

A concern I have right now—I've not fully addressed it—is I have to build this house in [the suburb of] Bolton. And that will be done because it is imperative that I do it in terms of my total plan—where your finances are going to come from, where you live, kind of thing. But it will also be, for at least a little while, my home. That's where I'll officially live. Bolton is forty minutes away from where my dad lives, compared to five minutes from where I live now. You see it is, in fact, an issue because the house I'm staying in I may have to sell, and while the new place is being built, I may have to be under a permanent roof for six months or a year with my dad. Without a refuge—that might be difficult, and it is a concern. I have some qualms about not having a refuge, even if it's just for six months, or like that. And I also have qualms, even when I have the new place, in terms of keeping the eye that I do keep on him when my refuge is now going to be forty minutes away as opposed to five minutes away.

BROTHERS

How much are they involved? The day-to-day stuff, really not much at all. The oldest brother's a lawyer, he calls my dad most every morning around eight o'clock, and he'll talk for three, four, five minutes. And he's the brother, when I take my father out on an excursion, I'll take him to that brother's for a Sunday dinner, which we do on an average once every two to three weeks. Occasionally he comes, but mostly he calls and we visit there. My other brother doesn't call as often, but he will call for very, very short telephone conversations of a minute, two minutes. He will make a point of occasionally coming by and visiting for an hour or so once every two or three weeks. He lives in Hamilton [about 45 miles away].

At this point, both my brothers are fairly well off. They're on their own treadmills. One brother is an ophthalmologist, makes and spends a lot of money. My other brother is a lawyer—doesn't like law—but has a fairly strong asset base. The cash is there, so our family has been very fortunate, for the most part, that way. There is affection for my father, but in terms of my mother, trotting my mother between hospitals and looking after all the things that had to be done . . . I'm always the one who has done that. They sort of acknowledge it, but it's not really required and the fact is there is a bit of a trade-off. For instance, I had my own condo and I sold it, but I'm living in this place that is a family asset, so there is a barter kind of thing, financially. There is an unspoken trade-off kind of thing. They know that I do it. I get some things back. But I would be doing it notwithstanding. That's not the reason [I do it]. It's one of those situations where everything is more or less on an even keel, nobody is too unhappy, nobody rocks the boat. Nobody's ranting and raving.

Some people can take emotional duress, the duress involved in whatever it is I've done. My brothers, I think, would not handle it well. My brother is a lawyer, he can be kind of adversarial, kind of tough. Put into an emotional strain, I think he would personally, like if his wife would get sick . . . there are people who you think on the surface are rock, but anything that is difficult, they probably cannot handle well. My brothers wouldn't handle it well. They have to, in a sense, emotionally distance themselves. They could not have really handled these things particularly well, I believe.

Exactly what they would do if I'm not around, is a question mark. My lawyer brother has always been willing to take my father in, as long as he had a separate space. A separate space is absolutely vital. He's building an extension at his house and he has, like, an apartment downstairs in that extension. If my father wanted to stay there, he could. There would be no difficulty as long as there was a separation kind of thing, room to breathe type of thing. I don't think my other brother could swallow that at all.

You know what else I also realized, about six months ago, while I've been contemplating building this house in Bolton? Moving my dad might be fine in theory, but he's been in that house for thirty-three years. Practical reality is that even though my other brothers are in Burlington and Hamilton, the right place to be for him is here, at his own home. In terms of geography, he's been in that place an awful long time. The reality is it would be very difficult for him to move. That is where I see constraint, given I have this place in Bolton, and that has not been fully addressed. And he's quite protective, I suppose, my dad, of his home. There were stages, like when he was in his pill stage, there were arrangements at various points made for people to come in and, you know, clean up the house, do the dishes. He really was quite intolerant of that. Kicked them out, kind of thing.

ON CARE GIVING

It has been a major part of my life. But overall, I would say I've had a very checkered kind of a life period and it's been simply one facet of it. I had a brief career as a film maker. That's what my schooling was. It was moving along just swimmingly for a while. Then I went to get my M.B.A., so that was kind of a quasi career, going back to school after many years away. Then there was a period where I operated as a land developer up in Timmins, Ontario, for the better part of a year or two. In the last little while I've sort of been building houses, and now I'm anticipating building one or two kind of monster homes and hopefully will have enough to live comfortably from that. So whenever people ask me what I do, I always say I've had a checkered career, and on a personal level the kind of incidents we're talking about here are only one facet of a checkered background.

But I've never really, really felt—except for brief periods of crisis— that it's been an impediment to my living my life more or less the way that I have wanted to. The only time I ever really, actually felt that at all was, I suppose, in the year after my mother died. It will now be two years ago on September tenth that she died. In the year after, and given my father's health and that there was nobody around, kind of thing, I felt for the first time ever, to my recollection, that impedance about being able to get away. And a certain amount of, "My brothers are going away, going away, dashing off here, dashing off there." And I sort of felt a little less able to do that because of my responsibilities as being the one that was sort of still living in Toronto while they were living in Burlington and Hamilton. Or going away weekends. But then last year at about this time, almost a year ago, I went away for two weeks to the East Coast and just tried to make a point with my brother that he call every day and I would call every couple of days. And he (Father) got along okay, he got along okay. And since then, I have felt much, much less reservations about going away if I wanted to or about his capacity for maintaining himself for a while.

Have I thought a lot about this role? It's not been a preoccupation of my thoughts. For the most part, most of the thinking involved has been of a functional nature: What's got to be done? How do I do it? The greatest part has been to sort of concoct the duplicities that have been sometimes necessary to keep things on an even keel. They extend to even now. My father takes this one pill that was originally prescribed to him, it is an antidepressant. It probably isn't really necessary, but there was a period when we thought that maybe it might be necessary. But he takes it even now. He believes, because I had to tell him [to get him to take it] that it was a sleeping pill and there was one time that he fell asleep really well from this. Because he's always said he never really slept well. That couple of times when it helped him to sleep well, he believed it was, and I sort of told him it was a sleeping pill. He believes to this day that it is a sleeping pill. And there are occasions now when he'll say, "I can't sleep because we ran out of my sleeping pills," when that's not what it was at all.

Do I worry about when my father is doing to die? Yes and no. I've thought about it a little. It's more of a concern with how it relates to my relationships with women. I was involved in a fashion in a situation in which I coasted for a long time. And it ended. I coasted a long time in that thing, so it took me a couple of years to recover, and it's really only been since the latter part of last year [note: a year after his mother's death] that I started dating again, getting back to the whole thing.

I'm probably more socially active than just about anybody I know. As a for instance, tomorrow I'm going out with one friend to *Fiddler on the Roof*. Friday I'm going to Ottawa for white-water rafting. Next Tuesday I'm going out driving about. There's another lady I've got to call tonight to see a club I read about called The Sketch Pad, sort of like Second City. This past Saturday I went to a jazz club called The Bermuda Onion to see a singer called Rainey Lee. I have a very, very active social life. More so than just about anybody I know, as I said. The previous week a friend came in from Owen Sound, he's an Ottawa fan, we went to an Argos game. I have a lot of friends. I cultivate friends. Most of the times if I'm feeling blue or lonely or whatever, the list of friends to call is long. If I go to things, like in the winter I went to an interior decorating course— which wasn't that great—I sat down next to a lady and we had an instant rapport. But I made a point of turning that into a friendship. And most of my friendships will go on for years.

There are perhaps a half a dozen I could have relationships with, right now, because basically I'm a pretty nice guy. Do I ever take women over to see my dad? No, in part because there's nobody, really. My problem right now is that I have found, dating women that I have an affinity with, as I put it, they haven't given me a buzz. The one who has given me a buzz . . . something is off there. There was only one, since I've started dating again, that I could have run with. But I'm working on that. So yes, it is a concern but if it ever came down to having a nice lady companion, I don't think it would ever be a problem. But yes, I have thought about it, I have thought about it because I probably still have to consider if I want a family. In part, what I have done—not because of this but simply because I have the time now—I've initiated the process whereby I'm going to become a Big Brother. That was something that when my mother was alive was not a possibility. It was never stress, but required a lot of time. There just would not have been enough time to be a Big Brother then. The whole situation now is one where I said, "Hey, I can do this."

FAMILY HISTORIES

I've cared for my parents very much. Yeah, I've probably looked after them more than is the norm. But do I feel any particular regret about it or have I felt constrained by it? "Constrained" is too strong a word. You've looked after your parents because they're your parents. It's something you do. I don't think I've ever felt any bitterness about it. If there are any foibles in my life, I don't attribute it to the fact I've had to look after them.

My parents were old school. You're married because you're married, kind of thing. My parents were married, I think, fifty-five years. My father came over from the Ukraine when he was quite young. My mother came over from the old country, which was the Ukraine, for the express purpose of marrying my father. My father saw this picture. My mother was a beautiful, beautiful woman. When I see pictures of her, that is a classic beauty she was. And my father just fell in love with the picture, and I could well see why he would. And he brought her over, arranged for her passage, for the specific purpose of marrying her. It wasn't a matter of working through. It was just what you did.

They lived for a while in the North Bay, Ontario, area, but for the greater part, it was in Trois-Rivières in Northern Quebec. That's where my father's halcyon days were, as a big fish in the Ukrainian community of Trois-Rivières, you know. I was there until I was seven, when one brother was in college here and my other brother was a couple of years away from college. So my father decided to move here as well.

The period immediately after moving here was an unhappy time for me. My father was quite miserable for a number of years, perhaps for a decade after he moved here, and always threatening to go back, which was always kind of a trauma for me because I didn't want to go back, because I liked Toronto so much. I was always a Toronto fan, even before it was in vogue to be a Toronto fan. From the time we started visiting Toronto when I was a little kid, Toronto was where the television was. In rural areas, like where we lived, TV hadn't arrived. I never had great aspirations for living elsewhere. But those had been my father's halcyon days and because of my father's natural negativity, he'd want to go back, go back, even though there was nothing to go back to.

I was this little kid who loved his parents. When my dad was in a bad mood, when I was seven to seventeen, roughly speaking, then there would be these fights that developed in the middle of the night because my dad was, you know, the way he was. And those fights in the middle of the night would start as whispers and emerge as arguments. I think they were actually quite—being my own psychologist here—those were quite significant in determining my personality traits. Because I was a sensitive kid even then and these were so, so traumatic to me. They were so traumatic that I think a lot of my distaste for being adversarial came from that.

FINAL THOUGHTS

I think I always really kind of loved my parents, perhaps more so than most. Because sometimes, in stories of my peers, you realize—to a greater degree than I would have thought—the absence of family love, of parental love, and of how many difficulties there are. And when you hear this theme over and over, it's kind of surprising, because to me it's kind of foreign. I think I really, actually loved my parents from a very early stage. Probably beyond. I don't know why I did because there was that period in my very formative years when my dad was not very pleasant. I think it was always love, and to some degree, obligation, but never a sort of resentment attached to that obligation. There was never any guilt. These are your parents, you love them and you look after them. They were good to you.

Some of my friends are just getting into it now. I have a feeling that my parents were older. My dad was in his fifties, I think, when he had me. So my parents were always older than those of most of my equals, or cohorts, or friends. To some extent, I've gone through something that many of them will have to go through.

Recommendations to others? As I have told a lot of people, get them [parents] on the list [for a nursing home]. Fast. If things are starting to go downhill, you know, when the whole process begins it is a long, downward process and at a certain point it just becomes overwhelming. For me, The Provincial was a godsend. For a brief period, my mother was in the Lakeshore Hospital, which was awful. Just awful. She was only there for a week. I said this was too far for my father because he wanted to get down there by bus and I had to teach him to get there by bus. For the week or two she was there it was just horrendous because the care was not good and getting there was bad. But when she went into The Provincial, that was just such a major, major relief in terms of good care and in terms of where my life was going, because it was getting more difficult. My dad wasn't great, my mum wasn't great. It was beginning to be a bit much. When they sort of came into the picture, it reduced it to a level which I could manage. So what I say to my friends is: "If you see your parents are beginning, given the difficulty of getting parents into some of these places, check out good places and get them on the list. Because there may come a time soon enough when you may need it."

Postscript

It seems to me that, in many ways, the little boy who asked nothing more than to be allowed to grow up in the city of Toronto and not return to Trois-Rivières remains the dominant character in Mr. Lypchuk's life. The young man's great trauma was his father's early dislike of Toronto, and the overhead threats that they would return to the small town in which the young Mr. Lypchuk was born. All Bill wanted was for his father to agree to remain in Toronto, to make his peace with the boy's city. And Bill Lypchuk the adult has dedicated his life to assisting his parents in their continued habitation in that city. If that requires a nursing home or daily companionship, so be it. One gets the sense, in talking with him, that it is this location, this town—represented for him by his father's residence in the family home—which is a crucial anchor in Bill Lypchuk's world. The little boy who hated to hear his parents arguing is the man who now dismisses his father's "negativity" as unimportant and beneath serious consideration. There is in Bill Lypchuk's story a sense of creating for his parents, as they once did for him, a world in the city, an "ambiance of living" built upon the miracle city the boy first new and loved.

I do not doubt his loyalty or his love. Nor do I suggest that he is not absolutely committed to a view of relations in which individuals care for their relatives. He does this not out of guilt, not as "payback" but, in his own words, out of love: "You've looked after your parents because they're your parents." He is honestly surprised by the distance between some friends and their parents, one increasingly evidenced by their conflicts over the possible necessity of future parent care. But it is equally clear that at this stage, and after almost two decades of parent care, that Mr. Lypchuk can conceive of no course other than continued supervision of his surviving parent. It is, quite simply, a part of his life and life's vision.

DRUG DEPENDENCE

The subject of elders' abuse of prescription drugs has received increasing attention in recent years from the medical, nursing, and pharmacologic communities. In the 1980s, researchers found that 25 percent of all prescription drugs in the United States were prescribed to the then 11 percent of the population sixty-five years of age or older. In addition, as individuals age, physical mass and bone density naturally diminish, and with these changes drug tolerance diminishes. The result is that what are normal doses for younger adults become overdoses for the senior. Thus, the potential for inadvertent misuse ("this is what I always took") increases as natural tolerances decline with body mass and self-prescription from the medicine chest in the home continues without thought or supervision. Self-dosage with prescription pills left in the house may represent simply an elderly individual's attempt to cure sleep disorders or depression. In other cases, it may be symptomatic of a depression so severe as to result in a suicide attempt. Many elderly say they keep pills, sometimes for years, as a potential suicide aid should they find their lives unbearable. The degree to which individual overdosing may be not accidental self-abuse but rather a masked attempt at suicide is not always clear.

Mr. Lypchuk is probably correct that his father's self-dosage was a means by which he could gain some personal control, medically, in a context where care of and hope for his wife had been removed from him. It was also, one suspects, a means by which the elder Lypchuk could dull his fears, concern and distress—emotions he could not express verbally—over his wife's deterioration. Clinical depression is not uncommon in the elderly, and for a man like the senior Mr. Lypchuk, watching a wife's physical degeneration while being unable to adequately care for her must have been depressing in the extreme. The sleeping problems Mr. Lypchuk senior suffered during this period are a common indication of stress and depression, symptoms the blustering, self-important Ukrainian would presumably be loath to discuss with anyone, even a physician.

The problem of drug abuse is complicated, in this case, by what some gerontologists call the "tea and toast syndrome." When the act of cooking becomes difficult because of physical problems like arthritis, or psychologically insupportable (because meals are, to many single elderly, traditionally communal and not solitary affairs), the fragile, aged person attempts to subsist on tea and toast. This snack becomes, in fact, a whole meal, with resulting nutritional imbalances, which may contribute to depression, lassitude, and cognitive problems. In cases where this type of inadvertent self-starvation is a factor, a hospital stay (with three balanced meals provided per day) may work as miraculous a cure as the one noted here, which was attributed solely to the withdrawal of unprescribed medication.

The problem is compounded in senior men, widowers who have absolutely no idea how to cook even the most basic meals. Just as many older women with no experience in financial matters find themselves unable to manage their money when left to their own devices after a husband dies, so do older men find themselves performing in apparently bizarre ways when required to cook. I have met men of the older Mr. Lypchuk's generation who, quite simply, did not know how to use a stove. The elder Mr. Lypchuk's use of a heating element to prepare a can of soup may result not simply from "cheapness"—his son's assumption—but, more important, from a total ignorance of cooking or cooking implements. If this was true in Mr. Lypchuk's case, it also suggests his mental problems stemmed not simply from problems with medication and depression, but also from nutritional deficits, which compounded their effect.

Mr. Lypchuk's assumption at this time that his father had "lost it" and was suffering from increasing cognitive deficits is not an uncommon conclusion in cases like this. One researcher, Marie Caroselli-Karinga, notes that among the elderly, symptoms of drug overdoses "may result in decreased alertness, lethargy, motor disturbances, falls and confusion. This confused state is often perceived and misdiagnosed as demential." What this story demonstrates is how a complex of problems—drug abuse, depression, patterns of nutrition and communication—can combine to create symptoms of cognitive dysfunction which, with proper home care and supervision, can be reversed.

5

The Only Child

Katie O'Connor is a forty-three-year-old woman living in Wilkes-Barre, Pennsylvania. Over the last twenty years, she has held a stunning number of diverse jobs—from dealing blackjack and working as a stand-up comedian to school teaching and working in a university admissions program. But what she is, by her own admission, is a care giver, a person who needs to care for others. The daughter of alcoholic parents, she nursed her mother through years of illness and now faces the prospect of caring for a distant, alcoholic, and physically diminished father.

It is possible that her father's sporadic incontinence is a side effect of medication. There are a variety of medications currently available for high blood pressure, but the use of some may be dangerous for patients with obstructive lung diseases such as the one her father has. So, in cases like this, physicians often prescribe diuretics, drugs that work by reducing body fluids through urination. Thus he may be right in blaming the medication for his embarrassment.

Further, the symptoms she describes in her father's case after knee surgery (coma, disorientation, memory loss) can result from a period of decreased oxygenation, an all-too-common result of improper anesthetic administration or inadequate monitoring during surgery.

The degree to which Mrs. O'Connor identifies with her mother's physical decline is understandable. The family's medical history of early heart disease puts her at special risk, especially because of her own tobacco use and history of heart trouble. We are too often and too clearly our parents' children in matters of health.

I'm going to go through taking care of my father. It is immanent. I am an only child. There is no one else to do it. I am putting it off as long as I can, but I am spending more and more time doing things for him, taking him places, and checking on him at his own apartment. So it's around the corner, his coming to live with us. There will be guidelines. I will not give up my entire life for him. He will have to understand that if I have places to go and things to do, someone else will have to sit with him. And if I can't get someone to sit with him for free, then I'll pay somebody. But I would never do it the way I did it with my mother again. Never. Because it was bad for her as well as bad for me.

My father, he is seventy-six, and he thinks he's twenty-two—but he's not. He has one lady friend who is in poor health. And they're kind of trying to take care of each other and, very selfishly, I promote that because it's easier for me. But it's getting to the point that he's getting too much for her to handle. My father and I had a set-to about this woman he lives with. I said, "Look. I bend over backwards, but the woman hates me." I said, "Make a choice." And I stayed away for the longest time. Well, then he got sick, with the flu or something, and she called me, and I went over. And there was a big, emotional scene. And my dad said, "I wish you two would get along." Well, that's like asking Saddam and Bush to go to bed together. But we did make a truce. I can't stand her, I'm very uncomfortable around her, and she around me. I make her just as nervous and unhappy as she makes me. But we just cope with each other for his sake. And, in a way, I wish I had just walked away. But I can't. I can't. Because in some strange way, I think before he dies, he's going to know that he has a daughter, and he's going to have to love me.

He's had cataract surgery, he's had knee replacement surgery. He has hearing aids. He's lost a tremendous amount of weight. His appetite is failing, and he has the usual complaints of constipation and fatigue, and he just doesn't feel well. "I don't feel like myself." He gets very aggravated, and the one thing that he wants . . . he keeps going to the doctor because he wants a pill. He wants to take that pill and get better, and it's not going to happen. The other day he called me, and he swore for twenty minutes. It took me that long to get him calmed down. I said, "Dad, what is the problem?" And the problem was that he's on high blood pressure medicine, and he went to the store, and he was trying to get home in time. He had to go to the bathroom, and he wet himself. Well, this was the worst possible thing that could happen, and so on and so forth. And I said, "Dad, this happens to the best of us once in a while. It's not like this is happening all the time." But rather than him saying, "I'm getting older, and I don't have much control over my bladder like I used to," he said, "it wasn't my fault." It was the blood pressure medicine that made him do that. You know, let's blame the doctor. Let's blame the medicine. Let's, for God's sake, not admit that we're getting older and we just aren't in control as much as we used to be!

He's seventy-six, and he aged tremendously after this bout in the hospital. He's still driving—not well—and he gets very angry. He gets winded when he walks somewhere. He's very tottery now. He lost a tremendous amount of weight, so he's very weak. And if he gets a cold, it's more like the flu. He doesn't like to admit if he's sick, and it's a really hard thing for him to accept. He will rage at himself. He will say, "I'm so stupid." Or, "I can't believe that I walked up the stairs." And I've heard him rage at me. I said, "Dad, I think you ought to go see the doctor about this cold rather than just let him prescribe an antibiotic over the phone." And then I reminded him, "Your lung collapsed when you were in the hospital. We need you to see someone." And he would get so angry. He would swear at me and hang up the phone, and I have had to lit-erally—physically—drag him to the car to take him to the doctor's. And part of me understands. It doesn't make it too much easier, but I do understand how he feels. He doesn't want to know if he's sick. He wants a pill, he wants to be twenty-two years old again. And he wants to have his muscles back, and he wants to be able to run the mile. And there is no pill for that . . . and I think part of his anger, part of his rage, is that he knows that. So why bother going to the doctor? Why bother listening to the doctor?

He worked for years and years and years, he worked for the state. He took his retirement very hard. He hedged it for a year, but there was no dodging it after that. He did not want to retire, but circum-stances being what they were with his job and the state, it was necessary. The state had to say, "You take this retirement now." And he didn't retire until he was actually sixty-six. He took his retirement and what I was hoping for was that he would travel. He loves to travel. The first year he was retired, he traveled. But he was involved with this woman, and I think the epitome of what she's like is that when they went to Hawaii—my dad was sixty-six years old—he was out learning how to surf, she was in the room watching Lawrence Welk [laughs]. He could have been active . . . I blame her a little bit. She's a very homebody-type person, and he got used to sitting at home and drinking with her. That's what they do. He had had periods of drinking—both my parents were alcoholics—he would have periods of drinking and then there would be periods when he didn't drink at all.

When I was in sixth grade, he left home for a while. My dad came from a family where there wasn't a lot of affection. He didn't know how to show affection. To this day he doesn't know how to show affection. And my dad does not relate well with people. He really doesn't. It was just easier for him, and more comfortable for him, to remove himself from the situation. The marriage was not good. And during the time of my mother's illness, they lived in the same house. They certainly didn't have the same room. They hadn't had the same room for years and years. And he just handed the care of her over to me and walked away from it.

MOTHER'S CARE

I was twenty-four when I started taking care of her. She had a heart problem and it was severe enough that the doctor said, you know, she can't clean or run the sweeper, or so on and so forth. And my husband and I moved in with them, because I said, "I have a choice here. I can either take care of my house, and just let her have another heart attack, or I can try and take care of two houses, and ours will be a mess. Or we'll just live together, and I'll take care of one house." So that's what we did. My husband was extremely supportive. He would say to me, "But she's your mother, and you're an only child." His background was that his grandmother lived with them—my father-in-law's mother—lived with them for twenty years after her husband died. So this seemed very normal to my husband: "You take care of your own."

A typical day, it would start . . . I had to take her pulse—she had a pacemaker—I would have to take her pulse and make her take her medicine, and she would fight me on that. "I hate taking the medicine, blah, blah, blah." Like a little kid, it would be a big deal. Later on, when my kid was in kindergarten, I would have to make sure he was ready for kindergarten, give him his breakfast, then I would have laundry to do and the house to clean. And my mother would want me to read for her. My mother would want me to just sit down and talk to her. And then she would inevitably say, "I can't believe you don't have the laundry done yet!" Or, "I can't believe you haven't run the sweeper yet!" Later on, as she got worse, I might have to give her a bath. I would have to help her to the bathroom. She never did reach the point where she was incontinent, until the last days in the hospital, which I'm very grateful for.

My son would come home from school. I would have him to attend to. I would have to keep an eye on him. My husband would come home from work. He would want to talk to me about his day. I would have to prepare supper. She would want a special diet; she would not eat what the family ate. My father—he was living in the same house at that time—we never knew when he was coming home, or what kind of condition he would be in when he came home. He was still working at that time. He was like a boarder, I mean, that was how removed he was from the whole situation. And I would fix two meals—one supper for her; one for my husband, my son, and me—and then have leftovers for my dad when he came in.

My son did not get as much attention as he should have—another ball of guilt for that—but I'm pleased to say that, at this time, he's twenty years old, he has a full-time job, plus he is putting himself through school and is very independent and successful. And I really think part of the reason is he had to be independent when he was a child, when he was young. He was only a year old when we moved in with her and he had just turned seven when she died. Well, he was going on eight. But he would help me with little things and he was my mother's pride and joy—he could do no wrong, which was another problem, because it was difficult to discipline my son when my mother was around. And you get to the point where you just tiptoed and wanted her to shut up! You did not want to hear her mouth about anything! And you would placate her.

She had a talent for making me feel guilty. It was a manipulative tool to get me to wait on her twenty-four hours a day. We would get into royal battles occasionally, over which I would feel guilty and she would claim to feel sicker, because I had put her through this stress. She may have felt worse, because stress is hard on you, but we both had the same temperament, which is bad. I wanted to buy a wheelchair, but she wouldn't let me. We rented one. Because she was going to get better. That's what she said. She was very humiliated about being in it. I think she equated the illness with old age and it really . . . because she was young—she wasn't old—it seemed to be aging her before her time, and she saw it as a humiliation. She would try and deny the illness. I see that now, I didn't see that then. I just thought, "She has to make everything hard. She has to cause a problem. She can't let anything be easy." And I was terribly angry at everybody.

She would do the craziest things. I would take them personally, like, "Why is she doing this?" Now I can sit back and say, "she was trying to come back. She was trying to fight and say, "I'm not going to give in to the illness. I want to beat the old men." For instance, I would set the table. She would come behind me when she was mobile and put other plates on, like I didn't pick the right plates! Now I can look back and see [she was saying], "This is my house! My table! I will set it. You don't have to do this for me." I didn't read it that way, then. And then she would sneak . . . she would get up very quietly—she had a bell that she would ring when she needed me—but she would get up and go downstairs at, like, four o'clock in the morning, and start pulling everything out of the cupboards. She'd decide she was going to clean the cupboards. And then of course she would get everything half out of the cupboards. The kitchen would be a mess and I'd hear her, get this, she'd say, "You need to clean the cupboards!" And that was very irritating. I know, now, that it was an effort on her part to be in charge of her own household, do what she always did—take care of things—and I don't think now that she did it to me deliberately. But I did then.

I had to quit my job, eventually. I was working just part-time, but my son was real small. I was very active in the church, and it got to the point that the only time I got out of the house was to go to church, go to the grocery store, or take her to the doctor. And that put a tremendous strain on my marriage, as you can imagine. But it reached the point where I was teaching Sunday school and I had to give that up. I was lucky if I made church services once a month. We lived close to the church, the church was two minutes away. I would make sure that she was settled, I'd put the phone by her bed, and she'd say, "If I get a pain, or if something happens, I'm not calling you. I'll lay here and die." She would try and make me feel guilty for leaving her. And I'd say, "I'm going to church! You know, I'm not going out to boogie [dance] or drink or party or have orgies, or anything. I'm going to church!" And it was, like, this was a sin, for me to leave her alone to go to church. Great Guilt. I felt terrible about it, but I felt resentment and guilt. And anger at her. But I shouldn't have felt the anger, that's what I thought then: "I should not be feeling this anger. My poor mother." So it just made a big ball of more guilt, is what happened.

I just kept on going. I had reached the point, the very last time she was in the hospital, I had told my husband that I was at the breaking point. I wasn't getting enough sleep, I was run down, tired, crying most of the time. And I said to my husband, "I can't do this. We're going to have to put her into a home." But we didn't have to face that because she never came back out of the hospital. He was extremely supportive, as much as he could be, but he also had every right to make demands on my time. Our sex life went down to nothing. I mean, I was too doggone tired to even think about it. I thought, "You've got to be nuts!" My husband was very supportive and understanding, but he became resentful, too. It was, uh, almost a relief when she died, which led to another big ball of guilt on that point. But one of the things that I find so amusing to myself, now, is that when I would have what are normal reactions to the circumstances that I was in, I would think it was bad. I would think there was something wrong with me. I felt I was selfish, and that would just compound the guilt that I felt.

It was, like, this was my situation. I had to deal with it. And I felt as if I was failing because I was angry, because I was resentful, because I felt miserable. I felt trapped. And my idea was that I shouldn't feel that way because this was my mother. I should just do this. "Nobody should do this except me." So I really didn't expect help from anywhere. Now, it makes me feel angry. It really does. I've had friends who were caring for an ill parent, and I've made a point of going to them and saying, "Get out of the house!" because I know what that means.

Our minister would come down and get into theological arguments with my mother. When she died, the church got on the bandwagon and they cooked—they came in with all this food and everything. But not once did anybody other than my cousins say, "Get out of the house. Get away from it for awhile." People from the church would call me and say, "How's your mother?" And, you know, I would say, "She's doing about as well as can be expected," or "She's about the same," or whatever. Not once did anybody say, "Gee, you look tired," or "Gee, I bet you'd like to get out of the house." No, not once did anybody do that.

I had an aunt who had to go for cancer treatments, and for some reason I decided I would take her. Because nobody else would, I said, "Okay, I'll do it." And I would hire a nurse to come in once a week to sit with my mother and my son while I took my aunt for cancer treatments. The only people who came in to give me a break . . . I have one cousin, he and his wife would come over, they would get over as often as they could. They had their own family, their own problems, but they would come over and say, "Get out of the house." And so my husband and I would go to a movie, and they would sit with my mother. And they are my favorite cousins because of that. But they were the only ones. People would come in the beginning to visit. As my mother went downhill, because I was with her on a daily basis, I did not see how emaciated she was, how really bad she looked, because it was a gradual thing over seven years.

I had a girlfriend come over that had been my girlfriend in high school. Hadn't seen us in years. I was sitting in the living room, and she said, "I'm going to go get a cup of coffee," and it took her too long. I thought, "What's the matter with her?" I went into the kitchen, and she was in tears. And I said, "What's wrong with you?" And she said, "Your mother looks so bad, I can't believe it." I didn't see it. And I remember taking out a photograph, one of the last photographs that I ever took of my mother—I couldn't look at anything of hers, no pictures or anything, after she died, but about five years after she died I looked at this picture and I thought, "She looks terrible. She looks like a skeleton." But at the time I couldn't see it, and I think if I could have I wouldn't have been able to take care of her. I would have been too emotional.

Then she developed cancer. She was only sixty-one when she died. I made peace with my mother before she died. We talked about it. And she talked to me about the mistakes she had made as a mother, and I looked at her and said, "Why didn't you kill me when I was thirteen, because I was obnoxious." I really was. But, toward the end, I think the nicest thing with my mother was she let me know she knew that it was hard for me, but I also understood it was hard for her. I didn't have any regrets when my mother died. The aunt that I took for cancer treatments, when she died . . . I have a cousin who was drunk when she called me up [crying], "I should have spent time with my mother." Yeah, yeah, yeah. On and on and on. I thought, "Yeah, you're right. You should have." And I did. That's the one thing that I'm real happy about, that I don't have any regrets about. I did it. I didn't pass it on to someone else.

For forty-three years I've wanted "Ozzie and Harriet," "Father Knows Best," "Leave It to Beaver." Because we can't go back and get that, just really having the knowledge that there was some type of relationship between us, some kind of relationship—because we [my father and I] are very much like strangers—I think that's basically why I keep going and doing for people, trying to get them to say, "You did a good job, you pleased me." But it doesn't mean anything to me when I hear it from other people, because I'm not hearing it from Mum and Dad. And that's who you needed to hear it from. I heard it from Mum. If I get to hear it from Dad, I think I would start to look around and appreciate the people that I do have. Then I think I could be satisfied. Probably even with my husband. He's a good man. He really is.

All the women in my mother's family don't seem to get past sixty-one, which is a little scary for me. And I have had a heart attack already. As I sit here smoking my cigarettes [laughs]. When she died, I had a period of time which was like, a midlife crisis, and I wasn't in midlife—thank God! I don't even consider myself midlife now—but it was a time where I would say, "I'm going out with my friends!" And I'd make my husband take me dancing and I just wanted to, I was trying to catch up for seven years. And then I started to get very involved in the church, PTA, band mothers, and so forth, but it was funny. My focus for so long had been on her, on taking care of her, and after she died for approximately a month I made daily visits to the cemetery. And when I got there, I wouldn't even know why I was there. A minister pointed it out to me—I didn't figure it out, he did—he said, "In your mind you're still taking care of her. You're giving her her bath. You're giving her her medicine. But she's not here for you to do that, so you go to the cemetery." Because there was an enormous void, and I didn't know how to fill it.

HEART ATTACK

She died in 1977. It's been fourteen years, but it's still very real to me. I feel as if I've had seven years of my life taken away from me, stolen, that I can't get back. When I had my heart attack [June 1, 1989] I was terrified and denied that I had had one. I felt a rage which has helped me understand her rage a little bit. I was so angry: "How could this happen to me?" And when people say to me, "Take it easy," "You've got to quit smoking," "Are you taking your medicine?" I get like a crazy woman, I get so angry. I will say to them, "I'm not a baby." And the more that this happens to me, the more I can understand her rage at me saying, "You have to take your pills," or "The doctor says you must do this." And I think that anybody who has an illness like that and becomes so dependent has that helpless child feeling. And we all talk about, "Let's go back to childhood." I wouldn't go back to childhood on a bet! I like being a grown-up, I like making my own decisions and doing what I wanna do!

I was in a big state of denial about the heart attack. In fact, I'm a legend in my own time at the hospital. I ran away from cardiac care. I got up and ran! And I kept telling them, "If I can run away from the hospital, I'm not in that bad of a shape." But they put me back into the hospital with a psychiatric nurse around the clock [laughs] because they thought I wanted to hurt myself. But I didn't want to hurt myself. I just didn't want to be there, and I didn't want to be sick. And I didn't want to get old. To me, having a heart attack is getting old. I took my blood pressure medicine, my heart pills for a while, and I thought, "This is crazy. I feel good." And I stopped. My blood pressure went back up, and one of the things my doctor said to me was, "Well, you know you have to take this medicine, you of all people should know that. I mean, it runs in your family. Your mother had this." And I said, "Yes, and I'm not my mother and I'm not going to lay down and give in to an illness." I didn't know I felt that way [at the time], but evidently that was a feeling that was there. Like, "Why are you giving in to this?" "Why don't you fight this?" I resented that, and when she developed a cancer with the heart problem and the hardening of the arteries, she could progressively do less and less for herself. I was required to do more and more.

FATHER

He went downhill just this last year. Actually, within the last two years, since he had knee replacement surgery, one of those "simple operations." Let me put it this way: he went in there a very healthy, active man, and he is now a tottering, frail, small man. I've noticed lately that his mind is not nearly as sharp as it used to be. Things have to be repeated. He has hearing aids, so he is hearing it. He's just not assimilating what's being said to him. Or he's forgetting. Before, I could call him on the phone maybe once or twice a week, or if he needed, you know, to maybe get in touch with me—or just wanted to see me—he'd call or he'd come over and drop in. Now, it's the phone calls. "I'm low on groceries. Can you go to the store for me?" "I'm not feeling well. Come over and see me." He called me the other day because the remote control for his TV wasn't working. He just forgot how to push the buttons.

When he was in the hospital, he was supposed to be in and out within something like six days. He was in for a month and a half. When he came out of the surgery it's still up in the air whether he had the d.t.'s [delirium tremens]—because he is an alcoholic—or whether it was a combination of the d.t.'s and too much anesthetic. But he was delirious, he was tied down in the bed. He has emphysema, his lung collapsed, he went into a coma. I was told at the hospital that there could be brain damage, that I might have to put him in a home, and so on and so forth. He has recovered, as far as the doctors are concerned it is a miraculous recovery. But during that stint he probably aged twenty years.

He was very close with some of his cousins, and he has acquaintances. He never had any real close friends. But now he has isolated himself to the point that it's just his lady friend and himself, because to keep the friendships going with his cousins, he would jump in the car and go see them and say, "Let's go out to dinner," or "Let's go to the ball game," or "Let's take in a movie." He can't do that now, and they aren't making the effort. They have their own lives, really, basically. When he was in the hospital, at first people came to see him. It was a turning point, because one of the things that happened—as he came out of his coma and came back, he was very irritable—he was very nasty, and he was also not lucid a lot of the time. People would go to see him; he wouldn't know who they were. They got disgusted, they wouldn't go back. If he was lucid, he was likely to be very irritable, say nasty things to them, almost as if he was blaming them for him being in the hospital. It was just anger coming out, but it's not easy not to personalize that, when you're the one listening to it! A lot of the anger was directed at me.

One of the biggest problems was that he was very angry that I admitted to the hospital that he was indeed an alcoholic and that, yes, indeed, this could be the d.t.'s. He still rages at me about that. And I don't think the man has been sober in twenty years. Really. He gets up in the morning, and with his orange juice, he has his vodka. Really. First thing in the morning. And he always says, "But I don't drink that much. I have a few beers." Well, a few beers to him could be a six-pack while he's watching TV in the evening.

And yet now I'm thinking of taking care of him? It's like an obsession. I just keep on playing the role. I can't get out. My husband has said to me, "Do you know what it's going to be like if he moves in here?" Yes I do, and I don't know whether I'm choosing to be a martyr, or if I am afraid what people will say if I say, "Dad, I can't take care of you. I have to put you in a home." And part of me says, "I'm an only child. I have to do this." It's a guilt thing, it's a guilt thing. He's my dad, what can I do? I think that a part of it is that— and this goes into all my therapy—that in a very strange way, as much as I'm not looking forward to it, part of me, the little girl in me, is saying, "Oh, Daddy needs me. Daddy loves me." He is finally going to say, "I have a daughter," because he has to, now. I don't think he would have been close to a son, either. I have a son, and actually at his birth I thought, "Now my Dad will be close to me because I've had a boy."

THERAPY

I am in therapy, I went into therapy about two years ago. I went in for reasons . . . because of my marriage and things that were going on. All I wanted was for him [my therapist] to give me back my coping mechanisms. That's why I went in. My coping mechanisms broke down. I couldn't do my little role playing. I was immobilized by all this. And I couldn't deal with it. But what I thought I had to deal with was my son's homosexuality. There was so much more, but that was the catalyst. At this point in time, he lives twenty minutes away with his lover. And if he talks to me, if they've had a spat or something, it's like he's talking to me about his girlfriend. Brad's part of the family, and I have come to the point that I'm not happy about it, but I accept it. That's the way he is. And I also know that it's not my fault [laughs].

I went in to the therapist and I said, "I don't have a lot of time and money to waste on this. I am the daughter of alcoholic parents, I'm having an affair, I've had a heart attack, I'm not in that great shape, but the reason I'm here is that my only son is gay, and I need to cope with that. You get me to cope with that, and I can handle the rest." [Laughs.] And that was—believe me—how I felt. That's really what I thought. As he started to get me to learn that I had nothing to do with my son's sexual preferences, we'd get into, you know, "Why did I feel that I was responsible for this?" He'd give me books to read, he'd give me studies to look at, he talked to both my son and to me, and as I began to see the facts, I'd [still] say, "Well, just because I *am* responsible."

And that's when he began to dig deep about, "Why do you feel this responsibility for everything?" Even my husband laughs about it. I'm one of these people who, if it's raining, I go, "I'm sorry." Like, I control the weather. The best line my husband has ever gotten off. . . somebody famous has died and it's on TV, I don't remember who, and he was walking through the living room. I had the news on and they announced so-and-so died, and I went "Gasp!" and he said, "And it's not your fault!" [laughs]. I mourned when [actress] Natalie Wood drowned, because I teach swimming. I thought if I could have been there, I could have saved her [laughs].

That's the way I see life. That I control, that I'm in control. If I am sad, I ought to be able to change it. If I am debilitated in some manner, then I should be able to exercise, or follow some kind of health plan and get my strength back. If I am angry about something, then I take action on it, even if it's the wrong action. I have to do something. That's what my therapist says, that it's a terrible burden I carry with me all the time. But that's how I see things. And, possibly because of growing up with two alcoholic parents, I still have this childlike belief that I can control a situation. If the situation goes sour, I have done something wrong.

I'm a person who's in control. I married a man that I can control. Whatever I want, I do. I'm not happy about that, no. But it is what I did. I don't have a lot of respect for my husband. He works for the state. I am in an affair that I've been in for four years and, basically, I don't care about this guy. Basically, it's almost thumbing my nose at my husband. Watch me, I can do anything I want to do. I'm in control, which is crazy, because I'm not in control. The fellow I'm seeing, I do a lot of things for him. He is very depressed, and he can't make decisions. He's in therapy. I appear to be the strong one, to help him make decisions, and so on and so forth. And he has said to me, "I do not know what I would do without you," "You are so wonderful," "I count on you so much," "I am so glad you're here." And when he does that, it makes me want to run away. And I don't understand that, but that's the way I feel. It's almost like I have to battle the odds, it's like if I get that compliment, well then, there better be another mountain to climb.

The funniest thing to me is so much comes out when you're in therapy. There's all this hostility inside me about when I took care of my mother, unresolved issues that I have buried that I didn't even know were in there. I think the best-case scenario is that I was angry at her about her illness. I certainly would not admit that to myself. I thought I was Joan of Arc, Saint Joan, Mother Theresa. "Look at me, how selfless I am, taking care of this woman."

We're working on it. We're working on it very hard. But it's basically . . . I think my therapist sees a therapist after I see him. I think he needs a session. But I know what I'd like to be. One of the things my therapist said to me, was, "How will you know when you are happy?" And I said, "I think it would be real nice to not care what anybody else thought about you. To just be happy with you." And I'm not. I depend on what other people think of me. "Oh look, isn't she a wonderful person! She took care of her mother." "Oh look, isn't she great at the church?" "Oh look, doesn't she do a good job?"

And that leads to the care giving. I'm not doing it selflessly, although some people see it that way. And I love that! I get off on that. But it's definitely not that I need to take care of these people. It's that deep down inside I think I ought to be able to change the situation. I ought to be able to control the outcome. If they're not happy, then I must find a way to make them happy. If they are sick, I must find a way to make it easier for them. I must help them through this. Almost as if I had caused the sickness, I had caused the happiness. And that just goes back to that childhood thing that if something is wrong in the home and you're a kid, you think, "Oh my God, I have to change this."

It's very, very common. I've gone to a lot of support groups, plus I used to work with socially and emotionally disturbed adolescents. I took a lot of psychology courses on it, and it is a very common thing when there is a divorce with young children, or there is constant fighting, or alcoholism, or problems in the home. Because the child is so self-centered, he feels that he is the cause and that he should be the solution. And children of alcoholics have a hard time growing out of this. We play roles a lot, because we think that everybody lives lives like "Ozzie and Harriet," so we learn to play a role so our friends think everything is fine at home. It's a real common thing among children of alcoholics. Not just alcoholics. Children that have been in a bad home situation where the parents are fighting, where there's abuse of some kind. You just get this internalized, "It's my fault." And as you grow into adulthood, that it's-my-fault syndrome turns into, "I must do something about this. I should have the power to do something about this." And you don't.

FINAL THOUGHTS

Part of me says, "What's going to happen to me when I'm seventy-six? Will I get like my mother? Is someone going to take care of me, or are they going to put me away somewhere?" I do not want anybody to take care of me and, truth be told, I do not want to be seventy-six. I'm forty-three and I don't want to be forty-three! But I don't think I would let that happen, for the simple fact that if I were to have signs of a heart attack now, I would not tell a soul. I would go quietly away and let it happen. Even tomorrow. I would do that. Probably gratefully, because I would think, "Okay, I've done as much as I'm gonna do here," and if I can't do—this sounds selfless but it's not, because it's my makeup—because if I can't do for other people, then there's no point in my being here. I don't want them to do for me at all.

The one thing I want to say is that I wish to God that they would do some studies and some courses on how to deal with this, this phenomenon in our country of people having to take care of their parents. Our nursing homes are overcrowded, it costs a fortune to get them in there, people for financial reasons or whatever are having to take care of their own, and there's not enough help or guidance around for them. And I think that, God knows, our government does studies on everything else. They ought to do a study and see how many people are out there, because I really think they'd be surprised.

What would I tell others? The first thing I would tell them, twenty-

twenty hindsight, is don't try and do it alone. I would tell them to seek some help, ask for help. From the church, from agencies, if they had the wherewithall to do it on a regular basis, have a nurse in, a visiting nurse at least one day a week. If they could afford it, at least two days a week. Take a break and get away from it. For two reasons. One, they need the break. And two, they need to establish their independence from that person they're taking care of. Because the person you take care of will eat you alive. I have never been able to do that. I make stabs at it.

Postscript

Psychologists with whom I've shared this case immediately accepted Mrs. O'Connor's assignment of blame for her own and her parents' perspective and actions on the family history of alcoholism. They call it "codependence," the need of one person to draw from another an affirmation of reality and worth. In 1990, it was being used as a catch-all phrase for a variety of personal, social and development disorders, including those resulting from tenure in an alcoholic family. Clearly, this woman has learned from her therapist, and creates a picture that places the responsibility for her actions on a dysfunctional family history.

But that perspective obscures another, equally important theme. Like her husband, Mrs. O'Connor also believes—strongly—that to be of a family includes by definition a responsibility for the care of its weaker members. There is a strong assumption in her story that caring for others in need is what an adult does, not simply to gain control but because it is the right thing to do. For example, after her aunt's death she notes her cousin's lament that she didn't do more. "Yeah, you're right," Mrs. O'Connor thinks. "You should have." Her cousin could and should have done more, both for the elderly woman's sake and for the cousin's as well. O'Connor can say what her cousin cannot: "I don't have any regrets. I did it. I didn't pass it on to someone else." The satisfaction she derives from that statement comes not simply from having fulfilled an obligation or discharged a debt but, just as important, from having resolved a whole series of interpersonal issues with her mother. Mrs. O'Connor acknowledges that she may have been a difficult child in her adolescence, while her mother acknowledges how hard it has been for her daughter to take care of her. They find, together, a way to seal the past and place it in perspective, something the cousin did not do when she could and now will not have the possibility of doing.

The importance of this is underlined by Mrs. O'Connor's insistence that when her father moves into her house, she will seek a similar resolution. By her account a cold and difficult man, he will be accepted reluctantly by his son-in-law and by this daughter who now cares for him at remove. The father's growing dependence will require, she says, less selflessness on her part and more acceptance from him of her needs. But he will be accepted, and during the tenure of their cohabitation she will seek from him some measure of personal understanding, some point behind or beyond the rages and angers and silences of the years, some time when both can put away the indignities of their shared past. "If I get to hear it from my dad . . . then I think I could be satisfied."

By emphasizing what may be a positive aspect of her decision to care for her parents, I do not mean to suggest that there is anything selfish or calculating about Mrs. O'Connor's actions. That she recognizes she can continue toward a healthy and satisfied life through caring for a parent who has nowhere else to turn does not mitigate the extraordinary empathy and understanding she brings to her charges. I am struck by her ability to simultaneously describe her own thoughts and actions, analyze her own motivations in the worst possible light, and yet maintain an extraordinary concern and empathy for these fragile and elderly relatives.

This may indeed come from her own experience with heart disease, with the denial and anger it brought forth in her. With this experience, she felt viscerally some shadow of what her charges feel in her care, knew herself what it must have been like for her mother to be frail while still young. And it is that experience, as much as the therapy, I suspect, which has given her such a broad perspective on the personalities and motivations active in this extended tale.

FOLLOW-UP

About six months after we met, I received a letter from Katie O'Connor apologizing for not having written to me for weeks. Referring to her father's care, she said she was "letting it all fall on his alcoholic girlfriend's shoulders." In this, as in most things, she saw herself as deficient. The crucial paragraph of that letter is included here:

Wow! Don't I sound like a selfish bitch! The epitome of my selfish behavior was reached on May 11, when I took an overdose of sleeping pills. Just call me "Babe," since I have the constitution of Paul Bunyan's famous blue ox. The doctors can't figure out how I survived, especially since I had it planned so well that it was eighteen hours before anyone had a clue to what I had done. I was fully prepared to wake up in hell, and as it turned out, I guess I did.

After hospitalization, intensive therapy, and a great deal of soul-searching, her life is turning around. "For the first time," she said in 1992, "I'm beginning to like myself." Her father's care was still an issue, but it was an issue that she knew she could not fully control or direct.

6

The Dancer

Jay Nakana is a former dancer and actor, now in his late forties, who runs a theatrical supply story in his native Honolulu. In addition, he works as a volunteer with local theater and community groups. Over the last decade of care giving, he has become overweight, while as a dancer, he was agile and lithe. He has also become a pack-a-day cigarette smoker. The youngest of four children, Mr. Nakana is the primary care giver for his eighty-seven-year-old mother, Agatha, who until recently spent her days with him at the shop. Physical infirmities now prevent her from leaving the home with that frequency.

What her son here describes as a natural outgrowth of his mother's age is more likely the result of a common type of cognitive dysfunction caused by ministrokes, sometimes called cerebrovascular accidents. His use of orienting questions following these incidents is a common and effective method used by physicians to assess an individual's awareness and also as a type of orientation therapy to focus the confused individual to a time and place.

For those unfamiliar with Hawaii, it may be helpful to point out that ethnicity is a major subject of humor and discussion throughout the culture. The presence of Fijians, Tongans, and Samoans mentioned here is only one strand in the multicultural fabric of Hawaiian culture at large. On the mainland, Mr. Nakana's generalizations and comments might seem to be the comments of a prejudiced man, but in Hawaii they would be seen as part of a long tradition of jokes and humor based on the nations of origin of local residents.

I would kind of just like to say that my name is Jay and I take care of my Mom, who is Agatha, and she is eighty-seven. About eight years ago my dad died at ninety, and so there was some beginning of caring for older relatives back then. He was very independent, my Dad, laid back—what was his world was his. And when he shared it with us, that was fine, but you know, there are just things he did himself that we never really bothered with. Dad was always an independent. He wasn't much of a communicator. He was a provider, a very caring, loving man. But he wasn't that much of a communicator. When his responsibilities became something that he couldn't handle, I kind of jumped in the picture and helped him. When Dad just forgot to file his taxes, that's when I started helping him. He prepped them, got them all together, but never took them in. Well, when he forgot one year, and the tax people came and said "Hey!" then I got involved. Then I started helping Dad.

I realized he needed help. So then I started doing the collecting of the information for the taxes. I found out who his CPA was. I didn't do the taxes; they did them. He had apartments, houses for rent. So then I got into the rentals, and stuff and stuff and other stuff. Then, when he passed on, Mom sort of—I don't want to say she withered away, but she sort of got disinterested in the normal responsibilities that she used to do so second nature. Like caring for the house, cooking. I've been the cook now at home for a number of years, although we have women that take care of Mom during the day.

She was kind of the breadwinner in the family in the sense that she was always out there, pulling for everyone. Whereas Dad was kind of laid back. Mom was always assertive; Dad was very passive. Strong passive, but passive. Also the fact that she was a schoolteacher. Schoolteachers are always fighting to always be on the ball. So anything that's not on the ball, they won't accept. So I try to not remind her about negatives, because that only pushes them, I think, back rather than acknowledging where they are. Does that make sense?

Right across the street in this white house there was an old, wonderful Japanese woman who used to take a walk every day. At least once a day I'd see her. She'd come with her cane, walk along here, she'd turn around, she'd walk around, and then she'd walk back. All of a sudden, she stopped walking. So then, when I asked the Japanese man who lives next to the building, "What happened to her?" he said, "They put her into a home. They couldn't cope." Three months later I asked, in conversation, "By the way, how is that old lady?"

He said, "Oh, she died." So I know that this disorientation was the demise of that wonderful old lady who used to walk around here.

Maybe fifteen years ago, I came back to the islands. I just thought it was time to come home. And one day not long after I came back, my parents and I went to see a relative in a care home. It's very sad, when you go to a care home. The care home is not taken care of very hygienically. It smells bad, it looks sad, and the people are not happy. I mean, you can tell from just looking at it, without even listening to things, that this is not a happy environment. Because the money isn't there, they've got to get cheap help. They've got to get immigrants, and the immigrants have a dialect [of English]. You have to be careful with older people. They can get disoriented very easily. So when you hear a dialect, and she's saying, "Do you Vant some Wa-Ter?" and Mom is going, "What?" and she's saying, "Do you Vant some Wa-Ter?" well, an older person gets very disoriented. And so Mother did say, when we came back from there, that she would never, ever want to be put in a home like that. And I always remembered that.

Remembering that Mom didn't want this, I remind my siblings about it—what Mom said—that she would never, ever want to be in a home like that. You see, both Mom and Dad used to come to the shop, to spend the day there in their later years. Part of the lifestyle here. Because she was always at the front door, she was, like, a fixture. People now will come in and say: "Where's that old lady?" or "Where's your grandma?" or "Where's your auntie?" or "Where's your mother?" When I think of Mom not being here any- more, I sort of flash back on my first experience in Europe when I went into a bathroom, the men's room, and there was a little woman sitting there making change. I never saw a lady in a men's room before that! Mom—she was like that at the shop, sitting there, waiting.

Why she stopped coming to the shop was that she had a blood clot in her thigh, and so she was in the hospital for a while as they tried to dissolve it. There are two ways: either operation or dissolving it, so she took the medication to dissolve it, which makes her like a hemophiliac. That means you have to be real careful, so we decided not to bring her back to the shop after she came home because she was still on that medication. So, because she'd been home for four months, and because of her age, things have slowed down. We don't want to bring her back to the mainstream. I strongly believe in keeping older people in the mainstream as much as possible, because once you take them out of the mainstream they start to wither away.

It was kind of fun watching them, my parents, way back then, when they both came to my shop. But then when Dad left and Mom used to come by herself, all of a sudden I thought it was getting a little too much for me. I had to take care of the rentals, I had to take care of Mom, and I had to do my own business. That's when I told my sisters, who are now retired—I have two older sisters—that I needed help. Since they in their retirement would prefer to take care of their own lives—both of them have husbands—it was agreed that maybe we should get help in. It might have been a feeling of guilt on their part, that we should get some help in.

We always had someone here at the shop to care for Mom. For the last five years we've had someone to care for her. Prior to that, I was doing everything, because she's older now and her eyesight fluctuates from sharp to fuzzy. Sometimes she'll amaze us by sitting in the living room and she can read the whole thing on the television set. She can still write her signature. Her handwriting is not as pretty as it used to be. My dad had wonderful John Hancock writing, of the old school. It's nice to see great handwriting because it tells you this is a great person.

MOTHER AT HOME

After that, Mom started having strokes, and her doctor said she would have numerous, many strokes. So Mom's forgetfulness did not happen until she started having strokes. Mom is eighty-seven. We never really know, and maybe we don't want to know. I think she's going into some early phase of Alzheimer's. The strokes that she has—this is what happens—she gets up from a long sleep where she doesn't want to get up, and she'll sleep and sleep and sleep, and when she finally gets up she's very disoriented. Because of the stroke. Another way is when she has these terrible headaches and she sleeps and when she gets up she's disoriented. When you live with someone and you care for someone you kind of, um, trial and error—you look and you work and you try and stuff. Then we've got to bring her back by asking her questions: "Your name? Your husband? How many children? Who are they? When were you born?" But then, part of growing old is becoming forgetful, and sometimes she does forget. But guaranteed, Mom is still terrific on multiplication tables. You can ask her any number and she'll just rattle it off. It goes with the fine handwriting.

Every so often she'll say, "I'll do the dishes tonight." And what do you tell her? "Mom! You haven't done the dishes for twelve years! So why are you doing it tonight?" And after I say it I really feel like a stinker, especially when I'm stressed out. When I have a busy day, I have a thousand and one things, and she wants to do the dishes! Or it's, "I'll cook dinner tonight if you'll put the rice on the stove." That kind of thing. You really feel bad, but sometimes you do things because you've been somewhere and then this comes in. I keep telling her, "Mom! Just enjoy your sleeping, eating, going places. Let us do the work." But you see, she's a fighter, because she was a strong, assertive individual it's hard for her to give up the things that she did before.

Many times she'll be upset that somebody feeds her. Somebody does feed her because otherwise she's all hands. Old people, they'll chew out the juices. Anything that's rough or very fibrous, they will just spit it out. [Ed. note: this may be a result of bad dentures.] I mean, my dad was doing that when he was still going out and about and going to lunches with us at places. You'd see all these little spitballs on the side of his plate. I don't think my dad ever ate with his fingers. My mom does spitballs too, but she also has elected to eat with her fingers. We were brought up to eat with a fork, and then pick up your knife and switch your hands, I mean switch them to eat [Ed. note: in the American as opposed to the continental manner].

A couple of times, and I don't know if it's just when she's lonely, she'll say, "Oh, come and jump in bed with me." But see, I never grew up jumping in bed with my parents, so I'll say, "Oh, no, Mom, this is your bed." She'll ask, "Where are you sleeping?" and I'll say, "In the living room on the floor." And she'll ask, "Well, why are you on the floor?" Well, you see, I've slept on the floor since Mom started having her strokes because one had to be more aware, to be closer. I decided to sleep in the living room because if I don't hear things I won't be getting up as much if she needs me. So for the last ten years, I've been sleeping in the living room on the floor. I can hear her easier.

When the time came with Mom and I realized that she needed help, it was the first time I'd ever seen *her,* you know, because, you see, we grew up where we never really exposed ourselves. I suppose a more liberal mother will sit in the tub with her children and bathe with them and stuff like that. But we weren't brought up that way. So it was kind of unusual and kind of odd, and kind of difficult for me. But after a while, Mom was so used to me that it was difficult to get her to let someone else bathe her.

To do opposite genders was kind of a shock to me. But it had to be done. You know, like, when babies do doo-doo it's "ooooh!" and when adults do doo-doo it's "ugh!" [laughs]. You have to do it, you have to clean it up. Clean it all out. You get used to it with parents. But it's a little more difficult because, see, with parents and especially with older parents—children can respond to you—parents don't necessarily respond. They don't know why they're standing there and all dirty, so at least children talk back to you. If anything, I think it's harder for an adult to confess to another adult that there was an accident. It's easier with children. Children accept it. Adults it's harder. It's harder for the person who's cleaning and it's harder for the person who got dirty. I mean, she's going, "Did I do that?" Kids are, "Mommy, I did this!" It's easier with children, harder with adults.

ON HOME AIDES

I would spend days trying to find someone to help at home within our means. I spend days and a week going through want ads, through the valley of [social] services, Catholic services, the numbers people give me. I know there are professional, professional people, but I know when Dad needed help in his last year that as a group the professional nurses, licensed nurses, were very, very accurate and very astute and very, very knowledgeable, but they were also very cold. We had various registered nurses to take care of Dad, but besides that, we had some what you call aides. And I find that aides, a lot of them are local people, they tend to have more feeling for the work that they do. So after Dad passed on, and we decided to get someone for Mom, I tended to try not to look for a professional licensed person because they seem to be without feeling, without humanity. They do their work well, but that's it.

Through the years, I've just lost my faith in the medical profession. I know there are still a few bedside-mannered doctors, which is important psychologically for anyone who is not feeling well. Part of getting better is feeding the right information into your system so you will get better, aside from the medication. I realize there are good doctors still around. Fortunately, my mom, she has wonderful doctors. But they move a lot, leave. And each of her doctors, as he went on to some other place, passed her on to someone else who was a caring doctor. But she was fortunate.

Aides, a lot of them are immigrants. A lot of them have different customs, different mores. People who have not been in Hawaii for a long time have lived with a different life-style. Let me just tell you about Samoans, and how they feel they can just go into people's yards, and, well, they think "What is mine is yours and what is yours is mine." That has been kind of a problem with one of the women taking care of Mom. We've always been brought up to ask. They've not been brought up to ask. So when mango season was around, they were just picking mangos and eating mangos like there was no tomorrow. It's not that I'm a scrooge about passing on mangos, but that I've been brought up to ask. So there are differences of lifestyle and mores.

This little story can be called "Retrieving the ivory earrings." It was this Samoan who was taking care of Mom and then she left and her sister started taking care of Mom. And this one became a real part of the family. She became so much a part of the family that if we went out, she went out. This time we had gone out to dinner. It was kind of dress-up night. I guess it was Christmas dinner. We went out to dinner and she was wearing these ivory earrings, and I looked at them and I went, "Those are the same earrings I gave Mom." So after dinner we went home and I went through all of Mom's things and I couldn't find them. So I went, "Where did you get those ivory earrings." And she went, "Oh, my sister gave them to me." And I said, "They're my mom's, because I gave them to her and they're not here in her thing." Well, of course, the woman wearing the earrings was really upset by it, but she gave them back. She was really embarrassed, but those are the things that happen. Then you think, "What else is missing?" Those are the things that happen. Is it because they're not getting enough, or is it because they feel they've become so much a part of the family?

HOME LIFE

If you'd like to hear the setup at home now . . . we have a woman who lives with us because, with her, then I can feel comfortable if

I have to go out at night or if I come back late for some reason. For a while, before she came in, it was really difficult. I became very antisocial because someone had to be around. Now, the setup we have at home, it makes it easier for me. Like, I'm going out for dinner tomorrow night. Or I can go to rehearsal tonight at the church that I'm working with that's going on this tour to Europe. I wrote the show, am directing it, costumed it, and that's why I'm going to Europe. I put the show together. Because somebody had to be around. So now we have a woman who's living with us.

She's Fijian and she works as a custodian up at a local high school. Because of her personality, I can rely on her and I feel very comfortable and I feel very safe with her. For a while, she moved away and I felt very uncomfortable and very unsupported. Then we had a whole influx of people who took care of Mom. One was an old lady from Hong Kong, and we had to learn her customs and mores, her dialect [of Chinese-accented English], which is very different. And we had a Samoan girl and she was wonderful with Mom. But she always wanted a child, so she adopted a child. My mother pointed a finger and said, "You're going to get pregnant." Sure enough, three months after she adopted the child, she had two babies. Then we had a black lady. Because we have our own life-style, it's easier to get people that can go with the flow. Then you're not bucking their customs and their traditions. You're just trying to say, "Hey, be careful with my mom." These obstacles become just another obstacle you don't need. Because taking care of your parent is stress enough.

The Fijian who lives with us talks about an experience when she used to take care of her grandmother. Now, you know, Fiji is British influenced, so she has this kind of British accent. As a kid she'd creep into her grandmother's bedroom and go right up to her to see if she was still breathing. Now I go in to check with Mom, timewise, two-thirty, three-thirty, four o'clock, or five o'clock. The reversal of roles.

We've got a Tongan woman now who comes during the daytime. We had her mother-in-law, who came during the evening. But it was a real stressful experience for me because she didn't speak English. Simple example: Mom would say, "I would like to go to the bathroom." The woman would say, "Yes, Mom." My mother would say, "I would like to go to the bathroom." The woman would say, "Yes, Mom." I'd be sitting somewhere at the table and say,

"Zola! MOM–TOILET–NOW!" She'd ask, "Toilet now?" I was going through this every day. It was inevitable; we had to get rid of Zola because of the language barrier. Communication. So now we have the Tongan girl's sister and they both speak English. You see the quality of each one who comes, and the most important thing is to see the rapport between the patient and the person who is caring for. So the girls we have now, rather than have them sit all day, we have them do housekeeping. Because you see, Mom isn't at the point where she's bedridden.

So the girl comes at six-thirty in the morning and that's when the Tongan lady leaves to go to work. And so the *wahine* [Ed. note: Hawaiian for female] then gives Mom her medication, which is at eight o'clock, and then she starts chores and gets her up, if Mom wants to get up. I really try to encourage her that she gets Mom up not too, too late, because I don't want Mom to just while away asleep all day long. It's better if she's clean, because, you know, Mom has diapers and she's back to pads, so rather than sleeping in a soiled diaper throughout the day, I want to get her up early. It's more hygienic. The thing I've found with a lot of people is their quality of personal hygiene. Like, the Tongan, my comb is your comb, or my toothpaste is your toothpaste, or my peanuts are your peanuts. So one day I had to tell them, "These are my peanuts, *not* your peanuts!"

The Fijian woman that lives with me basically takes care of Mom on Sunday and Saturday nights. Sunday we took her for a ride, went to the cemetery. She's not even interested anymore in going to the cemetery. I took a lei for my Dad's tombstone and we sat in the car and had lunch. Then we went to visit an old schoolteacher friend of hers who is still alive. And she kept saying on her walker, "Come in," and Mom kept saying, "NO." So from the roadway to her front door there's this conversation going on with two women yelling at each other in high-pitched voices, trying to communicate. It wasn't planned and we didn't want to go barging in on her. But she kept saying, "Come in, get out of the car and come in." And Mom kept saying, "No, I don't want to come in." Like a ten-minute conversation, which I thought was nice. We didn't call, we just drove by and said hi. She said, "Well, you must come back, Agatha, and spend the day with me." And Mom said, "And spend the night!" But you know that will never happen.

The only thing that gripes me is not my Mom, it's just the people who help her. They have to be flexible, too. I mean, if you change the pattern, like "Today we're not going swimming, we're going walking," whoa! They get very uptight about it. So now I see myself as the organizer, the house's keeper. I try to make sure that Mom gets a balanced weekly diet, that she's not eating the same thing. But I don't know. Is the woman who is watching Mom doing all the things that we told her to do? Sometimes we suspect that if Mom gets up really late, that she just has one meal. She doesn't have breakfast, she doesn't have lunch. She has brunch or she has either breakfast or lunch. Many times I've done the thing where, "This is what will be for lunch," and when I get home the stuff is still in the refrig. But you would think that you give people directions and they follow through with the instructions. I strongly feel that the wahine, the woman who is watching Mom is catching all the soaps. See, it's very touchy. What I will hate doing is, if this person that's taking care of Mom now leaves, is spending the time trying to find someone else. I certainly don't want a woman from Hong Kong again. I certainly don't want Zola again. You know.

ON FAMILY

It might be difficult if I were maybe a family person with children. I don't know. Caring for one takes up a lot of your time and you give up a lot of your time. I think because I'm the unmarried one and the youngest one, it kind of just naturally fell into my lap. Usually Hawaiians, at least our family, are always kind of close. But I don't mind it, taking care of parents. We're only able to do this because I guess you might say, Dad provided. I don't want to say he provided for Mom, but with what was left when he passed, we're able to do this. I know of friends who can't afford taking care of their parents, or parent, and put them away. Meaning in homes.

There are some hang-ups I have to take care of and I'm taking care of them. That's not important. But having the extra help is important. One way of getting rid of the stress is this—tobacco. I used to be a dancer—if they could see me now! [Here he gestured with his cigarette toward his body, indicating both his physical condition and his smoking.] Another way is to get into a totally oblivious state by watching television. Those are three ways of getting rid of stress. And getting out of the house.

Maybe if my sisters were in a bit more bad financial state, maybe we wouldn't be able to do this. Money we have, you know, would go to them. Yet they have their own lives. They're retired, I'm still working. Maybe they should be a little more helping with this situation. I mean physically, spiritually. But that's okay. I understand. They have a life to live. I mean, they're not just sitting back. They're in their early sixties, so they're still able to do things. One sister's husband has physical ailments. I know she'd like to come down, and she can come down from the Big Island because her son's a pilot; she gets a reasonable fare. She would like to come down more often, but she does have to take care of her spouse.

That sister lives on the Big Island and when she comes down it's, like, "I'm here! To help!" And I go, "Oh, forget it," because its the day-to-day things that are most important. Not that we should forget her, it's just that she doesn't have to be so assertive about it. I mean, when she comes I want to go somewheres else. I guess all of us in the family with the exception of my brother are very assertive. And when you have a bunch of assertive people, it gets very chaotic. The other sister, she's very family- and community-minded so she got involved in all kinds of things on her retirement. Volunteer here, volunteer there. Helping there, coming to see [Mom], so she's always on the go.

The other one lives here and she basically comes and checks in on Mom every day, four days of the week for sure. But you see, someone is with Mom, so she's coming in and checking on Mom when someone is there. And it's good when you have two people. My brother is in his late fifties, and I think he's become a recluse, so we'll just leave Brother where he is. See, for a while, before we got help, I was getting Mom up, I was bathing her, I was doing the meals. I felt, after the sisters retired, then I realized it was getting to be too much. I was getting stressed out with all the responsibilities.

FINAL THOUGHTS

Sometimes it's hard to watch because I realize what's happening and then you think about the future. Sometimes thinking about the future brings up a whole bunch of negatives, the fact that Mom's getting older, that she may not live . . . may not live another year. The fact that—how will I be when she's gone? I've been the last of the children and really connected with her every day and every night. I think she's become an integral part of my being, who I am. So will it be okay? Will I be all right? Will I be sad? We need to do short projections—today, tomorrow. It's just how the mainstream flows right now. I think what would happen if there was a big change in my life, but you know, as we get older, there are less changes. I think if there was a big change in my life maybe I'd want some more outs. But I'd not leave my Mom, or leave the situation that she's in.

Parents give a lot to their children, and I feel like I'm giving back. It's not that I feel guilty, that I have to give back. I don't feel that. I tell people how much parents give up for their children. I mean, I still remember growing up. My Mom—and this is true—she wore one pair of shoes until they just wore down. Then she got another. I mean she wasn't like this one woman who works for me who has forty pairs of shoes.

Mom kept all the letters and cards and stuff and paperwork that she had accumulated. But after Dad passed away, in editing things down, I finally threw away all the paper things. I did take out some of her papers, but her closet is still full. It can be thinned out so it is more accessible. I wonder if I should edit down Mom's belongings, because she probably won't wear them all. I would just keep the nice simpler things—something I've thought about. It just takes up more room, you keep dusting the same things. When we're getting her ready to go out, she doesn't know what she's wearing. But I tell her. Mom doesn't go through her things anymore.

Postscript

Mr. Nakana does not talk so much as perform. The two and a half hours we spent together were filled by skit after impromptu skit in which he would act out simultaneously the characters of various home aides, his mother, a nurse or doctor to illustrate some point. His whole approach is one closer to free association than to traditional discourse. This is not to suggest that Mr. Nakana is anything but perceptive and acute in his observations. The problem of communication between professional home aides, the elderly, and their families—in institutional or home settings—for example, is a theme in several of these stories. The dietary and communication problems faced in California by Mrs. Bee's mother and the language problems observed by "The Anniversary Girl," Mrs. Kumamoto, in nursing homes are both aspects of this same problem. What Mr. Nakana emphasizes is that the issue is not necessarily one of care-giver prejudice or care-receiver intransigence.

Conflicts with aides may in fact result from cultural differences or language problems. This is especially true in places like Hawaii distinguished by a large number of overt cultural and linguistic groups existing within a lingua franca of Pidgin English. The difficulties of a native speaker of Cantonese, Fijian, or Samoan attempting to communicate with a cognitively impaired Hawaiian-Japanese client are, while fraught with potential humor, also a serious barrier to care giving.

Like "The Miracle Pill's" Ruth Pfeiffer, Mr. Nakana details the problems inherent in balancing a care giver's often exhausting professional work schedule with the needs and problems that arise from supervising revolving shifts of home aide workers. The process, for example, of interviewing potential home-care aides, the need to acclimate them to the case and then supervise their actions on the job— all this is extraordinarily time-consuming and stressful. The alternative—insupportable to Mr. Nakana—was to place his mother in a nursing home. But as his story of the elderly Japanese neighbor demonstrates, Mr. Nakana associates that option with the death of the individual and, certainly, the death of relations with that fragile elder. I find particularly compelling and singularly moving his summation of the problems such a decision must involve. Nobody else has so clearly linked the issues of the elder's personal orientation, the problem of appropriate institutional assistance, the difficulties of distances separating family members interested in an elder's care, and the need to respect the preferences of the elderly person.

Clearly, Mr. Nakana's life is affected by his care giving role. He is overweight, far heavier than when he worked in theater, and smokes perhaps a pack of cigarettes a day. In addition, his social life, even though he hires home aides, is somewhat truncated by the demands of parent care. Care giving, coordinating schedules between aides, finding new aides, resolving home-care problems, dealing with his mother's physicians and the family issues are all time-consuming tasks on top of his professional responsibilities. And yet, Mr. Nakana takes real joy in his elder's care. He loves his role and appreciates seniors for their very existence. The rapid demise of an elderly Japanese neighbor woman following her institutionalization was, for him, a clearly cautionary tale. What drives him, at least in part, is an absolute insistence that his mother will not suffer a similar fate.

7

Allegiances and Alliances

Carol Bee is a schoolteacher who lives with her husband, Roger, and their children in Buffalo, New York. The family has three children, and the youngest, Martha, was nine years old at the time of the interview. A native of New York State, Carol's mother, Mrs. Ruben, moved first to California, where her son lives, following the death of Carol's father. Then, several ye rs later, following a debilitating stroke, she moved to Buffalo and her daughter's care. Carol insisted on the move because she was opposed to her mother's entry into a nursing home, and the woman's poststroke deficits (mobility, speech impairment, functional dysle:·ia, etc.) made a nursing home, in her son's view, a necessity. This interview took place in August of 1989, four years after Carol's mother moved to a house purchased for her by her daughter and son-in-law. It stands a half block from her daughter's.

What would you like to know? My life's story? How I got myself into this problem? Well, my mother has a saying, and I think it's true in every case: "A son is a son until he takes a wife. A daughter is a daughter for all her life." I think daughters are more inclined to be the care givers for the parents. That's why I had three children, so I'd have a daughter [laughs]. Someday this will all be Martha's. I don't know how it happens, but it does. Friends of mine have only one child and I tell them, "If you can possibly squeeze out another one, do it." These children are going to be relatively young when they have the responsibility for aging parents. And for one child it is very difficult.

There isn't a lot I can do, and I guess the reason is that I feel the situation is . . . , I brought it on myself. I wanted three kids. I can't blame anyone else. [My husband] Roger was my "victim" [laughs] and Rog hasn't changed too much over the last fifteen years. I invited my mother to live here. So I yell and scream a lot.

CALIFORNIA

My mother has had high blood pressure since she was a young woman. I think it's amazing she didn't have a stroke sooner, considering her blood pressure was up in the 200 range, you know. There is some weakness in her hands. But she's also arthritic. She's diabetic. She has carpal tunnel syndrome. She has a lot of little things. The major problem is her stroke was in the brain stem and it affected her balance. The fact that her nerve passages were knocked out really doesn't help the situation. One side of her face was affected. She seems to think she has a much greater problem with speech than she does. She's really very easy to understand. And when she's lying in bed and speaking she's a little slurry, and I tell her, "Sit up and talk right or don't talk to me!" But she can make herself understood.

And her attention wanders. The big problem is that she's not been able to read. Somehow her eyes have also been affected. She can see, but the words jump all over. She used to love to get into bed with a book, and she would read three, four hours a night, and that's been taken away. She doesn't have the patience to work a tape recorder. You know, she'll go from side one to side four and the story will make no sense to her [laughs]. "Did you turn the tape, Ma?" She says, "Nah."

When did she have her stroke? I think it must have been four years ago in the fall when she was in California. The following August my sister-in-law and my niece brought her east to visit me. At that time my sister-in-law told me that she and my brother were going to be looking for a "residence" for my mother because they could not manage any longer with her in an apartment and needing aides.

After her stroke, they put her in a rehab center and she worked harder than the younger people there to regain or at least get it [full mobility and use] back. Because of the severity of the stroke and where it was, where it affected her, she'd never get it 100 percent. And unfortunately, the way they work it there in California is that one morning my brother got a call saying, "You have to take your mother out." She evidently had not made the percentage of recovery that she was supposed to—for that week—and whatever insurance that she had was going to stop paying. So it was a hassle to get everything into the apartment and get an aide and so on. They started with agency help, but that got to be rather expensive, and then they went the route of, you know, advertising.

I don't think they were doing a whole lot for her, really. Not the rehab people or my brother and sister-in-law. In the time that my mother had the stroke until she moved here, my sister-in-law never even prepared a meal for her. Now, this is not a woman who has overwhelming responsibilities. Her kids are grown and most of the time she was working maybe three times a week as a teacher's aide. They would do ridiculous things. For example, Mom made out a shopping list and this is now six or eight months into it. She would forget to put things on the list and my brother would think she did it, so he would have to go again. To get attention.

Also, they didn't use a whole lot of sense when they arranged for care for her. In spite of the fact that my mother had lived out there for five or six years previous to this, my brother and sister-in-law still didn't seem to know what made her tick. Instead of taking her out and letting her go shopping one day a week so she could point at or say what she wanted, they'd go by and get lists, and because she'd forget to write down everything on the lists, she would need something else. But my brother always thought it was a ploy to get him to go out again. In some cases, I think it was, but I really don't think they did what they could have done to make it easier for them.

They were getting Mexicans to act as nurse's aides. Mexicans. She had some who were okay, but then she would end up getting people . . . One woman only lasted overnight because she was taking my mother's sleeping pills and medication. Most of the problems with the aides I still don't feel were my mother's problem. She might have been fussy, but the fact is nobody ever made her a meal. She lived on cottage cheese and canned vegetables. If any cooking was done—even in the situation that she was in, barely speaking and not being able to move—she did the cooking. One woman she had right off the boat from somewhere didn't know how to make Jell-O. I think if my brother didn't have the pressure of getting his own work done, maybe he could have done a little more.

BUFFALO

That August when my sister-in-law said they were starting to look
for retirement homes, I said forget it. I felt—and I still feel—that if
she had gone into a nursing home or any type of residence she would
not have survived the move because she is the type of person . . . her
home was always very, very important to her. Her *tchotchkes,* her
knicknacks, were always very important to her. The four thousand
pictures of her grandchildren that she has hanging up—very important to her; and I don't think she could have gone into a one-room
situation that was more like a hospital and survived. I really did not
think that would be possible.

Sometimes you just get lucky. At the same time she was visiting
here, a double [duplex] came on the market down the street. And
at that time I spoke to my husband, Roger, and said that when his
parents need help, the chances are very good that I'm going to supply
it. And, really, why should I have to do for his parents without doing
for my mother too? He's been okay about it. My aunt and uncle
loaned us the money for the down payment. At the same time that
I wanted to do this, I didn't think I should go into debt. It was an
expensive house. I knew the people who owned the house and, for
the purpose we wanted the house, it was important to them as well
that I get the house. They could have gotten a little more, but they
took our offer. They supported our decision. So my mother sent all
her furniture back from California and the pieces that looked so out
of place [there] just fit in so perfectly here.

AIDES

When she first moved here, I advertised in the paper and got
someone to live in. I know there is someone out there that I can get
for just a couple hours a day, someone with a car who can take my
mother where she wants to go. What happens is I get these people
and they spend all their time telling her their problems, and the fact
is my mother has a very, very sharp, a cutting sense of humor. When
she's on, she's hot. And she doesn't have patience for incompetents.
She doesn't have patience for people who do things slowly.

After her last live-in aide ended up in the psycho ward at Erie

County Hospital, I told her she really was too miserable to live with anyone. She likes to have her house to herself. The problem is when she has aides coming in, she wants to treat them like slaves. That's what she wants. I said, "You know, you have a companion. Someone who will sit and talk with you," but she doesn't want them talking. She wants to see, for her six, eight, ten dollars, an hour of heavy labor, which is not the point. And she doesn't need to have that done. She likes to be around younger people. She always has.

FINANCES

I really need to get her more aide service. Financially, she is in better shape than when she came from California. The rents and all the other expenses are cheaper here. When she was in California, her doctor wanted to see her every month to do complete blood work and so on, which ended up costing a fortune for her diabetes and whatever. Well, the internist that she's going to here, once every three months he sees her and once every six months he does her blood work. And the fact is that every time she's tested she's fine. So he says, why do it more often? It's expensive. So you know she really has cut down on expenses, but at the same time she's getting. . . . Well, I tell her and she thinks I'm not, you know, not very polite when I tell her that she's being tighter than a horse's ass. That she's becoming cheap. That it's time to spend more. At the same time I want her to spend more on getting aide time, I realize that she has a finite amount of money, and in the event she needs something later on, I don't want to say, "Well, she was fine and I made her spend all her money early on." Because you don't know how long this money has to last, it makes it very difficult to plan what to do now.

You do not know what a life span is, what kind of care will be necessary. And, as I said before, I find and I have always felt that it is easier when your parents really don't know who you are or don't know where they are and don't have the mental facilities, because I think then you can make, you can make decisions for them. You can even place them in places where they will get 24-hour care and yet you don't have on your conscience the fact that you're abandoning them. It's easier when they don't know what planet they're on. It's more difficult when they only have the physical limitations.

I think, maybe if I thought that if you wish real hard for something you'll get it, that then maybe, my conscience would bother me. Considering the things that I have wished for in the past. It's just that I say to myself, "God, it would be so much easier."

WAITING

When the phone rings at odd times, you're waiting for it.

Now, here's an example. She called the other day—"Hi! How are yah?" Oh, she's having a terrible time. She's having terrible problems. So I figure, what the hell could go wrong? She has another bladder infection? Her eyes are this or that? What part of her? Well, her aide who takes care of her dinner and takes her shopping one day a week—and I might add that I take her shopping at least once or twice a week myself—the aide's car broke down and my mother had something to photocopy and she was down to one quart of milk and couldn't get meat for the week because Barbara's car had broken down. And I find that my mother is so egocentric that this really is important to her.

You can go in there today and discuss any world situation with her. She knows the name of the leader of every country. She knows what's going on in Iran. She knows what's going on in the stock market. It doesn't matter to her. I mean, there are tremendous problems in the world. And the thing that bothers her and is so overwhelming is that she needs something xeroxed, which means she wants to send something in to AARP [American Association of Retired Persons], which means she could do this in six month's time. I'm supposed to come up with the answers. That I find aggravating.

I said to her this time, especially since my father-in-law is presently in hospital for a cataract operation and whatever, "You know, considering the world situation, I really don't consider those major problems." And then I said I would send over my oldest son Peter. "He'll go down and xerox. He can stop off and get your milk, and you have plenty of food in the house. But," I said, "you know what? It seems to me you can solve these problems yourself." And when I force her to, she does think of ways to solve these tremendous problems. Because she says, "Oh, she has such a terrible thing," God knows what she's going to come up with. And then when I find out it's . . . that she's down to one quart of milk instead of four quarts, which is what she likes to keep on hand for just her. Those things aggravate me, and I find them hard to deal with.

Sometimes it gets so that I'm trying to think, "Well, my mother hasn't been out for three days or so. I've got to take her for a ride. I should take the kids some place. I should do this for that one. I should do this for the other one." And along this continuum of things and of people I'm doing things for, I've no time to do anything for myself, because I feel at some point, well, maybe there will be time later for me to rest. I've always been one who could put off my rewards. I don't need immediate gratification. I can wait, but sometimes it builds up so that even though I don't even necessarily want to do anything, I resent the fact that I can't.

The problem is that when my mother is fine, she's fine. But if she passes out, if she has a seizure [a small stroke], someone has to be with her for the eight or twelve hours while she's real weak, until she recuperates. She can't be on her own. Because I never know when it's going to hit I just can't say, "Well, I'm going to take off because she's going to be fine this weekend."

I wanted to go visit a friend of mine who lives in North Carolina. It was a matter of trying to go when my mother was visiting her sister. And it just didn't work out. Then I have Rog, who doesn't want to take on any responsibility for the kids. So while my mother-in-law offered and she could watch them, now that my father-in-law is sick, I can't ask her for two weeks to watch the kids because she'll have her hands filled with *that* big baby. I'm really between a rock and a hard place, and the easiest thing is to say, "Forget it. I just won't go." But I don't say that easily, and I resent the fact that I can't go, and I just feel that over the last fifteen years that I've been married or twenty years that I've been teaching . . . why can't I just go away for the weekend? And I just feel that I can't.

My work really has been my salvation, the fact that I go out of the home. Not only do I make reasonably good money, but no matter what happens, I'm entitled to a 45-minute prep period a day. So for forty-five minutes once a day, Monday to Friday, I have forty-five minutes absolutely to my self. Now that's a hell of a reason to go into teaching or working [laughs] or whatever. But usually, I don't otherwise have forty-five minutes for myself a day, and there are things I know I should do. I should exercise more. I should get outside and do things. I have the time, I really do have the time. I'm not tired physically. I'm just drained, you know, emotionally and mentally. I'm usually the type of person who can force myself to do anything that I feel I have to do. Things that I don't want to do and things that I really resist doing. I can make myself do those things. But I have to be sharp, and that's the problem. It doesn't take as much to get me tired to the point where I cannot make myself do things.

AGGRAVATIONS

My mother passes out every once in a while. Knock on wood, she hasn't done it recently, so I'm expecting it. She has, like, a seizure and it only takes her twelve, twenty-four hours to recover and then she's fine. But it's never knowing when it's going to happen, you know, or when I'm going to get a phone call to please come get her because she's, you know, whatever. Or they need help. The hardest part, and it seems awfully superficial, is knowing that for as long as she's living here I can't go away for Thanksgiving, or the Fourth of July or Memorial Day, those traditional days when you get together with family. They're still important to her and there is no other family here, so I almost feel as if I'm tied here and can't escape.

I think the thing I really resented is that after my father died, my brother insisted she come to California so he could take care of her. She had five or six good years in California [before the stroke] that I felt were denied me and my children—his children were grown by that time—and when she really needed the care, that was it. It was too much for him. I really resented that. I resent him because he didn't do what he said he was going to do and he didn't do it as well as he was capable. Except for the fact that, you have to understand, my brother has no common sense whatsoever. My sister-in-law has two master's degrees in counseling and education and, uh, she hated teaching when she student-taught and hated teaching for the one year she did it. She lasted about three weeks in the classroom. She's now selling Thomasville furniture and loving it. She's a very bright woman who cannot deal on a day-to-day basis with things, and even when I resent them, I still feel they can't help being stupid. I'm just tired of doing it and the laundry and the picking up.

Do I still feel that way? Of course I do! I'm certainly not one to forgive and forget. I don't forget anything. He had her for the good times and, ah, in spite of the fact that he was supposed to be taking care of her, when push came to shove, he was ready to relinquish his responsibilities. The fact that my brother, until Peter's bar mitzvah, had not been here for two years—almost two years!—this is the son who swore eternal gratefulness for the care he got as a youngster and would take care of his mother—I've just been really aggravated.

I think part of it is that my mother does see that maybe he wasn't you know so, ah, terrific. Or maybe that he hasn't been the type of son he promised to be. When they came here for my son's bar mitzvah, my brother and his family should have stayed with me because I have more room. But I figured that my mother hasn't seen her granddaughters in two years. Let them stay with her. My mother could not wait for them to leave [laughs with satisfaction]. Couldn't wait to get rid of them. They're the same way they were in California. They didn't pick up after themselves. She's the one who did the cooking. My mother and I are both the type of people who believe that if you have to ask someone to do something for you that is obvious, that has to be done—like take the dishes into the kitchen or wash them—then you'd rather do it yourself.

FINAL THOUGHTS

I think personally that over the last three years my mother has gotten much stronger physically. That's not to say she could hold down a full-time job or that kind of thing, but there are four days a week she doesn't have anyone there in the mornings. She gets dressed herself, she gets her own breakfast, and most times she gets her own lunch. She complains she's tired, she's this, she's that, and I still have her do it, because at least she's in her own home and doing it.

The kids go there after school because they get home earlier than I do. There have been a lot of positive things just because the kids know they have another grandmother. Their Bubbie, you know. If I had to do it again, I'd do it again and I would get psychiatric care. No, I would do it again, because when it's good, it's great. And when it's not good, its not unexpected. That doesn't make it any easier, but it's not unexpected.

Postscript

Carol Bee is quite correct when she says her mother's condition has improved greatly since she moved to Buffalo. When she left California, the older woman was virtually wheelchair bound and unable to walk any but short distances or care for herself. Now she can ambulate with a cane and cook, and has become, if not self-sufficient, then far more self-aware and able than anyone originally believed would be possible. Although reading remains a problem for Mrs. Ruben because of a neurologic condition which will probably not reverse, she otherwise has been transformed from a virtually silent, taciturn, often unpleasant woman to one who seems set and certain in her place and with her family. She certainly can be acerbic and does, as Carol Bee insists, work on staying in touch with world affairs and with the world of her grandchildren.

Writing about the relation of elderly individuals to their children, sociologists Leopold Rosenmayr and Eva Köcheis described the ideal situation as "intimacy at a distance." Old people, they suggested, want to maintain physical distance—and thus independence—from their adult children without becoming isolated from them. In Buffalo, living about a three-minute walk from both her daughter and her son-in-law, Mrs. Ruben has achieved the appearance of the ideal. She is relatively independent, despite the need for home aides and attention from her daughter. Her grandchildren make her feel wanted and useful and needed. Since arriving in Buffalo, Mrs. Ruben has become a source of joy and an object of affection to her three grandchildren, who often visit her after school, run errands for her, and appear to genuinely enjoy her company.

The oldest son, whose bar mitzvah is mentioned here, developed an interest in cooking from his grandmother and learned to make traditional dishes under her tutelage. This affection is contrasted by the distance between Mrs. Ruben and her other grandchildren who visited from California. "She couldn't wait to get rid of them," Mrs. Bee says with satisfaction. But then, those young children had not seen Mrs. Ruben for several years—she was in many ways a stranger to them. Even when Mrs. Ruben lived in California, Mrs. Bee suggests that visits between generations were kept at a ceremonial minimum. For Carol Bee, the relations between her parent and her children is reward enough for her efforts. As proud as she is of her mother's physical progress, this social interaction between grand-children and grandparent is, for her, a personal triumph.

Perhaps the key to the Bees' success with Mrs. Ruben is that Carol Bee listened to and believed her mother, took her mother's complaints seriously. If Mrs. Ruben complained about an aide hired by her daughter, Mrs. Bee did not immediately discount the woman's criticism as the bitching of a bored old lady. She accepted from the start her mother's deficits and believed that with care, they could improve. Further, despite her statement that only daughters care for elderly relatives, she has consciously assured that all her children—male and female—know, visit, and help their grandmother. Carol Bee did not specifically promote the alliance of grandmother and grandson in the kitchen. But from the beginning, she believed that proximity would create areas of mutual care, concern, and interest. From this, she knew as an article of faith that good would come—both for her children and for her mother. That faith has been rewarded, and when asked if she would do it again, despite the frustration that the situation has created, she answered, "In a minute."

8

The Wrestler's Secret Yell

In 1988, Brian Leonard returned to his parents' rural West Virginia home to help care for a father whose multiple ailments and progressive dementia required constant home care from the family. Until his illness, Mr. Leonard's father had run a training camp for wrestlers where, in earlier years, his son had worked and trained. The story exemplifies the ambivalence children often feel during a parental decline. How Mr. Leonard felt toward his father, a man he had idolized, changes across this document and in his telling of these tales, from moment to moment.

This story is the only one presented here that deals explicitly with a parent whose illness is clearly terminal. But it is important to remember that when physicians insist that death is imminent, the elder often not only endures but recovers. Thus, while in retrospect this story is one dealing with the care of a terminally ill parent, this care stretched over almost two years, and even when dialysis was terminated, the father endured for a time.

For a while I was hit with rushes of emotion out of the blue. While walking, driving, sitting—I'd just burst into tears. Emotionally, I hit an all-time low. But that only lasted for so long. I guess I've cried myself out of it. Although my dad made a comeback after my sisters, my cousin Webster, his sister and brother-in-law, and one of his old wrestlers had come home or stopped by. Today, about two weeks since he's been unplugged, he's slowing down. Actually, tonight I feel strange. I lack words to describe this feeling that tonight my dad will die. He's sitting in a chair. An hour ago he gave his secret yell. I told you he yells a lot. My uncle says that yelling on the farm was common when my dad was a child—not arguments, but just communicating across the fields and orchard. Mom has become Margie (Dad's closest sister) to him, and I am often Ken (his older brother). Ken died a couple of months ago from heart failure. He died quickly, with a sigh, after dancing with his wife.

The worst part is dealing with Dad's senility. He's confused at least 95 percent of the time. He yells when he wants something, and he won't stop yelling until he gets it, or flops out of bed before yelling unceasingly more. Whoever spends the night with him gets little sleep. The last three nights I spent with him I got no more than a total of fifteen minutes' sleep combined. I try being a good son, but that doesn't last long since I lose my patience and we are at war half the time.

When he was my age he let himself go. I'm resentful he didn't take better care of himself. I'm resentful of the pain he's put Mom through the past nine months, and for her misery. Mom has been keeping him alive, yet he's been draining the life out of her. I resent my dad for being a glutton.

But I love him. I've loved him more than anyone. Now I feel like an asshole because I feel his condition has caused an inconvenience to me. What a selfish bastard I am! I resent resenting him, because it's his senility that has changed his character. There are moments when Dad is there, when he's Dad and he makes a humorous comment or asks a thoughtful question. But those moments are few and forgotten when trying to handle his obstinate, senile demands.

My dad has fallen apart physically and mentally. He seldom has the strength to raise to his elbow, to be handed a glass of water while lying in bed. He does manage to flop out of bed. Because he's 220-plus pounds, it's no wonder I popped my first hemorrhoid lifting him off the floor, onto the toilet, into the shower, to his cart, or into the car.

Hell, I'm really a jerk if I have to complain about a hemorrhoid. My dad has hemorrhoids, too, or else they're varicose veins around his asshole. He gets clogged up. It must be hell, because he'll go five days without shitting. When it won't come out my mom, dad, or I have to pick it out. My sisters don't have the stomach for it and, I have to admit, I almost blew chunks the first time I did it. His shit is like petrified loaves of knotted bread with the consistency of half-dried clay. The size of the logs is like half a large hoogie [submarine sandwich]. Although it's not at all appetizing to us, it is to our dog Randy. Now my mom and I throw the logs across the road into the woods or bury them in a pile of grass to hide them from Randy. If the logs weren't so big, we'd flush them down the toilet. [Ed. note: This is a dangerous and often an unnecessary as well as an unpleasant procedure. The problem can often be remedied by diet change, suppository use, enemas, or other less invasive procedures. At my suggestion, a health nurse visited their family, and with diet changes, this aspect of Mr. Hold's condition improved.]

Because of Dad's weakness, we rarely put him on the usual toilet. Instead, we carry a portable one next to the bed before lifting him over onto it. When he doesn't get his pecker in the hole, he pisses on the floor. On the thick carpeting. We think the carpet reeks, but our dog Randy loves it and occasionally rolls in it—even after the carpet has been cleaned.

When wrestlers die they're sometimes quickly forgotten, while great authors have life after death. But then, my father once told me, "Great wrestlers never die, they just smell that way." [laughs]

IMMINENT DEATH

In the past month I experienced my father's death five times. The first time was the last night he was hooked up to the [dialysis] machine. With today's technology, the doctors gave Dad a year of reasonable quality of life on the dialysis, but that hasn't been the case through the following [last] eight months. I began to feel bitter toward the doctors for keeping him alive longer than what was humane, at least in my mind, and he's my dad!

It was 4 A.M. and I was in an unforgivable mood. He was on the floor, yelling and wanting back in bed. When he locked, wrestler's grip around my neck, I bear-hugged him, lifted, and when he made no effort to help, I uncaringly threw him on the bed. When he landed on the mattress, on his back, he didn't move and stared at the ceiling.

He looked dead. I thought I had killed him. My body chilled under the skin. I became scared and guilt ridden. I couldn't get him to respond for half a minute, which seemed like eternity. When he did respond, he told me that I was a good son. I realized that I shouldn't feel resentful toward him any longer. My eyes swelled. That was my dad, before he drifted back into his scary world.

The second time was at Harvey [Medical Center] when, after a visit to the psychiatrist, he went into a coma. The doctors said his death could be at any minute and asked permission to do an autopsy.

But a few hours later he came out of it and was rolling on the floor after flopping over the bars of the hospital bed. When I arrived to bring him home, I found him tied in bed still trying to fall to the floor. He's had this feeling of falling for weeks, and it's so strong he makes himself fall.

The third and fourth times were when I was giving him a shower, and the fifth time was the day we made the funeral arrangements.

The doctors said that it would probably take ten days for him to die. On the ninth or tenth day, he seemed near death. My sisters came home and we made funeral arrangements. We decided to have a viewing, after talking to one of Dad's old wrestlers, before cremating him. There will be no plot or tombstone, and he's not going to be set on the mantel in an urn. We had first decided to plant a tree over his ashes next to our cabin at camp, but now I think we will spread them in the woods. According to our understanding, the ashes will be the thicker, calcium parts such as teeth and larger joints. My mother thought that the ashes would be like campfire ashes. We held a box of somebody's ashes at the funeral home which were, surprisingly, heavier than expected. Mom has a problem with thinking about Dad's ashes, especially if she'd be able to discern some of his parts. She said that she doesn't want to be the one to spread them, so I volunteered.

But when I told her that I thought this was going to be a neat burial, that I'd like to be buried in the same manner (it's almost like a Mongolian burial); this way the woods would be a living symbol of Dad, and since squirrels eat fallen antlers for the calcium and that Dad probably would be quickly recycled . . . well, I should have kept my mouth shut. Mom started to cry. She was no longer crazy about spreading his ashes. Now, instead, I will bury them in the woods. I seem to be able to talk about Dad's death easily now, but I have a feeling that when he does die, and I see him dead, and he lies in that coffin, and I hold and bury his bones . . . I think it will *not* be easy.

Once we made the plans and gave the information to the funeral-home dude, we went upstairs to pick out a coffin. I felt weird shopping for a coffin. I didn't like it. I have some beautiful cherry planks curing that a local sawmill cut from the logs of a tree I felled. I was going to make a table and a large set of shelves for my growing library, but I'd like to use it to make my dad's coffin. However, Mom doesn't go for that idea. When I found out that the coffin we had agreed on in the showroom [for the viewing] was the coffin to be used [in cremation], I waited for the others to turn their backs. Then I removed the price tag and hopped in with the intention of lying down. But when my sitting in it made sounds of ripping or stretching, I hopped back out. My mom gets embarrassed when her 29-year-old son screws around like that.

I'm seeing how much I'm like him. I hope I don't end up like him. I can't undo what's been done. I wish I could. I wish I could have my dad back how he was ten years ago. His death is slow. His mother, brother, and several friends who used to visit him are now dead themselves. I don't know who else he'll outlive.

After the death of his father, Brian Leonard went through a short, intense period of grief. Acting out that grief included "punching out" a local newspaper editor who ran what was, Brian felt, an unflattering and less than accurate obituary. Six months later I received the following from him in a letter:

The other day I drove my grandmother, who had been spending the holidays with us, to Altoona where a friend, Ronnie, was waiting to take her the rest of the way back to Sparksville. After a filling lunch of pot pie (West Virginia Dutch–style) and conversation (Ronnie-style), I walked Grandma to Ronnie's jeep. The door was locked, so I tried those on the other side while Ronnie walked back into the restaurant to look for her misplaced keys. Meanwhile, finding all the doors locked, I walked back to stand next to Grandma. She stood relaxed, facing the jeep, while a gush of urine spritzed her legs and puddled between her galoshes. I twisted my neck to better my view between Grandma's legs. When she saw me, she leaned over to gaze at her cataract and puddle. As soon as she leaned slightly, not knowing what to do or say, I did an about-face and walked away in hopes of saving Grandma from losing face.

I thought of saying something to Ronnie but decided against it. I just wanted to hit the road. On my way home later, I couldn't get Grandma out of my mind. After the caring for my father, the [thought of] caring for my grandmother if she were to start falling apart seemed a horrible ennui. Out of my own selfish and self-centered thoughts, I hoped that she would hold together at least until I got out of the country. I was planning a trip to China to finish my thesis at the time. But then I thought that maybe I was carrying this too far, maybe she's good for another fifteen years, that it was just her bladder that's going, and all she needs are diapers.

As soon as I got home I told my mother in case she thought that she should bring it up with Grandma. Mom laughed. She told me that Grandma never wears underwear and that she probably thought that she could get away with urinating outside, thinking I'd stay on the other side of the jeep, with no one else around—with Ronnie inside—saving herself from a trip inside to the rest room. I laughed in relief.

> *In November 1990, I received a letter from Brian in which he recounted a dream about his father that indicated that issues raised by the caregiving period had not been resolved. Earlier in the year he had married Daryl, a woman with whom he had grown up.*

In the dream it was autumn, or a warm snap in winter—I'm not altogether sure, not important. We were here at camp: me and Dad, Mom, Uncle Bill, Aunt Doris, maybe Aunt Marge, maybe some of my sisters, and Daryl. But Daryl was never really in view, just always holding my hand, standing beside me or behind. Dad and Aunt Doris and either Mom or Aunt Marge were walking around the lake, the women helping my feeble father. The rest of us were standing near the old fireplace in the center of camp, watching the others as they made their way at the far side of the lake (an impossible view in reality).

When they reached us, I was so proud of Dad for walking as far and as strongly as he did. Then everyone stood in a group, talking about things I wasn't listening to; Dad and I simply looked at each other. It was that old look we used to give each other. It used to say everything: I love you. No words had to be spoken; it didn't have to be said (although those words were often spoken, just not at *these* moments). As I looked at Dad I couldn't help noticing that he looked different. He wasn't really old. The white in his hair, his eyebrows, and his eyelashes didn't look real. Rather, he looked like his younger, strong, handsome self, but he'd just walked out of a grist mill.

As we stared into each other I felt my stare not only saying, "I love you," but "I miss you!" as well. He knew that, and we just continued staring as I began to shed tears, not breaking our stare, wanting not to hide them, but for him to know how much I miss him!

I woke up crying. Which woke Daryl. And when I explained my dream to her, I bawled. We were both awake when the five-thirty alarm went off.

Postscript

Terminal illness—the reaction of patients and their families to certain and immanent death—has its own dynamics, which may or may not relate to the complex of ongoing geriatric illness. At first, I did not want to introduce the issues of terminal care in a book whose emphasis is ongoing, future-oriented cases of elder care. But the conflicted emotions that Brian Leonard clearly articulates—"I love him," "I hate him" "I don't want to grow up to be like him," and so forth—are so much a part of the complex of elder care that I thought his statement important enough to include. Hating the physical wreck while loving the essential person who was parent is common, and perhaps hidden in many of these tales. Although others seem to share these feelings covertly, none have been able to speak with Brian Leonard's remarkable frankness. Margaret Nielson talks about the frustration she went through in caring for her grandmother and the blind loyalty that drove her to extreme care-giving measures. Mrs. Kumamoto's voice constricts when she remembers the way her mother tricked her into going to Japan and then constricts again as she talks about the years immediately afterward. But all through this conversation, she speaks of watching her mother and caring for her, loving what she was and accepting what she has become. Yet no one so explicitly (or graphically) sums up the emotional equations as Brian Leonard does.

Further, the rural context of the Leonard family and the physical world of wrestling that father and son inhabited together both stand in contrast to the largely urban setting in which most of the stories here are told. Indeed, it seems that Brian relates best to his role when he can be physical—picking up his father, demonstrating the secret yell, or doing some other manual act that gives his presence in the family purpose and drive. If physical activity is a part of the Leonards' rural world, it also provides a venue in which Brian can be involved with his mother in his father's care. The type of familial battles that mark, for example, Tina Harding's or Carol Bee's tales—or those detailed in *Mirrored Lives*—are absent here. But then, Brian is a prodigal son, and clearly willing to do whatever he can to help his mother care for his father in a terminal geriatric crisis.

This story emphasizes the degree to which physical problems are often manifestations of a family member's sensibilities more than of the patient's failure. Issues of bladder and bowel control, discussed here in Brian's nonchalantly graphic language, are a motif in many of these stories. Mrs. Kumamoto is unconcerned about her mother's bladder or bowel problems, and Craig Williams has become an expert on adult diapers, a subject on which he now lectures to Alzheimer's disease support groups with knowledge and enthusiasm. But it is inconceivable that Marie Dister, for example, would attempt as messy a procedure as the manual removal of feces. Alice McLeod felt that her grandfather's comparatively minor physical complaints demanded institutionalization, while other family members, used to these problems, were more amenable to home management. In *Mirrored Lives,* one brother chastises me for washing my father because, he insisted, "we weren't raised to empty bed pans." In all these narratives, it is the sensibility of a family member—not the elder's physical condition per se—that often makes the difference between continued home care or institutionalization.

Thus Brian Leonard's concern over his grandmother's bladder control at the end is especially interesting. Now a more urban university graduate, he is somewhat offended and sees this as a sign of perhaps another geriatric decline that could affect his personal plans and, as important, creates a dread he has no real words for. He calls this a horrible "ennui," perhaps an attempt to find some "educated" phrase for feelings he cannot otherwise express. In his statements, typically so direct, that phrase signals his ambivalence toward the rural, physical world in which he grew up, and the aging of that world. It is this tension that propels the story rather than the contrast between the urban, extended world he has moved to through university life and the slower, rural lifestyle of the father whom he admired. In this conflict I think his grandma's "falling apart" was more a symbol of the choices he had faced than a real problem to him. He was urban enough to notice and be concerned about the older woman's lack of bladder control and rural enough, "down-home" enough, to be able to speak of it frankly to his mother.

9

No More Christmas Cookies

Marie Dister is a mother of two in her early forties who is largely uninvolved in the care of her grandparents. Although she expresses concern for them—and admiration for their longevity—neither she nor her husband, Peter, direct their attention to care giving. Her story is included here in an attempt to provide a far different perspective from those presented in other interviews. It is offered, with "The Queen's Telegram," as an example of those more distant relatives whose concern for fragile elders perhaps exists but is not exercised in a significant way.

I have all my grandparents still alive, which I think is very amazing and wonderful. My mum's a single child, and she has all the responsibility for the four of them. My husband Peter has just one grandparent left. He doesn't have anything really to do with her anymore. She basically lives with her daughter—his aunt—who provides everything. So there's nothing really he has to do. But he doesn't want any part of her. He doesn't even send her a Christmas card. It's awful. And she'll be 91 this year. She's an amazing woman for her age, but unfortunate things have happened over the years, so they sort of don't feel close to her anymore. If that's the word. Oh yeah, I think it's that she's just sort of alienated their family. I think Peter's angry, that he still has a lot of feelings that he doesn't want to admit. I mean, he says, like, "Why should I start liking her now?" I mean, he doesn't provide any care for her at all.

It goes back to when Peter's mom and dad were going to get

married, and he was going into the war, World War II. He got married two months before going off to war. She was Catholic, he wasn't. One of those type of things. So of course Peter's grandmother refused to accept the marriage. She didn't go watch them get married or things like that. And things just happened over the years. She finally accepted Peter's mom, but, I donno, never really showed a lot of affection to the kids. Like, when we got married, or the other family members got married, she never showed up. She didn't show up. It wasn't important to her. She'd send the invitation back, you know, and at the "will attend, will not," the "will not" was typed in. So Pete didn't even invite her when we got married—I'm his second marriage. And Peter's sister, when she was married, she had to go down on her hands and knees and cry and beg her grandmother to go to the wedding. And she said, "But I need two hundred dollars to come to the wedding." Little things. And now she wants very much to get back into the family, and nobody wants her to.

I have one set of grandparents who live in a home, Rivell House on Sinclair Avenue. At first it was getting them from their apartment into the home. That was fun, yeah. My grandmother had broken her hip like three times and was sort of unable to get around. Mum couldn't come up there, to her, as much as she wanted to. And she, Grandma, was pretty fragile and she lost a lot of weight. Once that happened, the doctor put her onto a social worker from the hospital, Trying to locate some place for them. And that's how she got into it. I don't know if the social worker even talked about private home care, whatever. So that's when Mum said, "You know, either we have to get someone in here full-time or we'll have to put you into a home." So we decided to put her into a home. She couldn't have moved in with my mum and dad. It just wouldn't have worked. Maybe if my mum and dad had lived in a bigger house, but I don't think they would have even done it even then. I think it's just too difficult.

What do they want, my grandparents?

I don't know. I never really asked that. I don't think it would matter to Grandad where he was because I don't think he gets out. But she can talk to the other people. And she's not pleased with the food. She thinks the food is awful. My son would say that it sucks. And like, sometimes they get peanut butter and jam sandwiches, and she thinks that's horrible. I think she would have liked to have stayed at her apartment. I don't know, it wasn't a part of the deal. Could she have afforded to have someone come in? I donno. I don't know how expensive that is. Is it expensive?

It was sad. They both took some of their furniture with them. You figure, you work so long to accumulate these things that you want, you know? And then all of a sudden, someday you have to say, "Well, you can have this, dear. And you can have that." And you have to give it all away, or sell it all. That hit all of us really hard. Grandmum and Dad were always great travelers, but it seems like it's all out the window. It seems like they don't just, sort of, sit back. They didn't even keep their slides! They could have kept that! They could have kept that in our, in somebody's house! But she didn't even want them anymore.

It's sort of like, "All these good times that we had, they're all gone now. Let's just remember that we're sick every day." It can't be easy on anybody, I guess. If someone took everything I worked a lifetime for away from me, I donno. Grandma still sort of complains now, she says something about her dress being missing. She says, "I don't know what your mother did with my dress." And I said, "Well, I don't think she took it, Grandma." And she said, "Well, I don't know where it is." It's, I guess, her way of saying, "I don't like this." Over Christmas I stitched her a wreath, a Christmas-type thing, and she thought my Mum had given it to somebody. It's all very hard. She told my dad to invest some money [for her], and so my dad put it into some of those T-bills, you know? She kept thinking my Dad was taking her money from her. It's really hard on everybody.

It was hard for a while, because it was hard on her. Life wasn't good for her. She wasn't enjoying any part of her life. Grandad was sick. Now, every time that you phone her, you say, "How are you doing, Grandma?" And then she'll go [making a face], "Well, you know, there are some good days and there are bad days, but I married him for better or for worse. And I guess this is the worst." And every day we hear that. Every time you talked to her, she'd want to cry or something. And when you constantly call somebody and get the same answer you think, "I don't know if I want to hear this again." Even if you know what they're going through. And you think, "Oh, I know, but . . . " I have no idea how I'd be. It can't be easy for them, and I guess I can't expect them to be happy every time either, but I guess that's what we'd want for them. I mean, that you'd go in there and say, "How's everything?" And she'd say, "Oh, fine! I mean, don't worry about me!" Isn't that sort of how we all feel, what we want?

MATERNAL GRANDPARENTS

I think they, my parents, wanted some place that basically could provide good care for Grandad. I mean, like, he's on the respirator several times a day. And when he's having bad spells, they move him up to the fourth floor, which is more like a total-care floor. So he basically gets wheeled up there in the morning, gets his breakfast fed to him until he limbers up in the morning, and then he comes downstairs and they sit together in front of the TV. And they spend the rest of the day together type thing. So, I guess, maybe the choice was in getting her into a place where there was medical care for them.

My grandfather is a wonderful person, but he doesn't know how to do things. He said he made a grilled cheese, but he just took a piece of cheese and two pieces of bread and threw it in the oven. And burned it. I mean, he just didn't know. It's sad, it's really sad, that he wasn't self-sufficient in those type of things. But he was a great guy. He is a great guy, I should say. Years back, she was doing these things for him that she didn't need to do, I'm sure she probably laid out his clothes every day. She did all these things for him, but when she did go into the hospital for one of the hip operations, he was functional. He was getting up in the morning. He was able to answer a phone at ten o'clock. He could boil a kettle for a cup of tea. You know, he wouldn't make meals or anything, but he was pretty functional. And then when she came home again, I donno. He'd start relying on her again. And she'd just take up that role again that was too much for her. She couldn't do it.

Another thing, she took it upon herself to give him medicine, and she was giving him some of *her* medicine, stuff for her heart. I don't know if she gets attacks, or angina, or what it is. So she sort of thought he was frail that way, too. They were wondering if when she was in hospital, that was one reason he was doing so well. Because he wasn't being inundated with all this extra medicine. Everybody would say to her how well he would do when she was in hospital.

She'd go, "Nobody knows what I go through. Nobody knows what my life is like." And we'd say to her, we're not trying to say that you're not needed, [laughs] we're just trying to tell you that he is capable.

Grandfather has emphysema really bad. So he wakes up in the morning and he's, like, nonfunctional until about twelve o'clock. He barely can speak. And when he is up, he can get up and walk around with the help of a walker, but he gets really winded. I think she was doing a lot for him that she really didn't need to do.

About a year ago, they found a lump in Grandmother's breast. Here's someone who is eighty-eight years old, and they found a lump, so they thought they'd remove it. She was really concerned about my grandfather being in this room by himself. So she said to him, "Listen, I'm going to have this done. And I want you to know that if you're not capable of getting up in the morning, they're going to move you upstairs. And I don't want you moved upstairs. I don't want you going up to that chronic care ward because I'm afraid once you're upstairs, you're not going to come back down again. You're just going to slide. So for the next few days I want you to wake up, and I want you to get your clothes on." So the next morning she was wide awake, and from the bed across the room, he was going, "Hester, I need you, Hester," and he went on like that for ten minutes. And she wouldn't get out of bed. And it was the first time she made him be independent. And he was. Now she regrets it, she thinks he was faking it. All these years that she nurtured him into being this way, and now she doesn't like it. She's mad at him. It's really funny, I thought it funny.

I was really concerned because I thought there was no way she should have this done. Here she was, eighty-eight years old—no way she should go through this. I had this real aversion to the surgery. I thought, surely this was too drastic a measure. That she was too old. That it was very drastic. But she was recovered within a week. She was amazing. I was really proud of her. Especially at that age. And I was worried that she wouldn't come out of it because she got so disoriented for the other operations that she had with her hip. It was like, always a two- or three-day period that she didn't know who you were. She'd think I was keeping [my son] Steven outside the room and wouldn't bring him in. But it doesn't seem to have bothered her at all this time.

PATERNAL GRANDPARENTS

My other grandparents, she's eighty-eight and that grandfather's eighty-six. My mum and dad used to live across the street from each other as kids. That's how they met. So both grandparents are, like, quite close. We'd see both of them. And then, both grandfathers sort of retired around the same time. And then they just sort of decided to look into getting an apartment. My father fell off the roof one time when he was fixing the shingles. And then they all moved into the same apartment building together, so the four of them have always been together.

She's amazing. Just this last Christmas was the first Christmas that she stopped baking for us. She used to make a huge tin of cookies for us, but this Christmas she said, grumble grumble [laughs], no. She can't even come and visit us anymore. She can't get outside because it's too windy. She can't go anyplace that has stairs. She can't climb our stairs to go to the bathroom, so like they can't even come to our house to see where their things are that we've kept. I think she realizes now that this is where they have to be. My other grandparents are ninety and eighty-eight.

She's an amazing woman, though. But then, like, they've always had their house. Or apartment. But when my mum's parents were going through all this sickness and stuff, my other grandparents, they . . . I think at that time, when the one set of grandparents was in the home, that grandmother was jealous of everything. So I think she made it very tough for my other grandparents to come visit them. She was still very upset. "How very lucky you are to be able to stay in your home," kind of thing. They still come and visit each other once a month, maybe not that much anymore. And my other grandparents will take Wheel Trans over there. Which is really something.

Now my mum's mum will phone my dad's mum and ask, "How often do you hear from Cheryl (my mother)?" And I'll think, "Oh, give me a break!" Or she'll say to me, "Do you phone your Mum every week?" And I'll say, "Sometimes I call her or sometimes she calls me." But she doesn't like to get on the phone. But if I've gone to visit she'll normally phone me the next day and say, "That was really nice that you came to see us." That's the only time she'll ever call me. She'll never phone me out of the blue and say, "I just wanted to chat."

FINAL THOUGHTS

I just sort of thought that I had to call them [grandparents], to take the kids to see them regularly. If they saw the kids, they sort of forgot about their problems. My kids were real important to them. I'd sort of say to my mum, "Is there anything else I can do?" I sort of left everything in her court. I don't know if that was right or not. I thought it was hard enough for my mom to make the decisions she was making, rather than have me second-guess her. Maybe that was a cop-out, I don't know. Maybe she could have provided home care. Or I could have. I don't think that it's something that's really "in" now, that it's something that's discussed a lot. It's certainly something I would think about. But then, you need someone you can really trust.

For example, my neighbor's aunt. All the checks had been made to this one particular lady, Judy. And they figured from the end of 1989 until now, that there's been about twenty thousand dollars withdrawn from the account! But she doesn't need that much. She doesn't spend that much. But Aunt Rachel would write Judy a check for, say, five hundred dollars or something. She was a care giver for the lady next door who took it upon herself to come in and make coffee for Aunt Rachel, or make supper. Like, whenever the home care wasn't there [i.e., Meals On Wheels], she would sort of take over and have coffee with her in the morning, and cash her checks for her, and do the things home care couldn't do because home care was only there three days a week, and she was there to do laundry, cleaning, meal preparation kind of thing. So Judy did these things for her.

In the place we live now, in Toronto, we'd go right to our lawyer. But they live in a small town where everybody knows your business. So you sort of have a feeling that you don't want this lady's reputation ruined. And this woman provided beautiful birthday presents for all my Aunt Rachel's children. That's a lot of money! And there isn't even enough money in the account to bury Aunt Rachel right now.

We tend to go with the flow. My mum is very much like that,

too, she doesn't like to second-guess people. Like, you know, people must know better. I was going to say we're the first generation that does question, but look at me. I haven't questioned anything. Growing old? It's something I don't think about a lot. I don't want to grow old. Well, I'm going to, but I'm having such a good time right now, I'd like this just to stay for a while. Right now I don't think, "What am I going to do?" But it's a real eye-opener. You can lose it so quickly. Just to see how in control we are now, and how you can lose it so very quickly. I guess the time to get things in order is when you're in control. Here you think you'd like to look after your own affairs if things start to slip, but you should do it when you're having the good times.

Postscript

Marie Dister seems to applaud elders in the abstract—to take pride in her grandmothers' sheer longevity and endurance—but feels no personal responsibility for their care or maintenance, no real connection or relation with these seniors who once were so important to her life. She thinks her grandparents wonderful, but visits them only occasionally and takes no active part in their care. She understands that the transfer to the nursing home was tough on at least one and probably both sets of elders, but did nothing herself to ease the transition for them. The whole sense of her statement is that her desire for practical involvement in their affairs is virtually nonexistent.

In a very real sense, Mrs. Dister has so objectified her grandparents that, for her, they have lost their status as human beings. They fall into the category of past familial function. They are not real people because they can no longer do for her or her children what they did in the past. They can, for example, no longer bake tins of Christmas cookies, show slides of old trips at family gatherings, be counted on as individuals or couples to attend annual festivities which in previous years they dominated. They cannot visit her house on holidays. These, for her, are functional definitions of grandparenthood. As those abilities receded, so did any present involvement on her part with the people who once performed them.

These "amazing and wonderful" grandparents in whom she takes such pride are, in a real way, living memories: old, frail and largely extraneous to her contemporary world. A part of her hears the grand-mother's complaint—"I guess this is the worst"—and sympathizes with it. But she also feels burdened by it, as one would by any impolite statement at a social gathering. Significantly, what Mrs. Dister says she wants is to call or visit and hear, "Oh fine! I mean, don't worry about me!" It is not simply that she hopes for her grandmother's contentment, but also, I think, that such a statement would remove from her any feeling that she could—and perhaps should—have done something to ease her elder's old age.

The only way in which Mrs. Dister can begin to comprehend her grandparents' feelings is through the dismemberment of their house-hold and the dispersal of their possessions. "That hit all of us really hard," she says of her grandparents' loss of their home and its con-tents, and I do not doubt that this is true. She clearly is uneasy with the idea that someday all the things she has accumulated over a lifetime may be dispersed. That her grandparents would almost cer-tainly have preferred to remain at home, that the move of one set of elders caused a painful separation between four elderly people who had been first neighbors, then friends and finally families-in-law is not what she focuses on. Rather it is the loss of "things," not relations or the continuity of perhaps fragile but still active lives, with which she identifies.

It is in this context that her brief anecdote about Aunt Rachel and Judy makes sense. Mrs. Dister assumes that Judy somehow took money for herself. Mrs. Dister's concern is not the fact that outreach services are so inadequate that, sometimes, scheduled meals do not arrive. Nor does she consider that Aunt Rachel was, except for Judy's visits, bereft of companionship. What is truly inexplicable to her, I think, is that a woman like Judy would visit and offer care without compensation. Anyone who would do this, in Mrs. Dister's world, must have an ulterior motive and the missing money provides an easy answer (nobody apparently thought to ask Aunt Rachel about why she wrote these checks). This, however, is not an idea Mrs. Dister can entertain. To her, the disappearance of money must signal, instead, a confidence game played by the care giver, Judy, on Aunt Rachel.

10

The Queen's Telegram

Alice McLeod is a Vancouver public relations writer and the mother of three children. With her husband, Dan, she moved to Canada from England more than twenty years ago but has retained relations with her native land and family there.

Although she is assertively North American, elements of her story are clearly British. The "Queen's telegram," for example, is an honored British tradition. For a citizen's hundredth birthday, civil service employees gather information from which a personalized telegram from the Queen is fashioned. Generally speaking, in Great Britain's socialized medical system, the involvement of "social welfare people" includes a broad range of possible assistance—both medical and social. Invoking this category of aid involves no stigma, unlike in North America, where the word "welfare" implies a poverty of general resources. Indeed, because universal health care is a state responsibility, assistants from the social services are usually involved in cases requiring continuing home care, hospitalization, or institutionalization.

In a nation of immigrants, the problem of family members who attempt to deal with familial crises at remove, a situation that Alice McLeod's case exemplifies, is one that has yet to be fully studied from the viewpoint of care giver or care receiver.

We go back every four or five years to England and, that year, Grandfather was turning one hundred. So we were going back for his birthday. There was the whole deal with the Queen and the telegram. That was very important to him. We were interviewed by the social welfare workers and so forth to get the information for the telegram from the Queen, and there was a big birthday celebration planned.

He's somewhat deaf and somewhat blind, but he's not senile. He's really quite "with it." He can't cook; he's never cooked for himself. He's never really looked after himself. He's always had someone to prepare food for him. He's got a good sense of humor. He's really quite strong. You have to be strong to reach one hundred. You have to be stubborn, and bloody selfish [laughs].

All my family except my mother is in England, and all Dan's family is in England. We've been in Canada since 1963, since I was a young woman of twenty-one. But going back every four or five years, I've kept in close contact. Grandfather was coming up on one hundred and he had lost his son and his son-in-law, so he was living with his daughter, my aunt. My aunt had suddenly gone into a coma—she was in her early sixties. After a relatively minor operation, she had a major heart attack on the operating table. I had a very uneasy feeling that my aunt was going to die just at the time Grandfather was turning one hundred. And she did.

I told my cousins by phone before I came to England that I knew it was bad. I knew they were having a rough time. They didn't know who would look after him. My one cousin was pregnant and had a very small child and was quite ill with the pregnancy. The other cousin was having various family problems, so there was no one to look after him at that stage.

The social welfare people were unable to find homemakers to come in right away, so we were in a quasi-emergency situation. I left my own family with my husband's family down south in London and traveled up to the north of England to spend a week looking after my grandfather.

I had to clean his commode. I had to bathe him. He didn't want me to see him in his state, you know, with his [skin] ulcers—which I had to medicate—and I had to do all the nursing things for him.

Well, I decided to see the family lawyer, who knew the situation, and explain that this was an emergency and ask if there was any possibility I could get him into a nursing home. I felt I had to because no one else seemed able to make these decisions. There was no one else around to do it. My aunt in a coma was obviously in no condition to make a decision. My mother is not a blood relative and they don't get along well and she's here, in Canada, eight thousand miles away.

And there I was—the next living relative down my father's side. Who else could make a decision? There I was, on holiday, and I'd come eight thousand miles, but someone had to do something.

You can't leave a 100-year-old man alone!

I told my cousins what I was doing and I had their approval, but I didn't tell the old man, my granda', because I knew he wasn't going to be very happy. He found out that that was what I was doing and that's when the trouble hit the fan or, as we say, "the shit hit the fan."

He said to me he didn't know how I could do that, how anyone could put a relative into a home and how he would never, ever go to one of those places. And he's my grandfather and he's almost sixty years older than I am, and I can't tell my grandfather to go fly a kite! I really can't tell my grandfather to buzz off. I have too much respect for him. He started to cry in front of me, and what do you do with a hundred-year-old man who is crying?

It was pretty bad for everybody. It was devastating for him, but it was devastating for us, too. It was the most frustrating thing I've ever encountered and . . . it was such an emotional time. I can't really describe what it's like sitting there with a 100-year-old man whom you've respected all your life, crying his heart out and saying we didn't love him because we were putting him in a home where he would just wait to die. I said, "No, no, that's not it. I can't just leave you, and what can I do? I have a family to look after, and that family is eight thousand miles away. What am I supposed to do? I can't be in two places at once. My sister has a family. What are we to do? We have children to look after, and we can't just leave them." You can do it on an emergency basis—as we were doing—but you can't do it on a long-term basis.

We were doing a patchwork of whoever could come in and look after him. There was a strike on in the county and we couldn't get any homemakers in. He can't cook or prepare meals for himself. Everyone was sort of crowding around and saying, "Isn't this great? He's lived so long and we're all going to help out." But I thought: How long can this go on? It won't go on for more than another month, and then what's going to happen? There's no one to look after him.

My cousin finally said she would look after him, but then she had a nervous breakdown with the stress of everything that was happening and her mother—my aunt—dying and like that. So she had a breakdown shortly after this, and my other cousin was having a baby. As it turns out, it all worked out, and he's gone to my second cousin's in the south of England, but at the time I didn't know that was going to happen.

He had money. He had his nest egg, but you have to remember that he retired thirty-five years ago, and what money was then and what money is now . . . To him it was his life's work and his savings, but he wouldn't spend a penny and he wouldn't let us spend it for him. I kept saying, "Grandpa, you have to spend money to look after yourself, so that we can help you look after yourself." If he had gone into a home it would have been roughly £100 a week, so a lot of that money would have come out of his own savings. He would have had to use all his life savings. He had about £25,000 [Ed. note: about $60,000 U.S.], which—considering he had saved it all those years ago—was a considerable nest egg. But he wouldn't spend a penny! He kept saying, "It's not my money. It's *your* money. It's for you and the other girls." It was for the granddaughters. He kept saying, "That's your money!" and I was just flabbergasted by this attitude. I couldn't say, "Grandpa, it's not my money. It's your money." He wouldn't, couldn't spend what was left to him.

It was like a weapon, in a way. Not a weapon, really. It was like he was hanging on to the last vestiges of his heritage and that was what he was able to give us. I think, in the end, he may finally forgive me, but I don't know if he will ever really forgive me, because I was the one who had to do the dirty work. Someone had to do it. Why make everyone miserable? So I had to do it [laughs].

After a while, after the tension calmed down, I understood about the money—that it *was* him. It was his, well, last will and testament. It was what he had to give us, his life savings. It was his heritage. Suddenly I understood that [spending] it was like having to cut a part of himself off, a hand or a leg or a toe or something more important and he just wanted to keep himself whole.

And that *was* him, his money. That was what he was at this stage of his life. That was almost what he was reduced to. That was his dignity, and I couldn't take the final shred of dignity from him. He couldn't give up that last shred and, really, why should I ask him to?

Postscript

Alice is a physically distant relative who attempts to return home and "organize" care for her elder. The critical points of this short, almost anecdotal story are twofold. It illustrates how the physically absent relative will come into an ongoing geriatric situation or crisis and, on the basis of historic relations, attempt to take charge without understanding either the social dynamics or the individual needs of the patient. The immigrant or emigrant holds ties to his or her natal home and believes, despite often prolonged absence, that personal history creates a right and obligation to "set things right." In North America, it is frequently the absent but older sibling who returns to the family home for a week or so to "take charge" of a geriatric situation where other relatives have worked for months.

As Mrs. McLeod found out, North American–style crisis management is not always appropriate. In Great Britain, or anywhere families retain landed relations and strong community ties, other methods are often chosen. Within this extended family and community, it was impossible to dismiss the grandfather's wishes and use a practical but distancing "home" to resolve issues of care. The extended network that is operative in such families can bend to accommodate, a fact that Alice McLeod perhaps had forgotten in the years spent away from her ancestral home. She saw the "family" as those immediately involved, the "problem" as one of efficient care and the "solution" as necessarily involving official channels. Institutionalization was, for her, the rational and efficient resolution. Her relatives, however, saw the "family" as a broad network in which the grandfather was a valued member and the "problem" one of the aunt and cousin's illnesses as well as the elder's fragility. They sought a "solution" within a social network greater than Alice could conceive.

Although Mrs. McLeod insists she acted with the approval of her British family members, I suspect that her relatives did not agree but, instead, acquiesced to her plan. They knew changes needed to be made. After all, these relatives had lived intimately with her grandfather for years and, in the past, they may have discussed the possibility of institutionalization. But at the same time, they were more aware than was Mrs. McLeod of both the broader, ongoing family dynamics and also the fact that the grandfather's dislike of the idea would make it difficult to carry through.

Also illuminating is the issue of money and the different ways both Mrs. McLeod and her grandfather perceived its value. To her it was a practical matter—money is to be spent in the present for care—and only at the time of our talk, in talking about the money to me, she later said, did she finally come to understand that it was both her grandfather's past, the money saved over a lifetime's work, and his future, a proud legacy. Money was to her grandfather a totem of worth and, as an inheritance, a symbol of the future. With the best of intentions, Mrs. McLeod demeaned her grandfather's savings in his eyes by attempting to force him to spend it to pay for a "home." The connotations of being institutionalized and "just waiting to die" were, to her grandfather, sufficiently frightful without the added insult.

Mrs. McLeod is probably correct when she says that her grandfather may never forgive her for her actions during this episode. By beginning the process of institutionalization without even discussing it with him, she was in effect telling her grandfather to, in her words, "go fly a kite." To him it must have seemed a bitter betrayal by his closest living relative. Alice McLeod's story illustrates the tensions that arise between what an individual needs (food, clothing, and shelter) for existence, and what he or she may feel entitled to (respect, continuity at home and in the family). Michael Ignatieff analyzes these tensions in *The Needs of Strangers* in a discussion of Shakespeare's *King Lear*. He suggests that story is about precisely the type of imbalance that occurs when an elder's perceptions of what is needed to maintain a life worth living is challenged by a younger person's view of the minimum required simply to maintain physical life.

11

The Mattress Heiress

During the late 1970s and early 1980s, Margaret Neilson, then in her twenties, spent eight years caring for her ailing grandmother, who suffered from multiple ailments, including blood problems, mobility problems, and progressive cognitive deficits. Eighty-one years old, she was hospitalized twice during the care period for tests and once for a broken hip.

Even minor surgery on a serious skin ulcer, which Margaret describes in this account, is a fairly delicate procedure that most nurses would not contemplate performing. The success of her operation is something Ms. Neilson remembers with great pride even now, years after the operation occurred. She had told me the story several times before the interview, and for her it demonstrated an ability to do "anything" for her grandmother. In addition, I think, it confirmed her opinion that she knew better than anybody—relatives, physicians, aides or nurses—what her grandmother needed.

When I was small, the big thing was to go with my dad to my grandma's house on the weekends, and one of us kids was allowed to stay with her for the weekend. As she got older and she didn't like going to the store a lot—well, the grocery store was right down the street—so each kid got to go grocery shopping, or go banking or pick things up for her, and ultimately everyone had their chance taking care of her.

When I first went in there, she'd called me up on the phone and asked me if I'd come and stay with her because, ah, my father had apparently found her that day out on the floor of the porch at her apartment wedged in between the porch, the door, and the living room. She had fallen and couldn't get up off the floor, and he had to break the door in to get her out.

He had been coming every night to give her her medications because she would forget to take them. So she called me the next day to ask if I would please come and stay with her until she felt a bit better. When I moved in with her she couldn't remember what time it was, she sometimes couldn't remember the day of the week, she had no idea what year it was, but she could take care of all her own financial needs.

She was very businesslike in the whole arrangement, to begin with. She would not allow me to come and stay with her and help her unless she paid me. She was going to give me seventy-five dollars a week, because she and my father had agreed on that. She told me that if she got sicker and I had to stay longer that the figure would go up. Well, my father did not agree with that.

AGGRAVATIONS

When I first moved in she would forget that I was living there, and if I did not come home from work at quarter after nine like I said I would be home from work, she would lock the door. She'd put the chain on the door—everything. I'd have a key to the door, but with the chains on I couldn't get through, and she'd tell me that was my punishment for not being home when I said I'd be home. Then other times she'd forget, forget a lot of things. Then, when I'd remind her of them, she would get very agitated and say that I was being a brat and that she knew better than I knew what she was doing and that I shouldn't tell her what to do or what she had done.

She could be very aggravated [with me], which was a side I'd never seen of my grandmother. It was a complete and utter shock. We had terrible fights over stupid little things, even like a chest of drawers. When I moved in I had nowhere to put my clothes, so I got this little chest of drawers and I put it in the front hall closet because there was only one bedroom. She didn't want it anywhere and we had a terrible fight. She called my father up on the phone and told him I was abusive. She thought I was abusive because I brought this thing in that she didn't like.

It must have been the following March when she fell again. My aunt happened to stop over that time, and the lady across the hall had a key and let her in, and they couldn't get her up off the floor. They had to call me at work and have me come so I could help get her up off the floor. That's when we started getting aides in because we knew she couldn't do for herself. She'd try and go out, go down the stairs, do the laundry. She'd forget someone was supposed to be there.

When she broke her hip, that's when I had to quit school, because there was no possible way to keep up with her. She broke her hip in July. She broke her hip in 1983. She was basically doing things for herself, and one Sunday morning, she just got out of bed before my sister and I did. We heard this thud, and there she was, lying on the floor. She'd broken her hip. They don't think the fall did it, but that she got up out of the bed and turned the wrong way and broke her hip. So she went to hospital.

In the hospital, it was bad. They didn't get her up. The only time she got up was when I physically picked her up out of bed and got her out. As far as going for therapy, it was terrible. I went down there a couple of times with her and met them [the therapists]. They wouldn't push her to walk, and she had forgotten how. Within two weeks she didn't know how to walk anymore. She couldn't feed herself. They [aides] would come in and they would feed her, and she literally lost the ability to remember how to pick up the spoon and feed herself. She was incontinent—all the time—which she had never been before. She had had accidents and things, but never completely.

The family sent me away to rest for a week before she came home from the hospital, and in that week she did not get out of bed at all because, apparently, some aide had tried to do it by herself—help her up—and although she [grandma] was only four foot nine, she weighed about 160 pounds. So she was a pretty big lady and, ah, the aide had hurt her back fighting her, so they decided it wasn't worth the risk to get her out of bed. So while I was away, she just lay there. When I came home the day that she did, I found her in bed with her whole backside torn up. It was bleeding. There was what I would consider a diaper rash. She was allergic. She would just scratch herself up.

She developed a decubitus ulcer on the front of her leg, an ulceration on the skin the size of a half-dollar. When it finally did crust over and separate from good tissue, it was becoming necrotic. I was trying to clean it and remove it myself. My stepmother, who was a nurse, showed me how I could remove some of the tissue and try and keep it clean. It was getting so bad that we did ultimately have to take her into the emergency room and have it looked at. We had this one young doctor that cleaned it off a little bit and told me to put on these wet dressings, change it three times a day and this would clear it up, but if it didn't, they would probably have to do extensive surgery on her leg or, if she got gangrene, they'd have to have it cut off.

Well, for a week I did what he told me, and it got worse and worse and worse, because it had all that wet bandage against it and it was turning to mush and getting blacker and blacker and all the tissue around it was turning yellow. So I took her back to the surgeon who did her hip and he told me not to listen to anyone else. He showed me what to do and he took off one smaller black scab, but the bigger one he said was too involved and he wanted to wait a little while. I took her home and I took it off with my stepmother sitting there. I did it with a tweezers and a razor, a straight-edge razor blade.

We retaught her how to walk. She refused to walk with a walker, she said it was "indignant" [laughs]. So she used me or, if one of my brothers was there, he would stand in front of her and she would put her hands on each one of his forearms and use them as a walker. It got to the point where she could walk just with someone standing in front of her. But she did have a hard time getting up out of the chair, so she had to be pulled up to a standing position in order to move.

DEPENDENCE

She became my job, twenty-four hours a day with no break. Sometimes she used to make me so angry. She knew I was going out, whether it be grocery shopping, for a ride on my bike—she'd do something so I couldn't leave the house. She'd vomit! I'd feed her a meal and no sooner get one foot out that door but she would vomit all over the place, knowing full well I'd have to come back there and clean her up. And I lived by her bowel movements, I truly did. If she didn't have a bowel movement, I didn't leave the house because, when she went, she went all over the place. So I literally lived by bowel movements. I did, I did. And she knew it. I'd have to be very secretive if I had to go to the dentist. I'd hide in the bedroom talking on the phone because, if she knew I was going to walk out that apartment, that was it. She'd do something. She'd get this look in her eye. I'd say [to an aide], "Well, Nancy (or whatever), I'm going to go downstairs and start a load of laundry," so she wouldn't know I was actually leaving.

She also had a very bad habit, which started before she broke her hip, that if she did have a bowel movement in bed at night, she would hide it because she was afraid her mother would find it and she would be in trouble. She also, sometimes, put her hands in her mouth after she had picked it up, and I could always tell, because if I couldn't get her dentures away from her at night, it would be on the dentures. When she came home from the hospital, her dentures were covered with feces. Little kids do that, play with excrements, and she was back all that way already. It was just like having a little baby in the house.

Not being able to get her to understand, that was the hardest thing. Having to repeat things over and over and over. It gets to be that it's like she's your child and you're saying over and over again, "Don't do it! Don't do it! Don't do it. Ask if you have to go to the bathroom. Just let me know." And sometimes the stress gets so bad, you forget about the fact that they can't remember. That there's no way they can tell you, "I've got to go."

It gets so frustrating that, just like with a little kid, you want to spank them. You really do because it just gets so bad. But you can't. I mean, you can't spank your grandmother! My favorite thing was, I used to put my foot through the wall. I used to get so mad I would kick the wall. I was always plastering the hall wall up. I didn't break things, I would just kick the wall, and sometimes I'd get my foot stuck in it. Literally [laughs]. I had to take my aggravation out somewhere, and that was it. The wall in the hall was the thing to do it. With someone you're not related to, you can walk away from it. You're not there twenty-four hours a day. You can get out. You're not stuck. But when you're there twenty-four hours a day, there has to be an outlet.

Sometimes it aggravated me that I couldn't get more help than what I got. Like, if I would call my father and I'd absolutely need some relief and have to get out of there. I'd start hearing, "I'm a busy person. I have my life. I have my responsibilities. This is your responsibility. You wanted it." This was his mother, and it sometimes aggravated me that I couldn't get more [family] help than what I got. It would make me very, very angry.

And other people in the family—his brother and sister—wanted no part of it; their children, no part of it. They would just come once in a while, two or three times a year, and see her. You know, "Oh my goodness. She surely is going down, isn't she?" They had no idea what just a couple of hours out of there could've done to help. Not only that, but how much she missed it, too. She knew that people weren't there. They felt that she was completely gone and that she had no idea what was going on around her, but she knew. She knew people didn't come to see her. Sometimes there would be a bright light in Grandmother's eyes and she would ask, "Why don't they come to see me?"

As far as they were concerned, and unfortunately they had this attitude, my grandmother died a long time ago, because they felt that she wasn't like she used to be. I feel sorry for people like that. The big thing was they couldn't stand to see my grandmother the way that she was. They wanted to remember her like she used to be. To me this was part of life and you have to handle anything that comes along. I didn't care if they couldn't handle it. That's part of life. Things don't stay rosy.

MONEY

When we were young she was pretty free and liberal with the money, you know. She tossed it around pretty good. But when she got to be older, she told me, "You know I really don't have much money." And I knew full well [she did] because I was helping her with her books and I had to go through the trust statements and stuff like that. But then when my father took over taking care of the bills and things, he would say the same thing. "You know [whispering], your grandmother doesn't have much money!" [laughs]. She had a lot of money, though, her money and . . . , like a trust fund from my grandfather.

My grandmother was crazy when it came to money. She would,

ah, call the bank ten, fifteen times a day to check on the balance in her checking account. She always had plenty of money, she very rarely wrote a check—you had to really con her to write a check— but she would call and call and call [the bank]. And then she'd call the trust department to see how much money was in the trust fund. The funny thing was that she had books at home to take care of her stocks, all these accounting ledgers, she could do that. But she was always possessed about whether the balance she had was right. It would get so bad that they would actually call me at work and ask me to go home and take the phone away from her. Unplug it, take it apart, anything so she could no longer call them, because she was driving the trust department crazy and the checking department crazy.

I never argued with her about money. If she told me to cash a check, I would cash it. If she gave you a check for five hundred dollars, you didn't argue with her. You went and you cashed it. You had to bring back the money. If she sent me out to do things for her, I had to bring back exact receipts, and she wrote it all down in her book. But you could never find the money after you gave it to her. Like, if she gave me a check for five hundred dollars and sent me out grocery shopping and to the drugstore and to run errands for her, she'd tell me I'd have to bring back fifty ones and usually ten fives, two tens, and four twenties. She had to have those ones so she could pay the paperboy. She had to have those fifty ones. She would write down exact amounts of what had to be brought back.

But you could never find it. She never had any money when it came time to pay these things, you know? After she got very, very ill and broke her hip, my father and I went through all the accounts and he says, "Well, what are these checks written for—cash! cash! cash! cash!" Of course, I would have to countersign them on the back when I went to the bank. He would say, "What did you do with all this money?" And I'd be like, "I give it to her. I don't know what she does with it." We searched everywhere, but we could not find it.

We moved into an apartment, a larger apartment in the same complex. The boys, when they were walking down the driveway, dropped the mattress, and there it was. She had slit the mattress, a small part, pulled out the stuffing and then stitched it up. There it was. Every time she got money, she could not remember what happened to it. There were over seven thousand dollars in twenties stuffed into that mattress. And here, all along, everyone was looking at *me* like, there's something wrong here Margaret!

Because she had stitched it up instead of just leaving it open... I'd flipped the beds and stuff, but it obviously wasn't hard enough to make it pop open. She was just, like, "Where did that come from?" She obviously knew that was her hiding place when it came time to hiding money, but after that... well. But we had that kind of problem with her. Glasses and her teeth, too. Every morning was a mad search because I would put the glasses in the right place and the teeth in the right place every night. But in the middle of the night she got up and would move them because she said there were "sticky fingers" around that were going to "lose" them on her. Well, she used to call us "sticky fingers" when we were little because we would pick things up which we weren't supposed to, and she fully believed that all the children were still "sticky fingers," and still little and going to come in the middle of the night and take her teeth or remove her glasses.

She was a great paper saver. Napkins, toilet paper, everything. You'd find things balled up in little balls all over the place. And sometimes you'd find her glasses balled up in the paper towels or the Kleenex or something like that [laughs]. She could have taken them off an hour before and she could not remember where they were. So every time we'd look for something and find it in a new place, and we'd write it down. We'd just go through the list of looking around until we found what we were looking for.

WHY STAY?

Why did I stay? Because I loved my grandmother. I got to give back some of what she gave me. She gave me a lot of moral and emotional support when I was very young. She was always good to me and I could always, ahem, seek her out when I had a problem. It was the least I could do. If my grandmother didn't die, I would still have her home. I did everything, I learned how to run IVs, draw blood, do tube feedings. I can pump a stomach—I learned everything I could think of in order to keep her home.

I didn't want anyone else to take care of her because I knew how her mind worked, and even though she wasn't always completely there, I knew if she was ever put into a nursing home it would kill her, and I didn't really want her to die. I didn't. I'd worked in a nursing home and saw one lady sitting on a toilet who had died. Nobody'd come back to get her . . . and the look on her face . . . it didn't look like she'd died pleasantly, either. I didn't want something like that to happen to my grandmother. I wanted her to die the way my grandfather died: at home, with people around her that cared about her. But she didn't. They put her in the hospital and she suffered, I know she did, before she died.

Postscript

Some speak of the nastiness of the elderly, of, in M. F. K. Fisher's words, their "turning into a Nasty Old Man or an Old Witch." Certainly, Ms. Neilson's grandmother seems something of a harridan, and if not an "old witch," then at least a difficult patient. This was, Ms. Neilson says, "a side I'd never seen of my grandmother." The clear assumption is that the older woman's willful, sometimes abusive behavior—chaining the apartment door while her granddaughter is out—was directed consciously and with premeditation at the granddaughter. Ms. Neilson sees the whole of her grandmother's behavior as a fight for dominance, and certainly there is an element of a need to control in much of the grandmother's actions. By barring the door when her granddaughter was out and then complaining to her son about the daughter's behavior, the older woman clearly was asserting dominance and control in a situation where her position in fact was fragile and the ability to direct her own affairs increasingly limited.

It is more likely, however, that this was new behavior brought about by the grandmother's continued memory loss and resulting confusion. Her unreasonable anger over small changes, including her granddaughter's bringing a chest of drawers into the house for her clothes, is a typical symptom of a class of cognitive disorders causing agitation in elderly individuals whose need for constancy and order is based on an inability to adapt to change. It seems probable that even at the beginning, when Ms. Neilson first moved in, her grandmother actually forgot, day to day, that a companion and relative was living with her. She did not willfully lock the younger woman out of the house so much as forget that her granddaughter was now resident. Thus the older woman simply followed a habit of some years standing by locking up her home each night.

In short, the grandmother berated Margaret to mask her own memory loss. This would also explain how a woman who had cooked for herself and her family for more than forty years could suddenly develop clear dietary deficiencies. Certainly, she knew how to plan and cook balanced meals, but a series of physical and cognitive problems early in the older woman's decline made it impossible for her to carry out the tasks she had performed all her life. The grandmother's behavior in hospital—incontinence, refusal to exercise, anger—can be similarly explained. An inability to learn new patterns often results in a general confusion when the cognitively challenged person is placed in unfamiliar surroundings.

Some speak of the "narcissism" of old age as a means to explain the reluctance of patients to adapt to institutional surroundings. The implication is that the elderly's inappropriate behavior is regressive, that his or her decline is a recapitulation of stages—like the narcissistic—gone through during adolescent or childhood personality development. Thus the patient becomes "childish," if not childlike. Certainly this is how Ms. Neilson saw her grandmother. In retrospect, she says, "It was just like having a little baby in the house." But there is a danger in applying assumptions based on human developmental stages to the symptoms of illness in later life. Children go through stages they grow out of. They are toilet trained; they learn to function independently; they grow. Elderly people who are in need of assistance are in a clearly dependent role that offers no future release for the care giver, no potential of reciprocity for the hours of caring. To the caregiver, the behavioral similarities between a childhood stage and dependent adults physical deficit may be striking. But to the frail senior, the difference between stage and role, as Alice McLeod learned, is vast.

Perhaps we speak of the elderly as becoming childlike because in our society, only children are recognized as legitimate receivers of care. But to attempt to make an equation of dependent young and fragile elders is to do a disservice to both groups. The difference between stages of development and roles of dependence is absolute, a distance that cannot be bridged by something as trivial as the fact of incontinence as it is experienced by individuals living at opposite poles of life's physical course. What the elderly may experience—

whatever their physical limits—must be very different from the experiential world of a child.

After her grandmother died, Ms. Neilson began working as a nurse's aide in the hospital and as a home aide at the agency she first hired to take care of her grandmother. She is at present taking night school classes and hopes to enter medical school in the next few years.

12

Host or Guest?

In her forties and with two teenage children, Neolani and Martin, April Takahashi has for years worked part-time at her husband Paul's automobile garage in Honolulu, Hawaii. The historical context that forms the background of this and the next story, and the heart of their narratives, requires a brief explanation.

Until World War II, many Japanese-American families thought of their tenure in Hawaii as temporary and assumed that at least some family members eventually would return to Japan. Thus it was seen as important by community leaders and members alike to maintain relations with the home country and to assure, as Japanese culture demanded, that the family elderly were cared for. Traditionally, this was the responsibility of a family's oldest son. It was also not uncommon for Japanese families in Hawaii to send willful and delinquent children to Japan, where, it was generally believed, stricter socialization systems would cure them of their independent ways. So by sending April's mother, who was by all accounts unusually outspoken and strong willed, the family both fulfilled a familial obligation and followed the normal course of socializing a willful child.

The dominant role of host or parent is defined at the table in Japanese society by the manner in which food first is set out (for the family or guest) and then offered to them by the host or cook. The grandmother's insistence on offering to her daughter food the latter had prepared thus would be an extraordinary discontinuity, as if a guest at an American table sat down and said to the host, "See what I prepared for you."

My grandmother will be ninety-nine in December. My mother is, I think, seventy-one. My grandfather died of cancer of the pancreas . . . when was this? Maybe around '69. Somewhere around there. My uncles had bought some property in Nanakuli, so my grandparents moved there and did truck farming [after World War II]. As my grandparents got older, my grandmother had an accident one day. Climbing up a ladder, trying to pick some fruit. I don't know, she must have been hurt, but not bad. And she fell down. So they decided—the family decided—that it would be better for my grandparents to move into town with my aunt and her family. Their family has, let's see, my auntie, her husband, my auntie's brother, and the three kids. They took care of them [the grandparents] for quite a long time. Everything was pretty okay until a few years ago. Maybe two years ago, when my aunt had to have heart surgery. So she can't do strenuous activities. Then my grandmother moved in with my mother.

What does the doctor say about my grandmother? Just that she's old, already. I'm sure that she must have Alzheimer's or something because she's not, she's not . . . I guess she rambles a lot. Sometimes she can't recognize people. At times she knows who my mother is, but at other times she doesn't. In Japanese, the host or parent offers people food, but if my mother puts the food out for my grandmother, then my grandmother is offering it to my mother. You know, "Here, have this." My mother gets really angry. I guess she gets really frustrated.

Grandma needs constant care because she wants to do things, so she'll get into things. Like, whatever's on the table is fair game [laughs]. She'll start peeling all the bananas or she'll take instant coffee and put it in her soup, you know, and say, "Well, this is a strange kind of soup." She'll make a prune sandwich, take the pitted prunes and put them between two pieces of bread. Sometimes she'll take the unpitted prunes, too. She'll eat soap because she thinks it's food, you know? So we can't leave anything within her reach.

She can get around, she can crawl. But walking is difficult for her. She can walk a little bit, holding onto things. She grabs onto tables or holds onto the walls. She needs help with the bathroom and she wears those, you know, Depends. Diapers. Yeah, exactly what she calls them. She needs to be helped with everything because she'll, you know, if she soils in her diapers she'll pick it off and say, "I still can use it again." We got a portable toilet for her. She refuses to use it. For my grandmother, I guess it doesn't look like a toilet and she has a great difficulty relieving herself on something like that.

Mostly my going there and being with them is just that. Just being with them is the help, just having me to talk to. Me to complain to. I don't think I help very much. I guess it's still from my childhood, the feelings I get that I can't do things very well. Or that nobody can do things like my mother can. The thing with her is, you're supposed to know what to do, you know? She has to be the one to do it, to do it right. I don't think she does it intentionally, that's just how she is. With my mother, you're supposed to know what to do: to wash the dishes, wash the clothes, and do it in a certain way— the way she likes to have it done. But she won't tell you until after you do it. Then she'll criticize you. And she won't talk to the person about how she wants it done, she'll talk to somebody else about how this person did whatever.

Actually, though, you know, I like going out there. It is quiet and I can get away from here, from the responsibilities here. One month I'll go down several times and the next month I won't go down at all. When mother, she asks for help—maybe she has a doctor's appointment—then I'll go and babysit. In a way its a little bit difficult for me because she's my grandmother. Like, I have a problem if she would say "no" and I wanted her to do something. If I wanted to take her to the bathroom, then I would kind of let it go if she said "no," because she's older than me and she's kind of my grandmother, you know. My mother doesn't have that problem. In fact, she treats her mother more like a child. I guess it depends on if I get it straight in my mind that my grandmother is not how she used to be. I have to remind myself that she's not the way she used to be, but I have to think about what needs to be done and try to use persuasion if possible. That's something my mother has a hard time with, too, you know. She gets angry fast.

If my grandmother wakes up in the middle of the night and says, "Oh! Somebody came!" she wants my mother to go to the door to greet them, or else she'll try and go to the door herself. Instead of saying, "You know, I already took care of that. They're sleeping. I put them to bed already," my mother says, "Nobody came." She's angry. She says, "Go back to sleep. Nobody came." Whereas if she told my grandmother, "I took care of them. Everybody's sleeping now and they're warm enough," then my grandmother wouldn't worry about all these details. Because, to her, she heard somebody come in. Something in her memory, or her dream. Whatever. It's like it really happened.

My mother does a good job, she does a really good job of taking care of my grandmother. But it's a frustrating job because she has to get up at night, too, because my grandmother won't use the portable toilet and she has to take my grandmother to the bathroom. Mother gets very frustrated, but in a way I think she likes it. It makes her feel needed, yeah? She's had a lot of experience taking care of bedridden people.

JAPAN

Her older sister was supposed to go to Japan. Her father's mother was getting old and ill and of course she wanted her son to come back to keep the family home going. I guess it was an obligation that especially the eldest son had to take care of his parents, yeah. Mother's father was the oldest son. Since my grandfather wasn't going back, she [Mrs. Takahashi's maternal grandmother] wanted his oldest daughter to come and stay there, marry a cousin who would take on the family name and carry on the family in that area. But my mother's parents decided that their oldest daughter was too delicate and would surely die. I guess she was two years older than my mother. They just thought she was too soft, you know? That she wouldn't be able to take my grandfather's mother and life in Japan. My mother was very stubborn and outspoken, and they thought that she could handle that. They didn't tell her what she was going to do. They just said she was to go along to her grand-parents' wedding anniversary in Japan. So she went with her mother, thinking that she was only going to the wedding anniversary. When she got there, she found out that she wasn't coming home. That she was going to stay there and take care of her father's mother. She was very . . . upset. She was fourteen.

In the beginning she [April's great-grandmother] could walk and later on just crawl to get around. I don't know how long she was bedridden. My mother was very unhappy and gained I don't know how many pounds. She was quite fat. Obese. She went up in 1934 and came back in 1937. What the grandmother had wanted her to do was to stay there and get married. Although the property was my grandfather's, my mother's father's, he couldn't do anything

without my mother's permission because when my great-grand-
mother died, that's what she stipulated.

When she got back, my mother took care of another old person,
an invalid. A friend's grandmother who was Hawaiian. The grandmother was pure Hawaiian and the friend was Japanese-Hawaiian. I
don't know if she got paid.

NURSING HOME DEBATE

With families, they take it so personally what each says, because
each feels like they're not doing enough, or they did a lot and the
other person may not think so. And the other person has his own
guilt too, about not doing enough or about "I did plenty here,"
measuring out how much of their obligation they completed, you
know? A lot of it is cultural. I think the Japanese mentality is mostly
"face"—what do others think? I got brought up that way. What do
others think? I mean if someone is coming over, you have to clean
your house. You pretend that things are good. Others think, "How
cruel to put your mother in a nursing home." What are other people
going to think about you? It's face.

I've become interested in my Japanese heritage, our family there.
When I got back from visiting Japan last year, I found out my cousin—who is the daughter of the aunt who was taking care of my
grandmother before—was trying to arrange to put my grandmother
into a nursing home to relieve my aunt. What they were doing at that
time for my grandmother was one month with my aunt and one
month with my mother. But my aunt also takes care of my cousin's
kids. One is in school now and one is a toddler, I guess. Maybe a couple of years old. And it was really hard on my aunt because of her
heart condition, and after her heart surgery she really couldn't do very
much. So my cousin was trying to arrange to put my grandmother
into a nursing home to relieve my aunt. And she knew it would be
hard on my mother, too. When my sister got wind of it, the one with
the seven children, she said, "Hey, what's going on? I don't think anyone really wants to put Grandma into a nursing home." And I guess my
cousin felt like, "Oh hey, wait a minute. Now everybody thinks I'm the
bad guy, because everyone thinks I'm trying to get rid of Grandma." So
she got really upset, my cousin.

So my sister, the one with the seven children, she said she would go down and help my mother and take care of Grandmother, and that I could go down because I'm not working and my children are older. I only have two [embarrassed laugh]. My mother lives out in Nanakuli, and my sister lives over in Laie. She was going down once or twice a week and then she got really busy with her kids, because she's got seven, and one is in the band, one's in hula and, you know, Cub Scouts. All of that stuff. And her kids are pretty strung out, from college to first grade, so it's really difficult. With her church, also. She has a lot of responsibility there. Between the church and her own family, there's not much time for anything else.

Nobody wants to put Grandma into a nursing home because it feels so . . . because of that obligation of taking care of your parents or relatives. It feels cold. Exactly. And I guess other people feel the same way. And for my mother, she didn't want her mother in a nursing home either, because she said, "It's going to be too hard for me." She would feel like she has to go to the nursing home every day and help take care of my grandmother there and that would be hard for her. But especially after my grandmother got ill, it turned out to be hard anyway.

I think it probably would have been better for her, Mother, to put Grandmother into the nursing home. But the experience, at least for my mother and my sister—and whoever else, at least they can say, "Well, we tried." You know? They know what it's like to take care of someone who is old and helpless and can get into things. She needs constant supervision. It gives them an excuse or reason to put her into a nursing home.

MRS. TAKAHASHI AND HER GRANDPARENTS

Once or twice a year we'd go see them, because it was quite a long ride. By the time we were aware . . . that I was aware of who they were, I think they had already moved to Nanakuli. I don't know how long. It took a couple of hours at the least on the old Pali Road and no freeway then—we had to go through Waipahu and the towns along the way. It was quite a long drive. I remember the flowers they had, these purple flowers, lavender flowers [Ed. note: probably flowering bougainvilla]. That's what I remember about going there. And it was a very hot place. And they had pigs. They had a big bathtub outside, so we'd jump in there.

She was Japanese. She spoke Japanese, so we felt like she couldn't understand us. We couldn't understand her either. But she was always giving us things, some money and goodies—cookies or candy. So we always had a nice time when we were there. Sometimes we'd stay over and the back area was under a Christmas berry tree and it was open and had corrugated iron on three sides, rock on the bottom, and they heated the water over a hibachi, I guess, and put it in a big washtub and that would be where you bathed. In the open, and that was fun.

HUSBAND'S PARENTS

We're renovating the house and making more rooms downstairs because Paul's parents are going to come live with us, eventually. We put in an extra bathroom, and the plan is for them to stay upstairs, in our bedroom, and for us to stay downstairs. But the work is going slowly [laughs]. I think Paul's mother is in her late seventies and his father is eighty-three. They're getting old. His father recently had an accident with the car. He drives too close. He likes to get close to people, for some reason. His eyesight is not that good, and I guess his reaction time is not that good, either. He's not driving anymore; I guess Paul must have talked to him.

Neolani is sixteen now. She's going to be a junior this coming September, and I just started working again part-time, because eventually I think I'll need to get a full-time job or anyway spend more time out of the house, since they're going to be here. I think for me its going to be kind of difficult, although I don't mind having help with the cleaning and the meals [laughs]. I get along so-so. I haven't talked to his mother for quite a while, a few months. His father comes over and cleans the yard, but I don't go out and say hello and take a glass of water. I used to do that, but nowadays I don't do that. In the beginning we did a lot with Paul's parents, you know? Like every Sunday we'd go over for dinner. And that was just too much for me, because just going over for the holidays was too much. I kind of like being by myself. I don't like being close to my relatives . . . too much.

I want to do it because that's what Paul wants, but I know for me its going to be difficult. Even though, like, I have friends stay over every once in a while—and I want them to stay over—still, it's very difficult for me.

It depends when everything is finished, and I don't know how they'll feel about moving in because I think they kind of like their independence, too. It's kind of Paul's idea. I don't think they'll mind. If I had been a different kind of daughter-in-law. His father was born and raised in Japan until he was twenty, I think. He was left behind at the family home and raised by an uncle and aunt. They didn't have any children, but I think the thought was they would be returning to Japan—the family—so they left behind their eldest son, who would take over the family home and whatever. They weren't vocal about how they wanted things, or insistent.

FINAL THOUGHTS

That's how it is. They're older than you are and the older they get, the more they slow down and need care. I don't know if I can do with my mother what she does with my grandmother. I don't know if I can take care of a person like that. I took care of kids, but I don't consider myself a good parent. I guess I've always considered myself a little girl and still do. That's why people think I'm younger than I am. Not just my appearance. Maybe my appearance a little, but mostly the way I act, I think. They think I'm really young. I guess responsibility has always scared me. Being still a little girl inside, I'm not assertive so I'm easily . . . I think I would think, "How can I take care of this person?" It's scary.

I have a lot of problems that I guess I've not worked out from my childhood about this type of criticism. I got that I was cute, but that I couldn't do things. Both that I didn't know how and that I was lazy. That I was good for nothing. My father always said that, and I don't think he meant it in a derogatory manner. It was supposed to instill the fight in you to do something and be better. He was brought up in Japan, you know, because his mother died when he was about four. He lived there about ten years, so he was Japanese to me. And our relationship was pretty distant. Japanese: they coddle you when you're really little, they can hug you and kiss you and be real affectionate with little kids, but—I don't know at what age—they then become distant.

I've always been . . . responsibility has always been hard with me.

As far as Paul's business goes, in the beginning I was in there with him. I did his books, and then I started helping him with his work on the cars. With the installations or removals of the radio or antennas. I would do that also. But then I gradually started doing things less and less. Maybe only a couple of times a month do I go down to the shop and do anything at all. I used to go down every day. Neolani does some billing, answering the phone, perhaps once a week. Martin did also.

I just wonder how my mother feels about what happened to her, being sort of kidnapped. After she had us—there was five of us—she was sick and depressed a lot. I remember her in bed, reading books, not wanting to cope with things. Just like I do now myself.

Postscript

There are three separate stories in Mrs. Takahashi's narrative: her mother's experiences in Japan before the war, the family's current concern over the maternal grandmother's care, and Mrs. Takahashi's ambivalence over her household's expansion to include her in-laws. Although distinct, they are inseparable. Her mother's role was defined in childhood and it is clear, I think, that information about that experience were passed on to Mrs. Takahashi during her childhood. Perhaps she was threatened with expulsion (from the islands and nuclear family) if she, like her mother, was "stubborn." Cultural values of obedience, care giving, and respect are woven through the story. The Japanese-speaking grandparents of Mrs. Takahashi's childhood were distant, remote figures. Today Mrs. Takahashi's grandmother is seen largely through her mother's eyes, as indeed the whole tale reflects a complex of historical relations passed into the present.

Several weeks after this interview took place, Mrs. Takahashi invited me to her mother's house, to meet the other two women in this multigenerational tale.

13

The Anniversary Girl

Several weeks after my interview with April Takahashi, she suggested we visit her mother, Mrs. Mitsue Kumamoto, and her grandmother, Mrs. Akani, with whom she lived. Over the last decade, Mrs. Kumamoto has developed vocal problems that allow her to speak only in a hoarse whisper, the result, her doctors say, of clenched teeth and tensed neck muscles held rigid throughout long days and sleepless nights. They believed that this problem was a direct reaction to the stress of care giving, and that her voice would return when that role ended. Several years later, however, the problem had not diminished despite the eventual removal of her mother from Mrs. Kumamoto's house.

SSI is the Supplemental Security Income program, a part of the federal social safety net that aims to provide living expenses for its elderly recipients. It is supposed to provide support for those living at home with assistance, as does Mrs. Atani.

[Ed. note: Mrs. Kumamoto speaks a Hawaiian-English dialect whose grammar differs from "standard" American English. Rather than "correcting" a perfectly intelligible and, to me, expressive form of English, I've chosen to retain her natural speech patterns in this story."]

I was talking to a friend taking care of her grandfather who was telling me her father always said, " 'I'm never going to bother you folks. When my time comes, I'm not going to bother you folks. I'm going up into the hills and die in the hills.' But now, seeing how good I take care of grandpa, he says, 'Oh, now I don't have to worry about going up to the hills.' All my life I'm going to be taking care of other people," she says. "I don't have nothing to look forward to. Am I going to be like this all my life?" I told her what my experience was. I said, "Well, at one time I thought that way. I helped take care of Grandma. Take care of this, take care of that. But God must have put me on this earth to take care of others. To help." She says, "Well, maybe that's what I'm here for, too."

I thought, you know, I'd been taking care of Mama for three or four years now. I said, "No wonder I'm tired." But then when I actually sat down to count the years since I got her, it's ten years! When I brought Mama home, she was still able to go out in the yard, sickle the grass, pick the weeds. Just keep her company and make sure she dress warm. Clean, bathe, cook for her, and stuff. But see, well, I guess why I thought of the three or four years is . . . the three or four years since she became dependent on me. Really dependent. The funny thing is, up until the time I was seventy years old, I climbed the tree. I pruned the tree, leaned way over, cut the fruit. I used a pick and shovel and anything. Now, after I pass seventy, I feel when I exert myself a little bit I feel tired. Maybe because I'm taking care of mother. And when I climb the tree, I can still climb, but my feet get shaky. I feel slightly nervous. So I said, "Oh boy, I'm getting there." And I notice I slump.

ON NURSING HOMES

Sometimes it's getting to the point where I tell myself, "Maybe I should put her into the home." You know, when I help lift her and stuff like that, I can't straighten up myself sometimes! It takes a while for me to rub my back and then straighten up. So I say, "Chee, if I went down, who's going to take care of Mama?" All of our friends say, "You better put her in a nursing home, because you're going to fall. You're going to get sick." But I've visited nursing homes, you know. I've got friends who are in nursing homes. And when you go and there are visiting hours—everything is nice. People pay attention. But I drop in whenever I could, you know? They kinda didn't like the idea that I dropped in anytime of the day. But I tell them, "Look, I live far. And when I come to visit them, I come only because I have other things to do in town. So when I finish doing what I'm doing, I drop by to see them. I cannot come at the time you folks want me to come. Other than that, I cannot see my friends." And I notice that those who cannot walk are strapped onto wheelchairs. They can scream and yell and call, "Nurse, nurse, nurse, nurse," and all the time I'm there, maybe I'm there a half an hour, that person who call the nurse—nobody pay attention to the person.

And the lady is in the bed, and I'm sure she must be cold because she has only a sheet over her and she has that, you know, hospital gown with only a top, no bottom. So her bottom is bare with just a sheet over her. So I say, "Obaasan [Grandmother], aren't you cold?" She says, "Yes, but they don't give me nothing to put on." I say, "Why don't you say you feel cold?" She says she can't speak English. They don't understand her. I say to them, "You know, the lady is cold. She's just laying in bed and the blood circulation is poor. So she's cold." And they just say, "Okay, okay."

So when I'm all frustrated I think, "Ugh, going to put her in a nursing home. I think it's better." Then when I calm down, relax, I tell myself, "I cannot put her in a nursing home. I don't want her to go through that kind of thing where I visit my friends and see them ignored and everything."

MRS. AKANI

My father's mother in Japan, I didn't have to lift so much as I have to do with my mother. She was a very strong-willed woman, and she would crawl, she would pull herself to get to the bathroom. Even to position herself over the hole, she'd do. Only to wipe her, wash her, because she said her hand could not. All I did was bathe her, wash her clothes, and she'd put on her clothes herself. And I'd clean her bottom. She didn't want me to feed her. It wasn't hard. When they're bedridden, it's not as hard when they're not ambulatory. You get the sheet, lower them that way, clean the sheet, roll them again.

My mother is as a whole a good-natured woman. Most always smiling, laughing. Sometimes she says funny jokes. Like, my neighbor up the road, her mother-in-law was a cranky, terrible old lady. She found fault with everything and she screamed and yelled. The only time mother gets mean is when she's hurting. Its easier to throw her on a wheelchair and make her scoot back and forth, but then, I think, she's going to get weak. So I try to make her walk, slowly. She says "*Itai, itai* [It hurts, it hurts]. Let me go." But you don't want to let her go because if you let her go, she's going to fall. She might break her bone. And to try to make you release her, she'll try and lean over and bite anyplace she can get her mouth to. So I hurry her as best as I can and make her sit, so I don't get bitten. The other thing is that sometimes she gets stubborn.

But sometimes she surprises me. She goes "put-put-put-put" right along. In between I give her a cookie or something. But then she doesn't notice that I'm there. And she starts looking around, so I say, "Ma! What's a matter? You looking for me? I'm right here." "Oh, there you are," she says. "I thought nobody was home. I thought I was all by myself." See, half the time she's okay but sometimes she look at me and say, "Who are you? Who are you?" And I say, "Your daughter, Mitsue." And she says, "Really!" She is surprised-looking, you know?

Most times she's good, but once in a while she gets stubborn. And when she's very angry with me, I know this. You know, when I try and make her do something, like I want to turn her over. For example, to take her choppers out, it's a fight. "Please take it out. I'm going to clean and brush it for you. Mama, please! Otherwise you're going to start having sores in your mouth, and that's not good." I say, "Open your mouth, Mom, open your mouth." She'll close it, and when you try to force it she'll go [makes a face] EUGGGH [laughs]! She tries to bite you. I try to take it out and she goes, AAAGH [clenches her teeth]! I say, "Try and take it out yourself, then; push it out with your tongue. Push it out." She laugh, and it comes out loose and I pull. She wants to bite me! Her teeth fit her good, you know. Even the bottom one fit her good. And to get the top one, the suction off, oh! She bite me. But other than that, she's pretty good.

We try and put a diaper on her and she keeps going away, crawling. You have to chase her to put on the diaper. I tell you, a funny thing happened. I sat her on the toilet to make her BM. I said, "Don't you get off the toilet. You finish your BM. I'm just going to the kitchen to do something. I'll be right back." But then I thought I might as well take the slop out instead. So I took the bucket, came out, ran down the stairs, dropped it, came back—I didn't even rinse the bucket—I just ran back into the house. And there she was. She'd gotten off the toilet, scuttled on the floor, and she had the BM all on the floor. All to the back door. She was squatting right there and she made a pile of BM. I said, "Mom, I told you—please don't get off the toilet. Finish. I'll be right back." I said, "It didn't even take half a minute. Why did you do it? What is that over there!" Then she looked at it, then she looked up at the sky, and she said, "That must have been a big, big bird to make such a big dropping." I said, "Yeah, this big bird right here." But you know, sometimes she's like that. She comes out with funny, funny things.

DAILY ROUTINES

In the morning she gets up. I take her to the bathroom, she goes to the toilet, I wash her face, make her rinse her mouth, comb her hair, change her clothes, then take her to breakfast. Sometimes I try to let her eat by herself, but she can't deal with the food, so then I have to feed her. Sometimes it takes a long time. And when she doesn't like the food, she just goes pffut! She spits it out. Sometimes I like to give her vitamins and things. Sometimes she'll take it and sometimes she'll pffut! Even medicine. Even medicine! I know one time I got a certain medicine all over my face. Pah! And after that I take her to the parlor to sit down. Sometimes I put her on the TV. Sometimes she'll watch, sometimes not. Most times she'll fall asleep. So I try to go out, give my plants some water, come back in. If there's laundry to do I do laundry, sometimes pick up the house, whatever.

Most times, I try to go back to sleep because, nighttime, sometimes she doesn't go to sleep. On and off, she stays up, she gets up and stays up one hour, sometime two hours. Sometimes she goes, "I want to go toilet!" I say, "Mama, I just took you to the toilet. Just got back." She says, "Well, I want to go *shishi* [urinate] again." So there we go, and she cannot walk by herself so you have to hold her hand. But most times she'll crawl, or she'll scoot on the floor. She has a habit of, as she's going, she's mopping the floor with her hands like this [demonstrates a circular, mopping or waxing motion], like she's cleaning. And you'll give her a rag so she can do that. She hangs the rag up and she goes back with her hands. I say, "Mama, you don't do that. You go straight. When you come back from the toilet you can do that. NO." Every cranny, every corner she's scurrying.

So you have to *take* her to the toilet. Sometime's she'll do, sometimes she won't. So you wait, wait, wait, wait, and you're so sleepy while she's sitting on there. And she's not going to do anything. "Come on! Let's go back to bed." You pick her up, lift her up, wipe her bottom, go back in bed. She'll lay down. So I'll go wash my hands, come back, lay down. As I'm just falling asleep, she goes opening the doors! Scratching the floors, pulling the covers on her bed up high! You know the eggshell thing, the foam mattress used so that they don't have bedsores? She pulls *that* up on top of her like it's a blanket! She pulls everything out. Aaah. I can't go back to sleep. I have to go there, fix the bed, put her back in, lay down with her, and pat her on the back. Like a baby, you know.

Then I take her to my sister's house, one day. She has this daughter named May. And my mother was staying with them when May was a little girl. But all those years, fourteen years my mother was with my sister. Of course, May became a nice young lady by then. But about five years after she came with me, she hasn't seen May all that time. And she looks at May and says, "Who's this cute little girl? So cute! Pretty soon you'll get married, eh? I hope you get a good husband when you get married. You're so pretty, you should get a nice husband." And May says, "Obaasan, Obaasan, it's me! May!" She thinks, thinks back, can't seem to remember. May starts crying and says, "Obaasan doesn't know me any more." I say, "Ma, it's May, Yuki's youngest. The baby." She couldn't remember.

It's just like a little child, you know? That's the way she's feeling now. Does it bother me? Not at the time. At the time I think, "Oh well, it's not registering." But sometimes I'm sitting down trying to relax, unwind. And I think of the day's events, the things she did, what she said. Sometimes I replay it and sometimes I cry. I say, "Poor thing, to come to that." I hope I don't get to that point. I hope I can go before that. I told my children, "I'll find some way. Somewhere, somehow."

I spank her sometimes. I spank her sometimes on the *okole* [Hawaiian for buttocks]. She says, "You don't have to be so mean to me." I feel bad. Sometimes I cry by myself. I think, "She took care of me all these years, and look at me now. I'm getting all upset and I'm hitting her. Spanking her." My voice disappears. It just disappears. Sometimes [my daughter] Alice says, "Are you all right? Are you sick? Do you need help?" I say, "No, I'm just so frustrated that my voice goes." They say, "Oh, I thought you were sick." I go to shiatsu [Japanese massage] now once a week, but it's mostly for my back and my hip. It's tight . . . the stress. And picking her up, lifting her. Sometimes I'm just ready to fall over.

BUREAUCRACIES

One time she had pneumonia. But she wasn't sick enough to put into hospital. So I had to take her to Comprehensive [outpatient care] and have everything done. And I brought her home, then I took care of her. I said to Alice, "She's stayed awake and everything." I just said, "I need help somewhere!" I called . . . who did I call, now? I donno, something for the elderly [Hawaii Executive Office on Aging]. And they ask, "Just what kind of help do you need?" And I said "I need help for me!" I said, "I'm so tired. I'm so exhausted. It's hard to, you know, take care of her."

So they sent out a public health nurse, and they sent a physical therapist. The physical therapist said, "Well, I can't do anything because you're doing whatever she needs. She's ninety-eight and a half already. There's nothing much you can do." And the public health nurse said, "Oh, I don't have a doctor's permission, so I cannot help you. I just came to check on you. That's all" [laughs]. So I called Alice and she came help me. She was a big help, because then I could do what I had to do in between: relax or sleep or whatever. So it was a real help. Her sister came twice from Laie, but by the time she reached here—you know how long it takes—then she'd have to go home by a certain time, so . . .

I applied for help to the Leeward side [the local as opposed to the state office], and they said her application was denied because they do not have her correct birth date. I have her entry date into the U.S., and so I went to immigration and tried to get the information, and they said, "Oh, that's retired files. All in Washington. So it's going to take a long time before we can get the answer, maybe three or four months." Argh. But they took the paper, they put the stamp on it. They say, "Okay, we'll send you the information when it comes." So I went back and told them (at Leeward) what had happened. They said, "Whatever bills you have, whatever *de kine* [thing] for her you have, bring it." So I bring it. They said, "Oh, exactly how much does she get in Social Security and how much does she get in SSI [assistance]?"

So the next time I took the checks, and they made copies of them. I took her alien registration card, but they say, "That's not official. It's from the police department, so its not official." Then I took them her registry copy from Japan but they say, "It's not a birth certificate." I say, "In Japan they don't give birth certificate, you know!" They say, "We have to have a verification." So I went to the Japanese consulate. They have a record of Father coming into the country in 1907, but they don't have a date for Mama. They have a date on the father, so it's just like Mother came same time as Father. But actually, she came in 1911, '12 or '13. I don't know which one, and she doesn't remember, either. So I put the paper back to SSI and it's still denied. And they say if you apply—reapply—within 120 days then you don't have to go through making all those papers again. I got disgusted.

Then I got a new worker, a Mr. Yung. He was a little more helpful. He said, "You take this to immigration. You show them this paper and have them fill it in and return it." So I did. I'm still waiting to see what they're going to say. Meanwhile, the social worker told me, "Try to apply for Chore Service [Ed. note: home care or financial assistance available in Hawaii from the Department of Human Services]. If you qualify, they'll pay you for taking care of your mother and they'll supply you with, like, wheelchair, whatever things you need." So I applied on, let's see, May 29, I think. I filled it out, I sent it back. Then they had to process it. They called in between: "Oh, how much is she getting SSI, how much from Social Security? What else does she have? Does she have HMSA [a state medical insurance program] or other medical plans? Medicare or Medicaid?" Then I wait, and wait, and wait, and another set of papers came. I signed and dated them and sent back.

Finally, one day last week a man called and he said, "My name is Richard and I have your case. You know, I'm not sure. There's this something income, $360. What is that income?" I said I didn't know. He said, "How much money does your mother get?" I said that at the time she applied she was having $189 Social Security and then SSI, she was getting $44.44. He said, "Oh, your mother have SSI?" I said, "Yeah." He said, "Then there's no problem! It's automatic that you get your service."

But he said his Chore Division is separate from the D.H.S. [Hawaii Department of Human Services] welfare division, you know? So they don't have this, they don't have that. So finally I'm going to get some money retroactive to May 29, but he said it's at minimum wage, you know, $3.85. I said, "That's okay. If it's something, that will help me." And he said, "You're not going to have a forty-hour week. Nobody gets forty-hour week. The most anybody gets is twenty to twenty-five hours a week." I said that was okay. He said, "You know, bathing her, combing her head, dressing her, is not considered work. It's not considered labor." I said, "Well, what is considered labor?" He said, "Like, you take her to the park, you take her to the zoo, you take her shopping, to the doctor. That kind of thing. You take her out in the yard, the time you spend with her, you do things with her." I said, "Well, you comb her hair and *de kine* [that kind of thing], you do things with her!" He said those things are considered a normal, I don't know how he said it, duty type of thing. Feeding and stuff. Cooking is something different. Cooking is part of the job. Dealing with them is more frustrating than with her! And you ought to see the kind of questions in the application when you apply: how many people are in the house? You're only applying for one person! Sometimes I feel it is so asinine. Even for the Social Security supplement.

Listen, because Mama is living in this house, she's not paying rent. Then it's considered a $128 income for her. Now, because there's three people living in the house, you divide them (utilities) in three and add part to Mama's. It comes out to $360 together with her Social Security, so with the ceiling that Social Security allows, she gets $44.44.

JAPAN

I was in Japan for three years. I left here on September 9, 1934. At the time that she took me up there, it's her parents' fiftieth anniversary so they wanted her to come up. And she says, "I'm going to take you up with me." I was kind of happy that out of the seven kids I was selected to go up with her. But after the anniversary party was over and Mom was ready to go back, then she set me down and said, "I'm going to have to leave you here to take care of my mother-in-law for me because I cannot. You have to do it for me." What can I say? Did I want to stay? No, but what could I do?

Anyway, her father was a nice kind of understanding grandpa. "That's okay, that's okay, when things get tough, you just come stay with us."

It took a while, well, to come to terms with my grandmother and myself, because she was quite a sarcastic woman to me. She always say things which hurt you. Because you don't know how, you ask

her. And she says, "You're fifteen years old and you still don't know
how? What kind of mother do you have which won't show you
nothing!" Grandma had asthma and she had arthritis and she never
spoke softly or gently to make me feel good. Everything was sharp,
to the point. She'd say, "You're fifteen, so you don't know anything
yet." And you ask her, because you don't know, and she yells at
you: "And in the first place, I didn't want you to come. I wanted
your sister, your older sister, so that I could get her married and she
could settle over here." I said, "Good thing my sister couldn't come."
Anyway, she asked me to massage her, I massaged. An hour can go
by and you stop and she says, "You stopped. What are you stopping
for?" So you keep on massage, massage. Your fingers get tired, you
want to fall asleep, you start nodding, nodding. She says, "I didn't
tell you can go to sleep!"

So, anyhow, it took me a long time before I could become comfortable with her. There was Dr. Shimizu, who lived across the
valley, he sat me down one day. I went up to get medicine at his
place and he set me down. He says, "You look like you've been
crying." I said, "Yeah." He says, "You know, old people need to
be pampered. You have to kind of baby them and pamper them.
Even if she says things which hurt you, just let it slide off like rain
falling." He said, "She's a good woman. It's just that her daughter
got married, divorced, come back. Then the youngest daughter, who
was the best of all the children, died. The other child mortgaged the
whole place, took the mortgage money, and went off to Brazil. So
she's been hurt bad. But if you try to pamper her and try to be kind
to her, no matter what she says now, she'll come around." But you
know, being fifteen or sixteen, it takes a long time to learn to come
around.

The last half year things were okay. Until then, if things got bad,
I took off to my mother's parents' house. And there, my mother's
father tolerate me for one week and let me stay. Then he'd say, "You
have to go back because she needs you. You know? We don't need
you. We love to have you here, but we don't need you. She needs
you because she has nobody else. So even if it hurts, go back and
do the best you can and don't let things hurt you. You try your
best." So I go back, so I try and take care the best I can, and when
things get bad again, I take off again. That's how it went. And then,
finally, I think it was when her daughter came home for the second
time, after her husband had died, she came home and lived in the

lower house. We lived in the upper house. And from that time on, Grandma changed. Seeing her daughter there kind of upset her, because she and her daughter never got along. Her daughter was gimme, gimme, gimme, grab, take.

She used to make me go out to work. Even if she needed care, still she say, "I can crawl to the toilet. That's okay. And if you leave the food there [nearby] I can go get the food." So she sent me to this towel factory to sew the edges of the towel. So then I'd come home and find the yard all scattered with rubbish, stones. Come around the back door, the whetting stone is broken, things are broken. I knock on the door and say, "Grandma! Open the door. Grandma! Open the door." And there's no answer. I say, "It's me, I've come home from work." Finally, after about ten, fifteen minutes, she opens the door slowly and says, "Are you by yourself?" I say, "What's happened?" She says, "That was my daughter. Your auntie got angry at me. She threw things at the house. She wanted to beat me up, but I closed the door quick."

She wanted my grandmother to sign the property over to her, which my grandmother refused. It was in my father's name, because he was the eldest. In the end, Father came and stayed with Grandfather from March 7 to June 12. That's when my grandmother died. During that time, she told my father, "The property is yours, but I do not want you to do anything with it without her consent." That's *my* consent. "She will decide yes or no." Toward the end, she really leaned on me. It had to be me. My father would come and say, "I'll help you," and she'd say, "No! Get away from me! I don't want you. I want her." And I'd go help.

After she died, we stayed in Japan for another half a year, four months. My father, he took his father-in-law and me to Korea to visit my mother's sister who lived in Korea. And we came back. Then he wanted to go to Beppu [a coastal area on the island of Kyushu], so we went to Beppu, stayed about two weeks and came back. And we stayed at home for about a month and then began to get ready to come home. We went to Nara, Kyoto, then we came home [to Hawaii].

RETURNING HOME

In a way, I was happy to come home. And yet I felt I was an outsider. I wasn't comfortable with the family. And naturally I still had the resentment that they tricked me into going to Japan to take care of Grandma. I felt Mother took me up there. She lied to me, I felt. She didn't lie to me, she just didn't tell me what for. She just said, "We're going to this anniversary." [Laughs.] So I kind of flouted their authority [laughs again]. I gave Mom a bad time.

Oh, she was so angry with me. She just chopped my hair! Chop, chop, chop, chop! She say, "If I do this, you won't go out, looking like that." But I went out, I put a kerchief on and went out anyway! [Laughs.] I went out with groups of people, you know, so we wouldn't get into trouble. She say, "Hah! Maybe the other girls are all good girls. They don't drink and get drunk like you. They don't smoke like you." I said, "I like it, so I do it." In Japan, being with my grandmother, she'd say, "Keep me company," when we started to get together. So I'd have a jigger of wine. That's how I learned to drink! Keeping my grandmother company.

After I came back from Japan I was home for awhile. I didn't feel like going out to work or doing anything. Across the street had this family where this lady was taking care of her grandmother who was 101 years old. An old Hawaiian lady, she was a bag of skin and bones already. She was old, she had bedsores. She used to feel cold all the time because, I guess, the blood wasn't circulating good. She couldn't move. You had to lift her, put her on the potty. So Mary said, "Jeez, I'm so busy, why don't you come and help me take care of grandmother?" I said, "Okay, during the busiest time." They used to make box lunches for these Pearl Harbor people going to work. So when they were busy doing those things, then I took care of the grandma during that time. So I took care of her almost one year; then she passed away. Then I helped a lady part-time. So she could go out and do things, look after her mother, who was semiambulatory.

FINAL THOUGHTS

As I started to raise my own children, I realized what my mother had to go through. I kind of realized that all these kinda things I had to go through made me a stronger person. But still, it's a very stressful job. And I get upset. And I get angry at mother sometimes and I spank her. And I yell at her sometimes. And I scold her.

My mother said, she hopes she can go like stumbling, pfft. She always said, *"Kurute ikitai."* [Literally: I'd like to go out on a stumble.] And sometimes I'm watching and she feels so tired, she says, "Why can't I just go! I hear of other people working in the yard and, just go. I wish I could go like that." I say, "Maybe someday it will happen." She gets up in the morning, "Oh, I'm still here!" She say, she felt so tired last night, she think she die in her sleep. She says this morning, "No, I'm still here." But she tells me, "If I die, I don't want you people make any funeral. Don't make nothing big. Nothing, nothing. Just have me cremated, take me to the church, have prayers said over me. My children there, the grandchildren don't have to come."

I get to the point where I feel like I'm being a burden to my children, I'll do something. My sister's friend, she was a widow and she thought, before anything happened to her, she would give the son her house and property and the money, whatever money she had, and then he would take care of her. But she didn't do it in writing. Okay? He was still single yet. Then he got married, and it was still okay. But I guess the wife couldn't stand it. And one day, the woman came over and cried to my sister. She said, "You know what he told me? 'Mama, you have to move, you have to find someplace else.' " She said, "This is my home. You know, I gave it to you but still this is my home. I gave it to you because I had hoped you would take care of me." He said, "Well, it's in my name. It's mine now. My wife can't stand you, so you have to move." My sister told her, "Don't you dare move. You just stay in that house. You just stay in that house. You just make yourself invisible. Don't you ever get out of that house." And she's still there.

I liked it the way Mrs. Takata went. Long time ago, she came with her grandchildren to my house when we were living in Moilili. She brought her two grandchildren to play with my two children, my oldest daughter and my son. I had two at the time. And they played. And she said, "The vegetable man coming any minute so I better go home and take my pot so he can put the tofu inside. The two tofu." So after she went home, maybe fifteen, twenty minutes later, I heard, "Beep beep! Beep beep!" The vegetable man came. So I took my pot to go get my tofu and buy some vegetables, too. And, ah, of course it takes me a little time to get there because its like, ah, four or five houses down. Of course, I have to leave my children with my next-door neighbor and she says, "Oh, buy me my tofu, too." Then it takes me another ten minutes or so. I see this man, the man coming out from Mrs. Takata's house, and he's pale. I said, "What's the matter?" He say: "You know when I Beep-beep she always comes out right away with her two grandchildren. She didn't come out! You heard me make two time Beep beep! About five minutes later she still didn't come out. So I went to see. She's sitting on that chair and she's dead!" She had a heart attack, and the grandchildren were playing at my house. They didn't know. She just sat on the chair and went, ahhh. I hope I can go that way.

Postscript

Neither Mrs. Kumamoto nor Mrs. Takahashi has a great deal of time for the medical definitions or cared greatly for the technical names of the older woman's infirmities. "I guess she has Alzheimer's," both women shrugged when asked. "And she has that bone thing," meaning osteoporosis. Whether the dementia is caused by Alzheimer's or another pathology, it is certainly extreme. Mrs. Atani is typically and progressively disoriented. Several years ago she did not recognize cousins or grandchildren. Now she is largely unaware of her own hygiene or bodily functions. To the extent that she can get around, Mrs. Atani is a danger to herself. If doors are not locked, she will crawl outside. Electrical appliances are mysterious objects with which she, like a child, can injure herself. The stories of fights over cleaning her dentures remind many of caring for a very young and uncooperative child. But this is not a child; it is a mother and grandmother. The distinction is not lost on Mrs. Kumamoto. This is what her mother has become, and although she is in some ways childlike—and thus treated like a child—the distinction between child and adult is absolute. Spanking is, in her view, appropriate for one but not for the other, and when that boundary is crossed, the daughter feels guilty.

Although Mrs. Takahashi had warned me that her mother's voice was hard to understand, I was not prepared for the degree of impairment. Not only was it extremely low in volume—a clenched whisper is the best description I can offer—but it cracked repeatedly, especially when she became excited. Interestingly, as the interview progressed and she relaxed into memory, her voice improved a bit. The problem began when Mrs. Atani's ailments became severe and 24-hour care giving a necessity. Her doctors have told Mrs. Kumamoto that the impairment is a direct result of stress and that it will improve when her care-giving role either diminishes or ends. In addition, Mrs. Kumamoto admits to periods of severe depression as well as to moments of frustration so extreme that she spanks her mother, although she knows this is not right. And yet, she does call for help sometimes, asking both family members like Mrs. Takahashi and the state for assistance. Interestingly, when she began her trek through the labyrinth of state agencies, she was hoping for outreach nursing and home-care services. What she ended up with was a token financial compensation for her efforts.

That says more about social services, I suspect, than the necessities of the situation. A good physical therapist, for example, could have done much to assist in exercising Mrs. Akane's muscles and perhaps in improving her ambulation. Monies spent on a ramp for the front steps of the house would have made it far easier for other relatives to take the elderly woman out on excursions. At present there are a number of steep wooden steps which prohibit use of a wheelchair and require extreme caution when she is to be transported anywhere. This is the type of problem good outreach workers are trained to see and deal with, but it was ignored by the nurse and therapist who briefly visited Mrs. Kumamoto and her mother in 1990.

After recording Mrs. Takahashi's story, I wondered why and how Mrs. Kumamoto would care for a woman who had robbed her of those years at home and so cavalierly sent her to look after an old woman in a foreign country whom the young Mrs. Kumamoto had never met. I certainly did not expect the degree of tenderness and love this 71-year-old woman clearly feels and at times expresses for her elderly, frail, senile 98-year-old mother. I wondered if there would be a sense of triumph, a final dominance in the war of generations now that she was in control and the mother who took her to Japan and left her there had become totally dependent.

All this, of course, says far more about me than about the Kumamoto-Atani relationship. The actual situation is simply that Mrs. Kumamoto has learned to forgive if not forget. It is with real glee that she remembers the difficult time she gave her mother after returning to Hawaii. With great animation, she illustrated with gestures how her mother cut off her hair in an attempt to keep her daughter at home and within the bounds of decent behavior. But she also believes that it is her place to care for her mother now, and she accepts that the process that took her to Japan was not abandonment but a situation in some ways as difficult for her mother as it was for the young Mitsue.

FOLLOW-UP

About six weeks after these interviews were completed, Mrs. Atani fell and broke her arm. Mrs. Kumamoto said her mother "got away" from her, crawling to the door while her daughter was busy in the kitchen, and when she turned to see where her mother was, she had pulled herself up at the door frame only to fall and break the bones between elbow and wrist. She was then taken to hospital, where the arm was set, and Mrs. Atani was treated for several other, non–life-threatening problems. The broken arm led to a series of low-grade infections, a result of her depressed immune system.

At the urging of both physicians and social workers, Mrs. Atani was then placed in a nursing home. Her daughter said that Mrs. Atani's almost total lack of awareness, her need for constant supervision and care—feeding, hygiene, and so on—made it a practical and, indeed, necessary move. "Social Services is going to pay for everything," she added. With institutionalization, Mrs. Atani now fits within the definitions of bureaucracy, and financial support is available. Had a home-care worker or night aide been available, both women said it is likely that they would have kept Mrs. Atani at home. "Right now I'm trying to let go of her care," Mrs. Takahashi said to me after the institutionalization. Still, she visited the hospital frequently. Other relatives also plan trips to Mrs. Atani's bedside, so that most evenings a family member is present at the older woman's dinner time. Mrs. Takahashi made a "fabric book" with cloth pages of different textures and colors so that Mrs. Akani would have something to fondle, hold, touch, and consider when alone.

Although physicians had insisted Mrs. Kumamoto's vocal problems were psychosomatic—the result of "care-giver stress"—Mrs. Atani's institutionalization has not improved her daughters condition. Two years after Mrs. Atani's institutionalization, Mrs. Kumamoto's voice still had not returned to normal. Mrs. Kumamoto still visits her mother frequently, "at least several times a week." Interestingly, when April Takahashi goes to visit, it is often at the urging of her own daughter, who likes to accompany her mother on these trips.

Chorus

NECESSARY VERSUS CONTINGENT RELATIONS

One way to distinguish between the active care givers and less in-volved relatives whose stories are presented here is to distinguish between "necessary" and "contingent" relations. Care givers and their elderly are emotionally joined by "necessary" bonds which result in a determination to care for and be with that fragile individual. Mrs. Harding is necessary to her husband, just as Ms. Neilson's grandmother is somehow necessary to her. "I think she's become an integral part of my being," Jay Nakana says of his mother, "of who I am." But other relations living at a greater geographic and emo-tional distance—Ms. Neilson's father, Mr. Lypchuk's brothers—are joined to their fragile relatives only by "contingent" ties formed from the fact of a common genetic pool and a past history of proximate relation. Because these ties are primarily historical, they are not, in cases of a geriatric decline, strong enough to result in active personal assistance. Mrs. Takahashi, for example, makes it clear she feels a necessary tie to her mother, but only a contingent bond to her grand-mother. For Mrs. Dister, the world seems to be a place of contingent ties.

Family members may, like Mrs. McLeod, share a contingent tie to the fragile elder, but effective support only comes from those who have maintained a necessary bond with their parent, grandparent, or spouse. This distinction—necessary versus contingent—emphasizes the truth that families at large do not give care to the aging or infirm individual. Care givers, individuals who define a necessary relationship—a necessary bond—with their seniors, give care. Outriders who insist on the importance of family ties but do not actively involve themselves in care giving—people like Marie Dister—represent a different category of perception and behavior. This difference says a great deal about the individual involved and about us as a society.

"The way we conduct ourselves in relation to one another and to the world," R. D. Laing says in *The Voice of Experience,* "goes along with the way we experience each other." Each of our worlds is built over time upon the structure of meaningful relationships in which a person exists and in the design of which each relation participates. For these care givers, their adult world is built upon the continuance of an individual, upon a significant and continuing relation with the now old and frail elder. Thus, for each care giver, that relative remains significant. To be apathetic, not to act on the other's behalf, would damage the structure that supports not only the care receiver but as well the care giver in the world at large. "When the individual loses his [or her] significance," as Rollo May put it in *Psychology and the Human Dilemma,* "there occurs a sense of apathy, which is an expression of his state of diminished consciousness." It is because the care receiver does not lose significance for the care giver that the younger relation cannot be apathetic, must act on the fragile elder's behalf. It is this apathy care givers fight. They consider giving up their responsibilities, they think about what it would be like not to have responsibility. But they do not—cannot—give up their relations.

Clearly, some and perhaps all of these care givers do not understand the structure of contingent or functional ties that leads the greater society to abandon a senior who can no longer serve as he or she has in the past. Mr. Williams is angered and disheartened over the disavowal of his wife by their Washington community; Katie O'Connor wishes for help and respite which does not come from a community, personified by her minister, which applauds care in the abstract but provides little real support; Mrs. Pfeiffer seeks understanding if not assistance and is charged with negligence for her pains; the Hardings' daughter and son-in-law simply deny the needs of her parents—both the father's physical and the mother's emotional realities. Seeking support and help, Mrs. Kumamoto receives $44.44 a month. The difference between necessary and contingent bonds absolutely separates the worlds of care givers and those who do not actively participate in that care.

For these care givers, their need to act on behalf of the other comes from a belief in the value of the fragile elder as part of their own lives. In each case, their reasons can only be understood if one sees the care-giving relation both in the broader context of an unbroken historical relation and as the end point of a number of prior decisions and choices. In choosing or, in some cases, accepting, the care giver's role, these speakers have affirmed a view of self and other, an attachment that is neither financial at base nor economic at heart. Each care giver speaks of past actions, places, and events that have been shared with the individual care receiver. To maintain their attachment, to continue to experience the other, elder relative—whatever his or her infirmities—is to continue those shared memories of the past into the present. To refuse the time that care demands and concentrate instead on one's own career or needs would require the care giver to sever relations with the fragile elderly individual by making powerless those memories of the other. To make contingent a necessary bond would be, for the care giver, a traumatic and personally limiting transformation.

In the most profound sense, the care givers and care receivers of these stories are joined, cohabitants of a time and history that the care giver sees as crucial to his or her world. These speakers teach us that people may accept responsibility without feeling an external obligation or debt. Margaret Neilson is not singularly obliged to her grandmother, but she accepts responsibility for her; Alice McLeod feels obliged to arrange care for her grandfather but cannot accept responsibility for him. Although Bill Lypchuk and Jay Nakana are no more or less obligated to care for their parents than are their respective brothers and sisters, both have taken on the responsibility of caring. April Takahashi sees herself as responsible for and to her mother. Thus her concern for Mrs. Atani is based not on an obligation flowing down the matriarchal line, but rather on the strength of her commitment to a grandparent's child.

By saying that these care givers are responsible for rather than obliged to their elders, what is being described is not a debt but an attachment. The ties of memory or kinship have in these cases created a context of continuous and, for the care giver, profoundly shared experience. More precisely, the attachment, the tie that binds, grows out of an interpersonal history that joins individual care receivers and care givers as people. In all of the care givers' stories, these ties are a necessary part of their world, something so integral that they may not themselves perceive their importance. The relation of care giver to care receiver is a positive attachment affirming necessary ties, whatever the burden or frustration that may result from taking up the functional role.

Positive Attachments

Consider the examples of Margaret Neilson, Tina Harding, and Craig Williams as examples of historically necessary ties. "When I was small," Margaret Neilson says, "the big thing was to go with my dad on the weekends, and one of us was allowed to go to my grandma's house and stay with her for the weekend." To be the child chosen for an overnight visit at her grandmother's was a privileged respite. Margaret Neilson's sense of being as an *adult* is built on the strength of moral and emotional support she felt as a child with the older woman. As Ms. Neilson put it: "She was always good to me and I could always seek her out when I had a problem, and it [caring] was the least I could do." That mutuality—the child's memories feeding the adult's vision—has become a bond between the two women that Ms. Neilson does not want to sever. For the younger woman to deny her grandmother's needs, to allow her to live out her last years in institutional care, to refuse her own time and attention when asked to help, would have been to deny the moral and emotional ties, the necessary bonds that not only join them but, in some ways, define Ms. Neilson's present.

For Tina Harding, her husband is, and has been from adolescence, her world. He has been the focus of her life from the time of their courtship ("He was everything. He was so bright! He would tell me about stars, and things that I didn't know") through the years of their maturity, in which she fully participated ("If I gave him a dollar for lunch, fine."), to his fragile present. Although her husband is quite obviously a frail septuagenarian whose illness causes him to forget things, that is only the immediate foreground of a deeper perception she has of him, one born of a fully relational history. Tim exists for Tina not only as an individual in the isolated present, one whose problems can be dispassionately catalogued, but also as a man known through decades of shared life, a person whose best attributes over time cannot be easily dismissed. The Hardings are sustained, one by the other, through this one relation defined by marriage but confirmed through a mutuality which has deepened over a period of fifty-six years. She cannot separate the man who was from the man who is—both exist simultaneously for her. For him, she is not simply an object—a bride, a homemaker, or businesswoman—but all those things simultaneously, and more. They are not simply care giver and care receiver but, more accurately, each is the partner's absolutely significant other who in the past and today's present makes that person's life worth living. For Mrs. Harding to follow her children's suggestion and abandon their father to a nursing home would be to make what has been necessary to her since adolescence a merely contingent relation, and that would diminish not only him but her as well.

Perhaps nobody said it as well as Mr. Williams, who stated about his profoundly disabled wife: "I look at her now, realizing everything that she's lost, but I still see her as she was, too." The disheveled woman with Alzheimer's, the woman with whom he loved Hawaii, the community woman and mother of their children—all exist simultaneously for him. To care for one is to sustain the shared historical memories of those other women. "It's like having double, or maybe triple vision," a woman who assists her ailing and alcoholic father said to me. When asked who she saw when visiting her father in his apartment (which she maintained), she said, "I see this pathetic, helpless man. But I also see him as he was, say, ten years ago, when my children were small. And I see the huge man who didn't come to my birthday party when I was seven years old." The people of memory and the person of present time are to her forever linked. And so it seems to be for these other care givers.

Unresolved Attachments

In the stories of Mr. Williams, Ms. Neilson, and Mrs. Harding, care givers speak of the historically supportive associations that have bound them through time to their significant others—grandparent, parent, or spouse. But a tie can be positive or negative. It can be based on either an idyllic or a fiercely traumatic event whose meaning has yet to be integrated into an individual's private world. As R. D. Laing put it in *The Voice of Experience* "Attachment may be felt positively or negatively as being tied to the other by something or other. The time may be pleasant or unpleasant, desired or undesired, welcome or imposed, two-way or one-way. Innumerable variations of this theme are expressed in a host of metaphors. He's a noose around my neck. She's my lifeline. He's my anchor.''

Thus Brian Leonard returned to his family home not simply to assist his mother in her husband's care, but also to come to terms with a complex of feelings and memories involving his father. "I realized that I shouldn't feel resentful toward him any longer," Mr. Leonard said about seeing his demented and deathly ill father. "My eyes swelled. That was my dad, before he drifted back into his scary world." Clearly the resentment that he thus put to rest was not a feeling of recent tenure. His father was a wrestler and a powerful man who had let himself get fat while espousing a stature of physical prowess and care to his son. The effect of the older man's dissolution on the family at large, the difference between parental speech and action, is what the younger Mr. Leonard finally confronts: "When he was my age he let himself go. I'm resentful he didn't take better care of himself . . . I resent my dad for being a glutton, . . . but I love him. I've loved him more than anyone. Now I feel like an asshole because his condition has caused an inconvenience to me."

And so the son comes to accept the father's failings, to meet through caring the disparate parts of a parent's complex personality he has known across a lifetime. The adult's hypocrisy—do as I say and not as I do—which seems so intolerable to an adolescent, is accepted in maturity by the adult who knows how easy it is to fail another, how tempting it is to let demands pile up and goals be articulated that cannot be fulfilled. Brian Leonard comes to accept the power his father once had over the younger man's life by acknowledging the dissolution of that power as he, the son, comes through care giving to forceful maturity. In so doing, he is freed to develop a new pattern of relation integrating his own and his father's worlds.

Similarly, it is in this resolution of past trauma with present circumstance that the secret of Katie O'Connor's constancy is revealed. Her father's long absences, her mother's taciturn preoccupation— neither of these argue for a debt that the now middle-aged woman should necessarily feel herself obliged to repay. But unresolved issues rising from a childhood spent in an alcoholic household tied her to these parents in a way as profound as the bonds of happy memory that joined the Williamses or the Hardings. A conversation with her mother about their problems of years before freed Mrs. O'Connor in a fundamental way from part of the pain of her childhood. It is the potential for a similar resolution—and fear that one will not come about—that causes her conflict over the future care of her father. In a moment of acute realization, she says this clearly: "I think that's basically why I keep going and doing for people, trying to get them to say, 'You did a good job, you pleased me.' But it doesn't mean anything to me when I hear it from them, because I'm not hearing it from Mum and Dad. And that's who you needed to hear it from. But I heard it from Mum. If I get to hear it from Dad, I think I would start to look around and appreciate the people that I do have."

Here, too, one finds the essence of Mr. Lypchuk, who has remained available for his father's care long after his financially more successful brothers have abdicated any substantial role in their surviving parent's maintenance. But it was for these elder brothers that the family moved to Toronto, on their behalf—to assure inexpensive domicile—that the elder Mr. Lypchuk endured his earliest years in a city he detested but his youngest son dearly loved. The older boys came to Toronto to leave home, to be at school. But it was there, in the family house he now helps maintain, that Bill Lypchuk grew up. And it was in this house that he heard his father rage at night, that in early adolescence he promised the voices that crept into his bedroom that, were he only allowed to stay in the city whose marvels included baseball and TV, he would do anything he was asked. And so now, long after, he keeps that pledge, maintaining his father as he assisted his mother, assuring them in the city he once prayed he would be allowed to grow up and grow old in.

Ontological Securities

Those who seem to have been most successful as care givers are those whose lives are defined in relation across time. That which Katie O'Connor struggles toward, which Tina and Tim Harding together possess, and which Margaret Neilson and Brian Leonard come to in their respective care-giving tenures is a sense of "ontological security," an awareness of themselves in relation to others across time. "Such a basically ontologically secure person will en-counter all the hazards of life," Laing says in *The Divided Self,* "from a centrally firm sense of his own and other people's reality and iden-tity." By affirming through their actions a mutual history defined by relations shared with another—parent, grandparent, or spouse—these care givers simultaneously chose for themselves a perspective that admits neither depersonalization nor objectification of the other. To do other than be with and care for their aged and frail others would be to diminish the care giver's *own* sense of reality, identity, and worth. It is not simple compassion or base repayment but some-thing more profound that is here at work. What care givers share with their fragile elders is a sense of being in relation where the objective and functional role of parent, grandparent, or spouse is subordinated to the subjective and ongoing definition of self born out of a bond joining each to a truly significant other.

These are not relations born of pity on the part of the now powerful for those once strong, not charity offered in the name of family once old debts are repaid and obligation past. There are things and people, situations and moments so central to our lives that we cannot let them fall into oblivion without doing damage to ourselves. We re-member them—good and bad—and keep them before us. They do not, in our eyes, become either perishable or ephemeral over time. They are irreducible to anything else, not replaceable, not inter-changeable. They have a hard core that endures through time. Re-lations over time are, in these necessary bonds, more than passive memories dredged up from a now distanced and safely ordered past. Rather, care giving seems to be built upon a series of memories that are both retained and empowered through the proximate relation of care receiver and care giver. These memories become, through the daily assembly of mundane acts, a connection which is life sustaining.

Thus the frail senior is for the care giver not simply an icon from the past, a once potent figure of authority whose power has dimin-ished—a memory from long ago—but a being who, as part of the care giver's ongoing history, has an existence that is both sufficient and important in and of itself. Tim Harding can no longer dazzle his wife with the depth of his knowledge, and Brian Leonard's father will no longer dominate his son through the superior wrestling tech-nique or the greater weight (physical, social, and spiritual) that the older man once carried in his twin roles of father and coach. Perhaps, in the context of compassionate caring, Katie O'Connor will be able to diminish the power her father's periodic absences still hold over her. Clearly, Mrs. Takahashi has lost her fear of the distant, Japanese-speaking grandparents who once banished her mother, Mrs. Kumamoto, to a foreign land.

In all these cases, the elder is transformed from a potent, culturally defined role (parent, grandparent, or spouse) with the authority and power their positions once implied. Instead they become persons whose importance lies not in their function or their abilities but instead relies solely on the degree to which they are and have been a part of the younger, healthier person's life. In the end, what each care giver learned through caring is that one does not have to constantly improve, to become something stronger or better, to function as a moral arbiter or financial genius. It is enough simply to be, to exist with another.

One suspects that the inverse is also true, that for many there is no sense of being beyond the titles and powers and abilities of the person. Mostly this is seen in these interviews by reflection, in the speakers' statements about those who do not give physical care. When the elder's abilities and powers are gone, the sense of that person disappears for the sons and daughter of the Harding family, the Williamses' family friends. Marie Dister's grandmother, the woman who once baked Christmas cookies, has become a shadow of the past, an embarrassment unworthy of current attention. But the failure of these functionally defined relations denies the elderly person of memory, even as he or she lives on. Rollo May described this type of dismissal in *The Discovery of Being* as a "loss of the sense of being related on one hand to our tendency to subordinate existence to function: a man knows himself not as a man or self but as a token seller in the subway, a grocer, a professor, a vice-president of AT&T, or by whatever his economic function may be. And on the other hand, this loss of the sense of being is related to the mass collectivist trends and widespread conformist tendencies in our culture." The sense of being, as he understood, is never individual but always and ultimately relational. What the lives and stories of these care givers insist upon is that we may exist at any moment as a social or economic being, but we live over time in relation as members of a fundamentally communal species.

At this point we can only guess at the effect of fragility on the frail elder who is the subject of the care giver's concern. But Thomas H. Murray gives us a clue in his reading of Tolstoy's tale, "The

Death of Ivan Ilyich," about a man who, when faced with his own death, was terrified not by the immediacy of his dying but instead by the life he had lived. Stripped of both his position in the bureaucracy of officialdom and his roles of father and husband, for three days Ivan Ilyich screamed in agony rather than in pain, in terror rather than in fear. The cause of his distress was what he saw to be the meaninglessness of his life as it had been lived, the wasteland that vision mapped of his acts in the realm of human relations. In the language of existential psychologists, he "woke up," came to consciousness, and was terrified by the barren landscape of what had been his life. A man who had lived comfortably in conformity awakened to perceive as abhorrent and meaningless both the life he had lived and the self he knew. His anguish ended when his son grasped and kissed his father's hand as Ivan Ilyich's wife stood by in tears. Then, as Murray writes, "Ivan Ilyich discovered that there were still shreds of meaning in his life. Whatever the implied religious content of Ivan Ilyich's deathbed Epiphany, the concrete human event that touched it off was the loving touch of his son, and the tearful stripping away of the facade of his wife's propriety to reveal the simple sorrow and pity within."

It was at the point of that filial contact that Ilyich finally evoked a self defined by more than the trappings of ephemeral social and economic roles, found in himself the person who was known by and in relation to a wife and son who loved him better than he loved himself. Like the care givers whose stories are presented here, Ilyich awoke to a definition of self anchored in the other, a meaning far removed from the ephemeral trappings of the life he had lived. "Meaning is a crucial element in life," Murray concludes, adding that "the quest for meaning becomes particularly critical when meaning is most threatened, that is, when whatever has functioned as meaning is stripped away through disability, or separation, or severance from the world of economic productivity, or finally by proximity to death."

For the care giver, that meaning can and is defined in relation to the other who may be disabled, retired, sick, or frail. What is evoked is not a self that stands before the world defined by title, role, rank or economic resources, but a person whose life is defined in relation to those who are cherished and cared for. Anxiety has a resolution, and for these care givers, if not for their care receivers, the resolution lies in a subjective relation rooted in time's commitments.

Stress and Anxiety

The difference between seeing oneself or another as a "who"—as a being—or as a "what"—as a function—is the difference between subjective relation and objective definition, between necessary and contingent ties. To see beyond the objective title to the person is to be in relation with others for whom there is affection and esteem. Not surprisingly, how we address and perceive others is a reflection of our own values and sense of self-esteem, a duet and not simply a solo tune sung daily before the world. For those others who cannot make this leap, who do not accept the sufficiency of being in time, the elder becomes an abstraction, a shell that was, and is now devalued. If relations are nothing more than function (provider, guardian, moral arbiter) and interpersonal history is powerless, then all individual relations and futures are truncated and diminished to some degree.

By viewing the relation of care giver and care receiver from this perspective, the issue of care-giver stress, assumed by most to be a debilitating aspect of the role, is seen in a fundamentally different light. There is no doubt that the physical act of caring for an elderly relative would seem to have been at least moderately stressful for all the coauthors. Within this collection of care-giver stories there are examples of what most would consider to be profound examples of stress-related, care-giver deterioration. Most obvious are Mrs. Kumamoto's hysterical paralysis of the throat, Mrs. Harding's and Mrs. O'Connor's heart attacks, and the latter's subsequent psychiatric problems. Less serious but still significant are Margaret Neilson's habit of kicking the wall of the apartment she shared with her grandmother, Brian Leonard's bizarre behavior, Katie O'Connor's alcohol abuse, Jay Nakana's reliance on tobacco as a stress reliever, and both Carol Bee's and Jay Nakana's obesity. Further, most are, in Mrs. Pfeiffer's words, simply "worn out" and "worn down."

But it is unclear to me how much these symptoms are directly and solely attributable to the caring relation. Almost a year after Mrs. Atani's institutional admission, her daughter's voice had not returned. Mrs. O'Connor had a family history of cardiac illness and a life-style history that included tobacco and alcohol abuse as well as a weight problem that likely resulted from lack of exercise and a fatty diet. Given those conditions, heart problems were a virtual certainty for her whether or not she cared for a parent. Mrs. Harding is, by her own admission, a "Jewish mother," a worrier who for years has taken little exercise. At the time of her heart attack she was in her midsixties and, like Mrs. O'Connor, a statistical candidate for cardiac problems. Mr. Nakana's tobacco addiction and obesity may have occurred, even had his mother's care not demanded his attention, when he stopped exercising and accepted the long hours required by a small-store owner active in community theater. Carol Bee was a heavy woman long before her care-giving tenure began. On a survey matching incidence of illness to care-giving role, the relation of health problems to caring is assumed. But when examined case by case, a direct correspondence is far less certain.

This is not to deny that care giving is stressful. Had each of these individuals taken on a second, full-time job, their schedules would have been similarly overextended, and perhaps as prone to many of the same constraints. As Mrs. Pfeiffer says so cogently, the stress of caring stems, at least in part, from a lack of time to do things for oneself, from the disappearance of leisure time in which one can be at home and at ease with husband, children, hobbies, and friends. A world without relaxation is by definition stressful, whatever the cause of an individual's incessant industry. Certainly this is a fact of care giving, and not one I wish to dismiss. But perhaps more important than stress—a condition noted here as much by the absence of free time as the presence of a debilitating problem—all these speakers seem also to have suffered from anxiety of a fundamental nature. Anxiety is stressful, but stress does not necessarily include anxiety. The one is a physical state and the other a psychological and emotional problem. "Anxiety," as Rollo May defines it in *Pyschology and the Human Dilemma,* is "apprehension cued off by a threat to some value which the individual holds essential to his existence as a self."

The most obvious danger to a system of intrinsic, individual value is death, the extermination of existence and therefore of self. Another is the potential destruction of memory and the resulting loss of a sense of self, the removal of historical consciousness so that a person is simply a physical shell in which the memories, perceptions, and realities that have been shared disappear. This is the fear that Alzheimer's disease engenders in many, that they may become a vessel emptied not only of potential but also of historical memories, walking shells without the filling that seems to define life. Finally, anxiety can come from a sense of isolation from one's community, from a growing alienation brought on either by isolation or a sense of betrayal—as Katie O'Connor and Craig Williams suggest—when those whom one counted on refuse their help. Anxiety results when one's necessary ties are seen by others as merely contingent associations.

It is these fundamental anxieties—death, loss of memory, loss of community, and a resulting alienation—that each care giver personally confronts when caring for an elder. The aged relation may be sick, but that individual's condition has severe repercussions for the care giver as well. "She's getting older," Jay Nakana says of his mother. "She may not live, may not live another year. How will I be when she's gone? Will it be OK? Will I be all right?" As Oliver Sacks put it in *Awakenings,* "The terrors of suffering, sickness and death, of losing ourselves and losing the world are the most elemental and intense we know; and so too are our dreams of recovery and rebirth, of being wonderfully restored to ourselves and the world." It is not only the elderly patient but, as well, the caring relative who must come to terms with the loss of previously shared memory. The failure of an elder promises one's own decline. When even the most potent parent, grandparent, or spouse can fail, then one's own failure is inevitable. The existential terror this reality implies, the fear it can engender, is remarkable.

The once powerful elder's increasing fragility, and the isolation attending on that fragile state, affect not only the fragile senior's world but that of the care giver as well. The care giver's world shrinks as the care receiver's and care giver's shared universe of social and professional contacts is allowed to diminish. Mrs. Harding, for example, is distanced with her husband as their children pull away. Further, to the extent that care givers exist in daily proximity and relation to a frail elder, they go with their charges through the depersonalizing horrors of hospitalization and impersonal medical care. With their elders the care giver lives through elemental terrors, albeit at one remove. Some may hold hope for a new drug or a miraculous recovery, as does Mrs. Pfeiffer, but each must confront the fact that his or her charge is old and frail, and no matter what the care giver does, sooner rather than later the care receiver will die.

These are anxieties that modern society does not comfortably address. Their resolution requires each care giver to place the other to whom he or she is bound in a context where mutual histories—bad and good—are relieved. Stripped of the trappings of financial power, official position, and past familial function, the fragile elder's actions are remembered and at times perhaps relived by the care giver. In the forced proximity of this relation, old memories come to the fore and are reviewed from the current postures of power and caring that have altered the world of care receiver and care giver alike. Thus Mrs. Pfeiffer held, by the end, no illusions about the deficits of her cold father's personality; Mr. Leonard came to understand his father's worst failures as well as the old man's strengths. Mr. Williams could think of his wife as both a "liberated woman" and as a "dependent woman" tied to the house, admiring in retrospect both parts of the woman to whom he was married. Professional function and familial roles, like all contingent postures of social power, are seen to be temporary and therefore both transient and ephemeral. Like Shakespeare's King Lear, who sought from his daughters a retinue befitting the position he once had held, the formerly potent are now seen in their dotage to be nothing more than people like ourselves.

At the same time, the care giver must face personal anxieties brought on by assuming a position that is neither socially valued nor, by its very nature, defined as suitable employment. Some, like Ms. Neilson, must choose between work as it is normally defined (outside the home) and care giving, a position without social value or economic future. For those adults whose sense of self is bound up in their employment, this can be an alienating experience in itself. Others, like Bill Lypchuk, accept less prestigious, less future-oriented employment, and as a result assume a more marginal social position. Compared to his professionally employed brothers, Mr. Lypchuk is an underachiever. To the extent that care giving becomes a series of all-consuming tasks—Mrs. Pfeiffer's story is an example of this—it distances the care giver from his or her circle of friends and acquaintances, isolating the care giver at the very time when support is needed. Attendant on the role almost from its beginning is a social and professional marginalization ("worker" to "care giver"), which is at best isolating, more likely alienating, and certainly anxiety provoking.

Against this socially devalued role, in opposition to the whole complex of anxieties that it gives rise to, each care giver must pit the weight of a shared history. In opposition to another's decline, one has only a set of values, a sense of propriety strengthened in and by relation with the fragile, ill, often querulous and difficult—but somehow still important—care receiver, a person of memory who lies waiting and in need. Those values are what these care givers find it almost impossible to express. "I just did it," Mrs. Pfeiffer says. "You just have to do some things. You have to go the limit." Why, she doesn't know. "Because I love her," Mr. Williams says in explaination. But many who do not physically care for their spouses would argue that their love is none the less for their inability to function as nursing aide and companion. As if it were the most natural thing in the world, Brian Leonard returns, he says, to help his mother. But Margaret Neilson's father does little for his mother. Carol Bee's brother does less for his. It is hard for any of us to voice the deepest reasons why we do difficult and uncomfortable things that we know, somehow, are necessary and right.

Having lost religion as an explanatory force and having dismissed communities of lifelong residence as an anchor for our lives, we have no language with which to state the resolution that comes from caring. One hears reasons voiced by indirection, observes them more in the constancy of a speaker's acts than in the analysis each presents. "I just did it," Ruth Pfeiffer says. "I didn't think about it." In my association with these coauthors, a paragraph from Oliver Sacks's *Awakenings* continually came to mind: "It is human relations which carry the possibilities of proper being-in-the-world. Feeling the fullness of another person, as a person, reality is given to us by the reality of people; reality is taken from us by the unreality of unpeople; our sense of reality, of trust, of security is critically dependent on a human relation. A single good relation is a lifeline in trouble, a polestar and compass in the ocean of trouble. . . . [W]e are physicians to each other."

Those who choose to accept the care giver's role also accept, by definition, responsibility for another person, for an adult from their own childhood to whom each is linked by more than circumstance or birth. They are, in this, coming to a posture of ontological security in which their "being-in-the-world" is based on interpersonal values stemming from shared experiences nurtured across time, not on roles or functional associations (such as parent to child, working husband to homemaker wife, doting grandparent to spoiled grandchild), whose relevance diminishes in time. Through this choice comes a context in which the primarily younger care givers must face the essential, existential human anxieties of death, loss, and isolation.

What is returned by the experience is a feeling of reality, a knowing that one exists not as an isolate or a function but within the framework of ongoing, essential relations.

We all construct our worlds from both the precepts of society at large and from within a personal structure of meaningful relationships that each of us is free to accept or reject. Our worlds are created by each of us from choices and memories carried into the present. A care giver's world of active association, conceived across memories of past events, is defined by relation to and responsibility for others whose importance may be historical but whose presence is contemporary and real. If they survive, the adults of our youth will grow old and frail. That this change need not invalidate the world composed of shared memories—or render those past experiences impotent—is a lesson each person must test on his or her road to maturity. "This was still my mother who was sick," Bill Lypchuk says, "This was *always* my mother." We make our own worlds out of the matter of shared experience, and it is in the crises of elder care that one can see the strengths or failings of different approaches. The care givers of this book seem to say that whatever the anxiety encountered through their relative's fragility, the affirmation of those relations and the reality of shared experiences assures for each the continuance of his or her own world as well as a place in it for those significant if now frail others with whom each has shared time and experience over the years.

The result is an antidote to anxiety's terror that Kierkegaard called the healthy quality of "certitude." Those who accept responsibility for an elderly relative and those who do not may both know a sense of anxiety that stems from the issues of elder care. But certitude, an "inner quality of integrity," is attainable only by the individual who can choose for others. Rollo May calls this "consciousness," an active force as opposed to apathetic distancing from and in relationships. By choosing for and being with, certitude results. The solution to the primary anxieties we all must face comes not by distancing from a frail other but by acceptance and being in proximity to them *as they now are.* Through the memories aroused during periods of elder care, by making decisions based on the care of another, valued person rather than on one's own career or convenience, these individuals come to a point of certitude that is powerful and often liberating.

Thus Mrs. O'Connor could say with deep satisfaction to her cousin, bereft over opportunities lost during her mother's illness, that the other woman "could" and therefore perhaps "should" have done more for her elder relation. Katie O'Connor was not offering a social or religious value. Rather she was stating on the basis of her own experience that had her cousin done more for her mother, then at the point of bereavement, the woman would have felt less regret, less sense of failure. But her cousin's concern comes too late, and resolution with her mother is no longer achievable. As another care giver said of those who reject an active care-giving role, "afterwards, they have to live with that themselves."

If institutionalization of the elderly and the ill deprives them, in Oliver Sacks's words, "of their sense of reality and home, and forces them into the false homes and compensations of regression and sickness," we may speculate that care received from relations reinforces the frail seniors' sense of who they are and what, even in infirmity, they might become. Thus Carol Bee's mother improves remarkably when placed in proximity to her daughter and the grandchildren, who take on her care and ambulatory rehabilitation. Mr. Lypchuk's father recovers from depression and a drug problem whose resulting behavior, had his son been different and less committed, might have been seen as sufficient reason for his as well as his wife's institutionalization. But because of his son's insistence that his father has "a real place in the home of the world," the older man is sustained and can continue in the life he once built but now retains only through powers borrowed from his son. In each story recorded here, one sees the degree to which the acts of the care givers enforce the elder's sense of reality by providing a home, allowing the continuance of at least a part of their former lives.

There is a growing and extraordinary body of research that describes the degree to which sustained human contact, constant association with intimates and familiars, is health promoting and life sustaining. Recent studies published in the *Journal of the American Medical Association* in January, 1992, showed, for example, that people who live alone—those without social support—are more likely to die after a heart attack (or to rapidly suffer a second, fatal heart attack) than patients who live with others. According to another researcher writing in the October 14, 1989, issue of the *Lancet*, individuals with life-threatening cancers live an average of 18 months longer if they participate in support groups—if they act for themselves and for others—than those patients who do not so involve themselves. Over the last twenty years, health researchers and demographers have, as James House puts it, commented with "remarkable consistency on the overall finding that social relationships do predict mortality for men and women in a wide range of populations, even after adjustment for biomedical risk factors for mortality." Social relationships and familial contacts promote health and protect against disease by activating the anterior hypothalamic zone, thus occasioning the increased release of specific hormones while simultaneously inhibiting the discharge of others whose secretion would be unhealthy. It is this physiological response to the presence of a familiar individual that can also assist a patient in recovering from illness by decreasing, through these chemical releases, the effect of stress, neurosis, and hypertension, thus reducing the likelihood of physiological manifestations—ulcers, for example—of these states.

Here we see one possible explanation for the amazing tenacity, the incredible endurance displayed by of some of the care receivers this book's coauthors maintained. From the chemistry of relation came, perhaps, the ability of Mrs. Bee's mother to improve and endure once moved to Buffalo, the persistence of Mrs. Atani who remained at home for so long under her daughter's care. After his first life-threatening bout with chronic hepatitis, my father's physician said it was amazing that he had survived and suggested that I had somehow helped pull my father through. On the basis of this psychophysical research, we see that may have been more than metaphorically true.

As important, this physiology of mutual relation must, by definition, have a similar effect on the care givers themselves. That is, the constancy of contact with another, valued member of the family provides the care giver with a natural, chemical buffer against serious illness while promoting health in the care receiver. Opposing the demands of caring stands a natural, physical defense against stress and frustration. I think of it as the specie's reward for association. In the longer term, by allowing for a resolution of fundamental anxieties, and perhaps creating a pattern of lifelong relation with another, care giving teaches younger care givers like Margaret Neilson a way of being that itself creates a context for individual health and longevity. For those like Tina Harding and Craig Williams, who care for senior partners, there is both psychological certitude and a physical benefit in their continuing care of a frail other; physical and psychological association contribute to both care giver and care receiver's health.

Jocasta versus Oedipus

The anxiety one may suffer while participating in this role results from a profound testing of values perhaps held but never before actualized or articulated. The terrors that one faces with and on behalf of the elder—death, loss, isolation—are ones all individuals must eventually confront. By facing them with an elder, the care giver learns to accept a stance in which anxiety can be, if not mastered, at least placed in a perspective from which it can be controlled. Interpersonally, the lessons that are learned are born in the confrontation between present circumstances and older memories locked away in childhood. The indignities of childhood must stand, finally, against the reality of a now less-than-powerful figure who lies, too ashamed to ask for help, in a urine-soaked hospital bed. It is this ultimately necessary balance of banked memory leveled against present need that explains why, when asked to explain their contemporary situation, most interviewees focused on past history in their statements. The acceptance of history and the ability to perceive the truth of one's own—and the other's—past acts is a powerful good.

The importance of self-knowledge, itself the acceptance of past acts as they were lived, is the message of our oldest tales and myths. Consider, for example, the story of Oedipus. Bruno Bettelheim says in *Freud & Man's Soul* that the point of the myth is not that the young man unknowingly slept with his mother, Jocasta, but rather that neither he nor she could at first acknowledge that act. The gods' punishment was not visited upon them because they enjoyed sex together in ignorance of their biological relationship, but for the failure on both their parts later to accept the historical fact of their mutual desire and, more important, the self-knowledge that congress represented. Jocasta perishes because she is unable to face the truth, let alone accept the consequences of her own behavior. Oedipus is freed when he acknowledges the nature of his antecedent relations with Jocasta. Bettelheim argues that the myth's importance lies not in its emphasis on sexuality but in its focus on the degree to which self-discovery and honesty can free individuals from the pain of the past.

All children have complex and conflicting feelings about their parents as individuals and as role models. All children grow up with unconscious desires and suppressed angers resulting from acts committed against them—often unknowingly—by parents, siblings, or distanced relatives. For those like Mrs. Harding, who married young, one can imagine that across a life of fifty-six years there have been various conflicts repressed, "put away" until a day when they would well out of memory and onto the scales of daily decisions about a crucial relation. But the message of Oedipus, and the moral of these stories, is the degree to which we all must learn to confront our histories while remaining in relation with significant others. Having faced our own failings as well as those of a crucial other, each of us can then move forward to a stronger, less terrifying world. In this way, Mrs. Kumamoto remembers her actions upon returning to Hawaii, Katie O'Connor her adolescent behavior, Mr. Lypchuk his fearful childhood. Similarly, Mrs. Pfeiffer accepts her mother's failings, Mr. Leonard his father's dissolution, and I recognized my father's reliance on values I could not hold. From the perspective of self and other, care givers relive and confront through relation to the frail other specific truths and conflicts that—like those of Oedipus and Jocasta—have been long repressed.

Here, from *Freud and Man's Soul,* is Bettelheim's interpretation:

What forms the essence of our humanity—and of the play—is not our being victims of fate, but our struggle to discover the truth about ourselves. Jocasta, who clearly states that she does not wish to discover the truth, cannot face it when it is revealed, and she perishes. Oedipus, who does face the truth, despite the immense dangers to himself of which he is at least dimly aware, survives. Oedipus suffers much, but at the end, at Colonus, he not only finds peace, but is called to the god and becomes transformed.

And so it is with these care givers, excepting perhaps Katie O'Connor, who can neither accept her childhood nor, ultimately, her past as it so far has been lived with others. But most care givers do learn through their uncomfortable roles, do discover truths about themselves as ultimately fragile beings whose only strength may lie not in the fact of their individuality but rather through the power of sustained association. I suspect that the anxiety and discomfort that these lessons demand are something few would trade away if it meant losing the knowledge gained through that endeavor.

Perhaps these lessons were learned more painlessly in other ages and in other cultures. All of this may have seemed natural when a house was perceived not as a primary investment but assumed, instead, to be a home; when necessary rather than contingent or tangential ties bound us together more naturally. In that past, in that society, it was assumed that generations would live together and the progress of youth to maturity and through the body's decline was natural and would be both shared and learned in association. But modernity's longevity has been purchased at the price of residency; economic mobility has replaced a concentrated social vision of mutual benefit within the community, the neighborhood, the family itself. Simultaneously, we have gone from having an elite of treasured elders to a nation that sees its elderly community as a largely unproductive burden. In that change, what has been lost is a vision of the individual in relation as an entity worthy of society's time and people's care. Thus it is left to the one in five or seven individuals who agrees to become a care giver to rediscover these truths without assistance, comfort, or compensation.

Contrasting Viewpoints

From this perspective, it is possible to distinguish between care givers and those who choose not to give care, between individuals who accept relation to an elder as necessary and those who define their relationships as contingent and merely functional. Care givers feel *responsible for* rather than *obliged to* those they choose to care for. This sense of responsibility is based not on the perception of a clear and simple *debt owed* but instead on a reservoir of shared experience *amassed* across the care receiver and giver's mutual history. For these care givers, the fragile elder is and has been a social partner, and thus the relationship both care giver, and presumably the care receiver, together seek to preserve is one based not solely on historic role or function but instead on mutual and shared support over time. Because the relations that bind care receiver and giver are neither role driven nor functional at base, the decline a frail elder may experience through the decrease of physical or cognitive abilities may affect but will not necessarily diminish the care giver's sense of responsibility for the other. The caring relation is based not on a *contract* that balances past services with future compensations, but on, for want of a better word, a *covenant* in which debt, duty, and obligation are superseded by notions of mutuality and responsibility. The word has become almost exclusively religious in its usage, and for that reason I hesitate to use it here. But no other word or phrase so well suggests a bond over time, a relationship based not merely on debts accrued or obligations contracted but instead on a mutuality lived between human beings.

The parent, grandparent, or spouse thus remains a *being* whose importance is taken by the carer as a *given,* and is not seen as an *asset* whose *value* must necessarily diminish as physical powers decline. The importance of the care receiver cannot be abrogated, bought, or sold. He or she is a part of the shared life, of mutual history, and of the whole, messy complex that has brought carer and frail elder forward together to the present. The care receiver is therefore first and foremost a *person,* not an *it,* a subjective *being* rather than an objective *role* with a future-oriented, developmental function and value. It is because of this centrality of relation, this insistence on the person behind the role or disease, that the carer is concerned with far more than the frail elder's needs for survival—housing, food, basic medical care—all of which can be provided in an institution. To the extent that care receivers remain individuals of emotional and historical importance, they are, in the minds of their care givers, entitled to those human necessities of community, companionship, love, stimulation, and choice (within the capabilities of the body and mind) that, for us all, make life worth living.

Even when it becomes medically impossible to maintain a person at home, neither the severity of a physical disorder nor the fact of institutionalization truly severs the ties that bind these care givers to their care receivers. Mr. Williams still visits his wife's bedside. Mrs. Pfeiffer still feeds her mother her evening meal, traveling each night from work to the older woman's institutional bed. Mrs. Kumamoto's attentions to Mrs. Atani continue despite the older woman's residence in a long-term care ward. Even in extremity, the care giver's relation to the unaware elder does not end. It is clear to me that these care givers continue to visit not simply to comfort their elders—who are unlikely to recognize their visitors—but because the presence of their relations gives the care *givers* support. Proximity to even the cognitively deficient, memory-damaged other assured these husbands, grandchildren, and daughters a sense of continuity, and this became, for the speakers in this book, a necessary source of continuing strength.

Some insight into the non–care giver's perspective may be gained from the statements of Marie Dister, Alice McLeod, and April Takahashi. Those who do not continue the relationship see their elders primarily in functional roles that, since they can no longer be fulfilled, diminish the relation that has existed in the past. To the extent that elders can continue the activities by which they were previously defined—baking cookies, handling finances, fixing the roof, making familial decisions—their value and that of the shared relation is maintained. It is, to put it another way, a *fixed reference* and not a *necessary mutuality*. During a geriatric illness or decline, when the ability to fulfill these functions or roles diminishes, the elder—and thus the relation itself—is reduced in importance and value. The frail relative becomes all history, all past, because he or she can no longer sustain the functional aspects of the present relation.

Thus, for functionally oriented relatives and friends, care for that elder, which may require a heavy commitment of time and financial resources, is perceived as, at best, an unremunerative burden based on a sense of obligation and duty. It is in this way that the previously sustaining, historical relation is transformed into first an obligation and then an unrecoverable debt. There is no way the elder can hope to balance the scales—unless one accepts the notion of a primordial debt (the idea that the fact of biological parentage defines a never-ending filial obligation)—and the function of caring becomes, since no other perspective is possible, an unproductive liability. At this time and from this perspective, the frail elder may be efficiently stripped of the entitlements of community, respect and even a pretense of mutuality, retaining only the right of existence, albeit perhaps in an institutional setting. Put another way, the non–care giver balances his or her own development—financial and personal— against the elder's fragility and need. If the latter impedes the younger person's career or life-style, the burden is too great and mutuality is rejected in favor of, at best, efficient, professional care.

THE ONTOLOGICAL PARTNERSHIP

By making common cause with a fragile elder known throughout a lifetime, the care giver accepts an ontological partnership, a relationship in and through time. The power of this partnership is evident not only in my coauthors' stories, but in other descriptions written by those who faced signal crises involving a beloved other. For example, consider the published experiences of Janet Kaye, a lawyer and journalist who has described her feelings and experiences during a familial crisis. Before visiting her comatose father in the hospital, Ms. Kaye used a series of sensory talismans to evoke aspects of their life together, each associated with a memory of shared passions or events. "I'd been petting dogs or crushing leaves or eating chocolate each time before seeing him," she wrote. "He loves animals and gardening and sweets. Maybe, I thought, these smells could cut through the horrible competing odors of antiseptics and decay pervading his room and permeating our clothes, our hair, and even our bedding. Maybe he'd think chocolate and dogs and gardens were worth coming back to." Perhaps. But at the same time the crushed leaves, petted dogs, and the taste of chocolate also evoked them to her, brought from her memory a host of experiences that could serve her as counterweight to the reality of the passive and inert body of her father, who lay unconscious in a hospital bed. It is in this way that the care giver faces illness, loss of self, and death with the care receiver, and thus comes to know anxieties that are part of the human condition, anxieties first encountered, in this context of caring, through the mirror of the valued other.

Ships in the Night

From these stories I draw a lesson of different and opposing psychological scales, of different measures of individual volition, which contribute mightily to the way we are or wish to be as individuals in the world. By what constant can a person measure his or her actions? By what standard do we act? Care givers in this book take one scale and measure, non–care givers use another. The former see themselves as shipmates on a boat, acting with and for their crew mates, choosing between alternatives based on a personal scale defined and determined by relation with those others with whom they are, in the old navy phrase, "privileged to serve." To continue the analogy, non–care givers act as captains of solitary vessels, pilots of no–crew ships within a convoy. Each may act for another out of largesse or because of a contractual obligation, but otherwise choose in their dealings with others from the perspective of immediate productivity ("Can I keep on course?") and future function ("Will I achieve the desired destination?") rather than historical ties.

These two very different postures are supported by two very different worldviews. The non–care giver's is grounded in a linear temporality that assumes implicitly that all people and groups necessarily move forward, that experiential time by definition flows only in one direction—forward. To the extent that the focus of concern is the individual who matures across the life course, this is the obvious frame in which explorations of decisions and choices must occur. From this perspective, each person is a ship en route from past to future. Each ship is on a journey whose purpose may be uncertain but for which progress toward the destination is a crucial goal. Each vessel in the convoy has primary responsibility for its own progress, and on any convoy's voyage, some ships will reach a destination together, while others will be lost along the way.

When the elder becomes frail and unable, his or her inabilities are no longer able to support the progress of the convoy at large. At that point, these older, individual vessels become a liability to other convoy members, an impediment in the journey of more able troopships and carriers. Chateaubriand's metaphor becomes a reality and, quite literally, "old age is a shipwreck." To the extent that the frail elder's need interferes with the younger, still-active person's journey, that support becomes counterproductive, and a distancing occurs as their paths separate from that of other convoy members. Since each person is primarily responsible for his or her own sailing, for his or her own progress, those elements that would delay the trip must be dismissed.

But for the care giver, we are not ships efficiently passing in the night. The care giver experiences time as an areal spectrum in which past memories and shared experiences are an integral part of present-day relations. By "areal" I mean a plane in which all the directions within the experiential plan are open to the individual. "Progress," at least as it is defined in terms of career—by Mr. Lypchuk's brothers, for example—becomes less important, for those who view life in this way, than the wealth of accumulated, shared experiences that have marked the individual's progress with others to the present day. This relational frame suggests that in navigating time's river, the lessons and incidents learned at each past bend of the water course can influence current and future decisions along the river's banks. Those memories are real, pertinent, and accurate guides to the relational world that exists in time.

Care givers act with, for and from the perspective of a broad, historical scale of action. Non–care givers choose on the basis of a narrower scale whose focus is the present with an eye to the future. It is the long scale that allows one to be with and for another, and this means ultimately that one can also do and be for him- or herself. A patient whom Oliver Sacks treated for encephalitis lethargica with the drug L-dopa stated the nature of this relation succinctly in describing her disease. "I can do nothing alone," Mrs. T. said. "I can do anything *with*—with music or people to help me. I cannot initiate, but I can fully share." It was as a result of the disease that she and other patients were frozen in time and place, removed of their mobility until another touched them, threw them a ball, in some way "activated" their will so that, for that incredibly brief period of activity, they could *be*—using, in Sacks's words, the volition of others.

The coauthors of this book, like Mrs. T., act not as solitary individuals but as communal beings, activating and empowering their fragile elders. Their will to act, to be in the world, springs not from economic equivalences or the pressure of social norms. Rather, it comes from and builds upon communal histories. Unlike Mrs. T., these care givers can initiate, but like her each must fully share with another if that initiation—and their own lives—is to have meaning. As their elders become unable to act—lose volition and the scale by which individual decisions and actions occur—these care givers initiate all the more, lending both their own volition and perhaps their own measures of memory and shared experience to the will and need of another, the more frail partner. In a very real way, the individual "I" is not so much formed as empowered and given meaning by the historical "We," which for each carries on as a real force into the future. Thus, each acts to assure that both "I" and "We" can be continued.

Graphically, the ties that bind can be represented as a Rubik's cube in which each face of the experiential whole is composed of the elements of time, place, self, and relation (or mutuality) to another. This relational complex is composed of memories joining the past and the present. The experiential whole supports and influences decisions of care givers regarding their relations to care receivers. Shared past experiences influence contemporary choices and decisions affecting both care giver and care receiver. Each facet of the cube's face is a memory, a past event or future hope that exists not as an isolated decision or choice, but within a frame composed of and tied to a complex of past experiences in which others have been crucial and active. Time in this frame is not simply progressive, not a line or course necessarily moving forward, but rather an integrated element of location placing people together in their shared lives. Certainly individuals grow from childhood through adolescence, achieve physical maturity, and—if they survive—eventually know the decline of old age. But that biological progression exists as background against an areal and emotionally inclusive relational frame in which a history of shared experience has at least equal value.

Each facet of the cube can also be seen as a part of the whole relation, as a trace of incidents across interpersonal history, or at least across the time of shared relation. Memory across time is, in this way, integrated. As in a Rubik's cube, no single facet can be changed in isolation. Each is a part of the composite, the

Memory as a Rubik's Cube

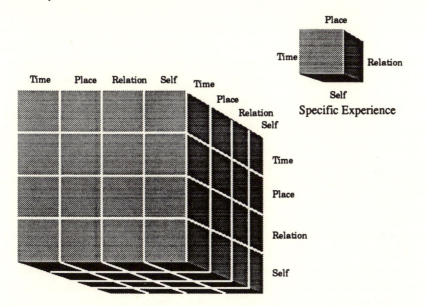

whole. To change one locus, to excise one cell or line, means to twist the whole into a different pattern. Thus, to use Ms. Neilson's story as an example, varying facets may stand for times she visited her grandmother as a child or for days during adolescence when she learned to bake in the woman's kitchen. The reality of relation is created by thousands of such memories, which are not simply past but remain a part of shared existence and thus, for the care giver, a part of the active present as well. For the care receiver, whose future is rooted in the past, these incidents—and the individuals who participated in them—may become exquisitely real once again. We know, for example, that Alzheimer's victims may relive past life experiences long buried in their memory, may experience again relations from childhood. This occurs not simply during the progression of cognitive disorders that attack short-term and recent memory, leaving past memories intact, but at least to some extent and more generally in frail elders who find themselves ill, isolated, confused, and without mobility, independence, or hope for a return to physical strength.

Thus, the anxiety of another's death might be visually imagined as the potential removal of specific cube facets, the weakening of a crucial, relational pattern that defines and holds in place a critical set of care-giver memories—those related to the now fragile care receiver. What the care giver learns is to accept that the death of the other, who shared these pooled events of memories, does not necessarily mean the death of the memory or of the previously shared emotions that accompanied it. Through the relation affirming that incidents of memory are, in fact, shared by the one with whom the events occurred, we may hypothesize that from this perspective the care receiver gradually learns to accept the possible diminishment and eventual death of self. Death may extinguish one's own self, but the cherished other will remain, and therefore so do the memories that seem at times so precious a part of the elder's constricted world.

A year after his father's death and long after his father's dementia began, news reporter Gene Warner wrote that "his death allows us to remember and celebrate his life once again. We could put a deck of cards in his casket—an old family joke, because one of his card-playing friends is buried in the next plot. We could look at old photos and try to ease the mental images of the skin-and-bones shell of a man who lay on his deathbed for three years. And we could laugh about the good old days. . . . In a mystical way, we have our father back." During his parent's illness, Mr. Warner was constant in his concern and care for his father, who remained at home and under the ministrations of his wife and family members. What returned— what remained—was the man of integrated memory who had perhaps been overwhelmed for a period by the physical reality of the fragile and demented man Gene Warner and his mother cared for. The result of his caring was the ability, a year after his father's death, to hold the memories of earlier joy and final fragility together in a single vision, to perceive a unity between the man who had been, the man who was, and the future that Mr. Warner himself might experience were he lucky enough to live an equally long life.

Warner's tale, like Kaye's quoted earlier, describes responses to critical illness and death as an integration of old memories and old associations within the present time frame. During his father's last years, Gene Warner worried that he would never again be able to remember this parent as other than the enfeebled man who lay lost to his world, his family, and his self in a hospital bed. Standing in opposition to the comatose patient or the "skin-and-bones" man however, is the person of shared experience. It is that person of complex memories with whom both Kaye and Warner faced respectively the illness and death of their parents. More generally, it is this association in time that is the end result of the actions of the care givers of this book who chose to confront a fragile elder's illness. For Mr. Warner, what has been graphically if simplistically represented in the next illustration as a distorted cube—one in which memories are removed (causing other distortions in turn)—has been healed through this process. The anxieties of frailty, loss, incapacity, and death have been faced. The result is a perception in which both shared past and recent, enfeebled memory are joined into a single perception of being in the world.

The stories of Warner, Kaye, and my coauthors make of these communal, experiential squares within the relational Rubik's cube not a calculating motive for caring or a cause for obligation but simply the building blocks for individuals involved in a shared life. Any one association or memory may become, for a period, a part of life's background, half-remembered and perhaps without apparent power. But sometimes that half-forgotten memory will become activated, proving to be a touchstone when one is faced with a geriatric crisis or death. In other words, anxiety is opposed by placing before the *fact* of death or incapacity a *face* of remembered, shared experience. And it is this experiential linkage—not obligation—that carries any one individual into relation with another, and perhaps, in the case of death, beyond oneself. It is finally, at least as Warner, Kaye, and the speakers of this book describe it, as if a convoy vessel had taken on crew members from a disabled and sinking ship. The crew members saved represent shared memories, which become a strong and vital part of the remaining vessel's complement. Much is lost, but with those survivors the new crew is stronger than the old.

Life's shared times become the glue with which communal experiences are cobbled together into an areal perspective, one in which place becomes a necessary proximity allowing relation to transform into integrated memory. Decisions between care giver and receiver thus are based on a complex of historical incidents and relationships, accessible to them at any point because they are part of the whole life experience. The physical progression from infancy to old age certainly occurs, but it occurs within the context of relations built in history.

If, however, we see ourselves as individuals living solely in a progressive frame, "moving on," then it is almost impossible to see relationships as anything but hatch marks on the life span of an individual. One is young and lives in the family, goes to school, grows up, moves away, gets a job, and starts a family of one's own. People of the past may be sentimental attachments, they may move along with one for a period, but if one is going forward as the frail elder is falling back, then to stop the progression of work or one's own personal life seems an unnatural regression. From this perspective, the frail elder is truly a burden, a weight slowing progress toward work advancement or a growing family's vacation plans, an impediment to the long line of development which, we assume, is the individual's birthright. Relation to another is merely part of life's progress, and progress is a step from then and there to here and now. In contrast, relation as conceived by the care giver constantly draws on the well of experience to define the present, building a life out of incidents defined by proximity and shared incidence.

The non–care giver's vision of self and world sees each person as an isolated individual in time, one born in and to a family but without the opportunity for anything but tangential relations or truly shared

Rubik's Cube II

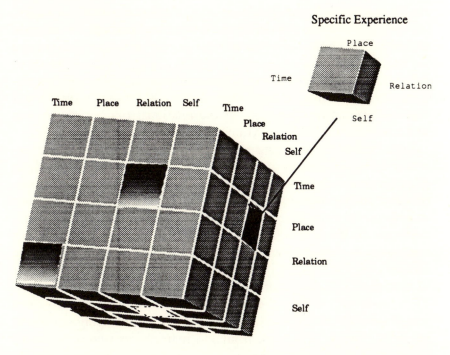

Specific Experience

Unresolved and unaccessible memories distort a series of cells.

experience. It is as if, at any moment, we are looking at others from the deck of a boat or the seat of a car, and while we may be able to distinguish others whose faces are familiar to our past, the best we all can hope for is proximity within an unassailable solitude. The past—in which others took part—is there to remember. But that past has no power to guide, instruct or inform. Even when others participated in a remembered event, that memory is not accessible as anything but a past experience whose power does not continue into the present, just as today will not influence in any emotional sense the future.

The more we move in space, seek separate residence, and build communities away from elder relatives, the more difficult it is to move from the time line of individuality and progress to the mutuality of relation. Practically and theoretically, if one imagines a single cube extracted from the whole, the face of time within that single part might be subdivided into four categories—all day, daily, sporadic, infrequent—to define the levels of intimacy between giver and receiver. Those who visit and attend on a frequent basis will be generally more tied, more in touch with a fragile elder than those who visit their seniors on an occasional basis. Care givers are distinguished by increased frequency of contact and proximity. These together strengthen and confirm the relational ties between selves past and present, older and younger. They also define the degree of practical relation that caring requires.

It is in the complex of the relational cube that one best understands the degree to which—despite lack of social support—care giving becomes a self-validating experience. Just as secure adults see children as real, biologically viable entities with their own histories and desires, so too do developing children experience themselves as real and alive, as responsible to and for those with whom they share history and affection. It is this sense of mutuality, as opposed to one of individual progress, that the care giver preserves and builds upon. The grandmother who baked, the spouse who supported, the parent who coached—all are retained as active and affirming agents in the complex relation each adult brings to maturity and continues with the now fragile elder. Indeed, one might define maturity as the integration of past memories into a sense of relation that is consistent and combines the complex of interpersonal histories into a secure adult self. By choosing to care—even when the incidents of memory are not idyllic—the care giver is forced to accept historic truths and can seek freedom from those faces of the cube that retain fears and anxieties from childhood or early adulthood.

The accompanying illustration attempts to make this clear. Unlike those who insist on the individuality of life's journey, those within this family continue to share a complex of mutual experiences that reflect an ongoing and interdependent association. At any point, the individuals share, at least in part, the strength of these associations, and this strength informs their decisions and allows them access at any moment to a broader and historically deep communal vision. The exception is an estranged son or daughter, who for whatever reason has chosen a separate path and thus remains away and outside the historical context that allows his relations to continue in time together. But in that estrangement, the distanced child loses the lessons and strengths mutuality may bring.

Shared Experiences

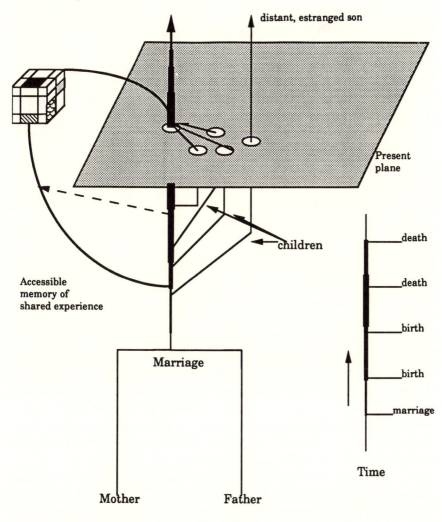

Oppositions

What is being suggested, in short, is two opposing life views in which the perspectives of those who choose to care for fragile elders can be contrasted with the definitions of those who decide that meeting the physical needs and social demands of an aged friend or relative is not a valuable use of their time. From the care giver's point of view, memory can be conceived as being like the random-access memory disk on a computer network to which care giver and receiver are linked together. They share the same history and can access, via their communal memories, a store of active experience that compels each to act in regard to the other. Thus, the peace that Margaret Neilson felt as a child with her grandmother in that woman's house is directly relevant to her decision, in the present, to care for her grandmother. In a similar vein, Katie O'Connor must ultimately access with her mother the problems of the younger woman's adolescence, which will create an opening for the older woman to say, "Well, I made mistakes as your parent, too." Both may finally acknowledge and at least partially resolve, in the caring relation, the troubled history they share.

For those like Marie Dister who are not care givers, who live by separate life paths, those stores of experience are "read-only" memory, something that perhaps can be remembered and reviewed, but not something that could be accessed and applied to the present world. For her—and one presumes for others like her—history is open to only one degree of freedom, accessible but not manipulatable in the present. The idyllic past is gone as anything but a nostalgic whisper. For individuals like Mitsue Kumamoto, however, the history with another is open to far more than one degree of freedom. Despite her mother's severe cognitive impairments, Mrs. Kumamoto sees in Mrs. Atani the woman who left her daughter in Japan, a young mother struggling to raise her children, the wife working in a still rural Hawaii, and finally a woman become frail and old. All these women who were—and are—her mother across time are part and parcel of Mrs. Kumamoto's decision to be with the woman of the present time, to maintain her, and thus their association, into the elder's frailest years.

The thematic structure of the care giver's life is both integral (integrating past and present) and inclusive (complete in its associations of individual, memory, and association). Time and memory do not simply become progressive, a ticking off of hatch marks on the life course, but operate on the basis of a relational structure in which a depth of shared experience—bad and good—is both accessible and real. A worldview that is inclusive and plenary, like the ones illustrated by these care givers' statements, also admits of no necessary direction. But this does not mean its experience is any less rich or less full. Mr. Lypchuk's brothers grew, moved with the family to go to the university in the city, then moved again to set up professional offices and separate homes. Bill Lypchuk, on the other hand, remained with his father, whose relationship to him is perhaps the most integral one in this youngest son's life. He too studied at the university and worked a variety of jobs. He now builds homes for a living. But Bill Lypchuk's life is not lived like his brothers in simple progress from dependent child to distant, independent, successful adult. Rather, it is lived within a historic and changing relationship that compels him to act from within the complex of a familial, interpersonal history.

The Williamses may have moved to Hawaii in an attempt to reinforce the memories and to recapture the experiences of their idyllic, shared life of earlier years. But unless they, and especially he, saw life as inclusive (plenary and areal), open in all directions from the present plane, such a move would have seemed not simply impractical but foolhardy. For those whose perspective is linear, those for whom history is open only at the point of progressive freedom, the idea of this return to Hawaii would have been inconceivable. This is not to suggest that by returning, Mr. or Mrs. Williams lived in a cyclical time. Instead, I believe that for Mr. Williams, whose view of life and relation prohibited abandonment of his wife to disease, moving to Hawaii meant moving away from friends and a society who shunned them in order to reset their ongoing and shared lives in a place where not only had they been happy in the past, but their associations and relationship would be accepted in the present.

What results is a philosophy in opposition to the functional definition of human worth that argues we, as individuals, are no more or less than our socially recognized, economically tabulated function. But the stories in this book insist that as human beings we are more than one-person ships in society's convoy, each ship moving forward purposefully, each with its own destination and function. When one ship is crippled and cannot sail, its disability does affect the others, who may render assistance not because they "must," but because they want to. The language used to compare these two opposing social perspectives—one functional, one relational—is summarized in the accompanying chart.

PERSPECTIVES

Non-Care Givers   **Care Givers**

Time

- Linear, unidirectional. Only a single, immediate direction is open.

- Progressive perspective. A future-dominated orientation.

- Areal and multidirectional. All directions within the plane are open to emphasize the individual.

- Plenary perspective inclusive of past and present.
- No dominating orientation.

History

- Open to only one degree of present access.

- Open to more than one degree of access.

Memory

- "Read-only" memory. Memory does not allow present activity to be based upon it.

- "Random-access" memory. Actions can draw on and from a wide range of historical associations.

Resulting Relational Structures

- Individualistic—contingent ties.
- Progressive perspective.
- Functional relations.
- Contractual model of relation to others.

- Relational—necessary ties.
- Inclusive perspective.
- Socially defined associations.
- Relations with others are covenant-based.

What is suggested by the coauthors of this volume, observers like Oliver Sacks, and writers like Kaye and Warner, is an alternative to society's generally accepted definitions of individual action and volition as both functional and progressive. In this alternate vision the valued tie to a significant other known over time is the defining characteristic of the human being. Care giving is something these individuals do because to do less would require exchanging the richness of the areal perspective with its many points of historical access— its perspective of life's value in shared relation—for a linear world in which the doors of emotionally rich, interpersonal history are battened down to nothing but a single and impotent point of immediate access. Grandma? Oh, yes. She baked good cookies, didn't she? Father? Well, he was an astute businessman in his day. To accept such a point of focus is simply not how my coauthors perceive the world.

What they teach by example does not lend itself either to quantitative analysis or simple generalization. There is no value, no benefit that can be measured in dollars and cents in this role. We are, these speaker say, creatures of our own history and characters among others who populate that time. The necessary path is not necessarily constantly up and onward, away from the home and onward to a better job. All of us may have the will and choice to write our own narratives, but if in the writing we delete those who have been close members of our lives, we then choose a path that makes individual progress, often voiced as a professional goal, a single objective that severely limits learning and living in other, crucial ways.

This leads the examination of the care giver's world perilously close to debates on what is typically called the "fact of human nature." Are we functionally defined, opportunistic individuals whose nature it is to take advantage of others, or are we more social beings who find in relation the purpose of our being? These questions can only be noted here with a single observation: If I understand these care givers in their stories, what distinguishes them is not selflessness— although from the outside that may seem to be their essential characteristic—but a definition of self that begins with relation, starts with a single, historic other, and then builds and chooses on the basis of that definition. Those who choose not to care for the other either accept that relations are first and foremost functional and opportunistic, or place their faith in the physical artifacts of material success, a decision that distances them from certain types of interpersonal concern. The other definitions and contrasts follow from that essential fact.

APPLICATIONS

The Gilberts and the Williams

The opposing paradigms presented here may help map a path through the ethical morass that in recent years has grown up in the area of euthanasia and "mercy killing." One can, using these cases and this analysis, better understand the motive powers of elder abuse in its various forms, including its most extreme form, the killing of a loved one because of his or her physical or cognitive deficits. In general, elder abuse may result not simply from frustration or stress but, more important, from an inability to face the anxiety inherent in the care giver's role. The failure of one who is no longer able—the requirements of caring for those who once were strong—creates a tension whose only outlet may find its expression in violence. Mrs. Kumamoto's spanking of her mother is a simple example. She knows it will serve no disciplinary function, that her mother will not learn from the pain. Spanking is done for the daughter's release, as an outlet for her anxiety and fears, not for her mother at all.

Less trivially, these paradigms can be applied to aspects of the current debate over euthanasia and the supposed right—some would say obligation—of elderly to die rather than continue in a fragile state. Compare, for example, Craig Williams's story and that of Roswell Gilbert, a retired electronics engineer who, about the time Mr. Williams was preparing to move to Hawaii, killed his wife of fifty-one years because of her degenerative Alzheimer's disease. On the surface, Mr. Gilbert and Mr. Williams shared a number of characteristics besides their roles as loving spouses of partners suffering from this progressive, cognitive disorder. Both were professional men with apparently mature networks of family and community support. Both had successful marriages of long tenure, and both, by all reports, were deeply attached to their wives. Both men were the dominant partners in the marriage.

And yet their ultimate responses to the disease were diametrically opposite. After first administering a sedative to his wife, Mr. Gilbert shot her twice with a Luger pistol, later stating at his trial that he killed his wife as an act of love and mercy that she herself desired. In trial testimony he was described as "a private and selfless person who was completely devoted to his wife—so much so that, in the end, he gave her the gift of euthanasia that she wanted." Roswell Gilbert became something of a hero for his acts, while Mr. Williams, who insists on continuing care for his wife even into the advanced stage of a degenerative disease, lives today in near total anonymity. What can be learned from comparing these two cases?

For the Gilberts, the loss of a quality of life, which accompanies this illness, along with the knowledge that physical and intellectual decline would inevitably increase, was insupportable. According to testimony given by the Gilberts' daughter, her mother was "a very vain woman; she never opened the door without checking the mirror." In that vanity she saw herself in a series of attractive roles: as mother, wife, and hostess—as a woman in the present whose capabilities justified a future. When that sense of ability was threatened, she attempted to hide the fact of her disease, first from her husband and then from their family and community. When she could not perform as she had in the shared past, when they could not be as before, when the future seemed to hold nothing but retrenchment, then she asked for and her husband gave her a death. Her murder was perceived by them both as a means of terminating a life that, while continuing, had simultaneously already ended.

By way of contrast, Mr. and Mrs. Williams shared the fact of the illness from the beginning. In a real way, it was not simply *her disease* but more completely *their condition,* something that affected them together. Neither partner shrank from the range of symptoms it represented. Both insisted that the illness was a part of *their* life, their shared experience. For Mr. Williams, his wife's condition did not mitigate the value of their relationship or its continuance. She remained to him, and despite the illness, as she had been—a person with whom he was married. Each partner continued, despite her disease, an integral part of the other's life. For them to have taken any other posture would have been, at least according to Mr. Williams's statement, to invalidate what in the past had been shared by them both. So he changed his life to accommodate her needs, and together, during the disease's early years, they built as large a body of shared experience as possible.

In this way Mr. Williams strengthened their historic ties while affirming their present relationship despite his wife's growing infirmities. When members of their community were unable to accept the deficits resulting from her illness, Mr. Williams abandoned not his wife but those who defined her—and therefore them—by function rather than history. As Mrs. Williams's condition worsened, the couple moved to Hawaii, a place that represented to them both an idyllic time in their past. He was thus able to accept her physical failures and memory deficits to the degree that he increasingly anchored their relationship in the complex of historical memories and a present built on and from both their shared history and the fact of her disease—their condition. He became an active participant in the Alzheimer's and Related Disorders Association support group to which they both belonged, further affirming through that membership their unity and his own activism.

In contrast, Mr. and Mrs. Gilbert denied the fact of *their* present in *her* disease and, seeing no future, used the murder of one partner by the other as an appropriate release. Perhaps Mr. Gilbert secured in memory the woman he had loved, but the price they paid was those years which, for the Williamses, were, if different, then continuous and strong. For the Gilberts, independence and progress were everything. To be infirm and dependent, to be "unable," marked an insupportable present and an intolerable future. Without the areal perspective of the Williams family, the Gilberts had no other point of access to their shared life except the one that said: "We cannot do in the future as we did in the past." The attractive and well-kept, independent Mrs. Gilbert of history was being replaced by the disheveled, dependent person of her disease. In that change both Gilberts faced fundamental, existential anxieties that they could not overcome—alone or together. Neither Gilbert was able to draw from and act on the basis of shared memory and history, to conceive or create in the present a context that would draw on and affirm that past relation—precisely what the Williamses achieved.

Of paramount importance in the Gilbert story is the fact that Mrs. Gilbert withheld information about her condition from her husband. She wanted to hold out against infirmity for a present which, while fulfilling, was ephemeral and transient. She could not speak of her own failing condition, thus perishing, one might say, because of both her own and her husband's inability to confront a disease that brings mental as well as physical decline. By acknowledging and accepting the fact of the disease—their condition—the Williams family learned to live with it, and perhaps even to be enriched by the experience. But this acceptance came through a sense of relation, by integrating the complex of shared experiences into a present perspective and course of action. It is this rich complex that the care givers' stories, as a body, bring forth.

The epistemological loneliness that all encounter when faced with disease is fought by the Williamses from the base of an inherent ontological security, a sense of shared time, which enables them to find ways to build upon past experiences in the present situation. Like Oedipus, the Williamses expressed their concerns, discussed their acts, confronted their world, and in so doing, survived. Like Jocasta, the Gilberts did not discuss, did not integrate, and therefore became caught in the division between the healthy past and a present cohabited with progressive disease. Thus, Mr. Williams can accept his wife's disabilities and can be involved in her life from the onset of the disease in a way that he may not have been involved throughout much of their married life. After all, he traveled frequently on business during the years of his career. She stayed home. The Gilberts could not conceive of a similar relation in which appearance and function, while diminished, were less important than mutuality. As a result, Mrs. Gilbert perished at her own request and by her husband's loving hand.

To one couple, the trappings of individuality—attractiveness and self-sufficiency—were essential. Life moved on or was terminated. To the other couple, life was more complex. Relations were built on and through the past, and thus, even in the adverse circumstances of a dementia, they could endure. For the Gilberts, the death of the wife was the sinking of a disabled ship in a convoy that could no longer proceed or turn back. The Williamses did not consider that option—they traveled and lived together as shipmates. To put it another way, Mr. Gilbert could not conceive of so magnanimous and generous an image as waving from the shore to his ever more distant wife. Mr. Williams could imagine nothing less.

One could say with some truth that Mrs. Gilbert perished because of a lack of imagination. She died, one might say, from a congenital inability to conceive of life in other than optimal circumstances. Sociologist Elsie Boulding says, "You cannot work for what you can't imagine." But imagination, like courage or a generous spirit, does not just spontaneously occur. It comes from a specific view of the world, from an order of life and human relations across years of experience and reflection. These narratives suggest that what we can perceive as possible is determined, at least in part, by how we live

with others in the world and in time. The flexibility which comes
from an aerial perspective, like that of Mr. and Mrs. Williams, leads
to options which were for the Gilbert's inconceivable. For them,
function and order in the present were crucial and, unable to imagine
acceptable alternatives, Mrs. Gilbert perished as a result.

To the extent we endorse the Gilberts' view, we accept the terrifying message that each of us exists alone as a separate individual
defined by a function whose continuance is always at risk. If the
mirrors of self-esteem do not return an image of capability, the fact
of historical relation will not be sufficient, and death becomes the
only answer. Between those who dismiss a fragile relative by reason
of limited function and those, like Margaret Neilson, who accept a
historical relation as a motive for present action, stands the division
between the Gilberts' choices and those the Williamses acted upon.
Perhaps there is no more powerful argument for the act of caring
and an affirmation of the fragile elderly than Mr. Williams's ability
to grow with his wife in her decline. In the same vein, the murder
of Mrs. Gilbert stands—as the tale of Jocasta has for centuries—as
a cautionary tale for those whose lives are a productive convoy toward some hidden goal.

The Humphrys

The Gilbert case has been much discussed as an example of the
dilemmas euthanasia poses, of the moral quandary some feel when
loved ones are perceived to be diminished by illness. Euthanasia is
"assisted suicide," the aiding of an individual in the taking of his or
her own life. Recently, the suicide of the Hemlock Society's Ann
Wickett Humphry provided additional insight into this subject. The
society is a nonprofit organization that advances the right of individuals to terminate their own lives in the case of terminal illness or
intolerable pain, and publishes information on methods of self-
termination. The author of *Double Exit,* Humphry painted in her
book a powerful portrait of her parents' double suicide, an act en-
couraged and witnessed, if not actively aided, by Humphry and her
husband, Derek. But later, after she developed breast cancer and
went through surgery, radiation treatment, and chemotherapy, Ann
Wickett Humphry became progressively troubled by her actions.
What had first been described as being "for" her parents ended up,

in her eyes, as actions done "to" or "against" them. "She felt guilty and remorseful," her closest friend, Julie Horvath, told *New York Times Magazine* writer Trip Gabriel. "She went back and forth. It ate at her."

According to Gabriel, Mrs. Humphry said before her own death that although her mother was not "ready" to die, she had pressured the older woman to die with her husband. The memory of that assisted suicide—and of her mother's doubts—troubled Humphry long after her book was published portraying the "double exit" as an example others might follow. Diagnosis of her own illness several years later was followed by a divorce from her husband, who, Mrs. Humphry felt, pressured her to die rather than be a "burden" in the messy protocols of cancer treatment. What Humphry found she wanted for herself was support from her husband and her friends while she fought her cancer. It was her illness, but she had hoped it would be "their disease." Instead, Gabriel says, her husbands response reportly made her feel "really chilled to the bone because now it was my life and my dying, and it was kind of like 'Good, get out of the way as quickly as possible.' There was none of this 'Jesus, hang in there, I want you to be here for me!' . . . I knew I was being pushed out of the picture."

Ann Wickett Humphry wanted to live and fight, at least until it might be clear there was no hope left. She came, it seems, to identify with her mother, whose death was, she said, hastened by her, her own husband, and her father. And when she herself became ill, her mother's death "ate at her." Perhaps her inability to live with her parents' decline, her inability to have their frail age part of her life was what was disturbing. Her memory of them was dominated by the final moments of their suicide, and the example that set for her— the lack of her support for their living and her advocacy of their assisted deaths—became an intolerable burden and regret. Unlike Gene Warner, who came to see his father as a whole history living in the son's memory—young strong father and frail old together— Ann Wickett Humphry was left with nothing but questions about her actions in relations to her own mother's demise. Like Jocasta, the truths she was forced to face through her own illness became, for her, ultimately unbearable. Perhaps she came to know firsthand how her mother may have felt. Ann Humphry's message at her own end was that one must live for and with those others of experience if, in extremes, we are not to find ourselves isolated and alone. If by one's own acts one does not affirm relation, the skills and strengths one needs to endure the anxiety of personal illness are difficult to develop, and the loss of love can be overwhelming and more deadly than the disease itself.

ALLIED ARGUMENTS

In considering the lessons offered by my coauthors' stories, I find myself drawn to the writings and position of Carol Gilligan. A psychologist, she argues in her book, *In a Different Voice* that separation and individualization are the perspectives traditionally taught to society's male children, while females in our culture are trained to express the values of relation and responsibility. For Gilligan, the historical differences in socialization have been due to patterns in which males learned a future, progressive, and rational balancing of function and role while, from an early age, females were taught to perceive relation and mutuality as the primary virtues. The male self thus becomes tied to the frame of an individual, rational effort within a progressive and productive society. The female child, on the other hand, is instructed to operate from a perceptive pattern in which relation to others is a primary virtue. The female frame is areal, plenary, and historically open. Men buy houses, women live in homes; males come home from work, females learn to cook and prepare the holiday dinners to which family members are invited; men forget birthdays and anniversaries, women honor these dates with gifts and cards. These two very different ways of being can be seen as deriving from two different views. In one, function or role dominates as historical relations and experiences are devalued. The other is a broader, relational model in which the community of historical memory becomes the bedrock of care, care giving, and appropriate choice. The life patterns resulting from each of these two different ways of being-in-the-world lead to very different moralities as they are expressed in action. Both models are learned social patterns. In both, individuals grow, mature, and die. From both perspectives, one acts with (but not necessarily for) others. The result is that males tend to reason from law and women to argue from relation.

What the coauthors of this book suggest is that men and women can and may at various stages of their life choose the relational and the mutual perspective over the progressive and functional. The assumed, historical division assigning males a focus of work and progress while ceding to women control of relation is not hard and fast—men can and do choose to care for others (Mr. Williams, for example). Women can define themselves in terms of society, work, future (for example, Mrs. Dister). Mrs. Gilbert might indeed have wanted to end her life because she could no longer look herself in the mirror and see tidy self-sufficiency. But that inability to accept the disease's decline was the end point of a way of life and being that defined worth in terms of values that the care givers in this book do not share. The difference between the Gilberts and the Williamses is the gulf separating those who see individuals as functions whose value lies in a progressive life course and those who adopt a perspective that makes the relation between people a potent, growing history.

SELF AND SOCIETY

Some, including the prestigious Hastings Institute's Daniel Callahan and former Colorado governor Richard Lamm, have argued that it makes sense to deny the elderly certain types of essential medical treatment because their present contribution to society does not warrant the same sustained care that younger, healthier individuals might receive. The latter returns an investment, while the former does not. To the extent that the contemporary social language focuses on economic definitions and a vision of its members as "functional" and "progressive," the elderly by definition will be perceived as an expendable drag on "productive," working citizens. Their presence therefore will be at best merely tolerated within the social and political fabric. That this perception is in no way factually true, as Binney and Estes make clear, is not the issue. Seniors no longer perceived as contributors and existing without an assigned productive function are *assumed* to be an impediment and an obligation both to relatives and to society as a whole. What one has been and done is, in this view, unimportant. What one can do tomorrow is what matters. Were life a wagon train, the elderly would be the cart with the broken axle or wheel.

From the vantage point of this functional, ultimately dehumanizing perspective, society would do well to ignore the elderly (and all those made fragile by disease) when they are no longer economically useful. When productivity decreases, these critics argue, then the elderly must rely on the beneficence, benevolence, and charity of their juniors. It is not simply that old people are assumed to be valueless because they are no longer serviceable as workers but that, in a more frightening way, they are no longer perceived as truly serviceable fellow human beings. A progressive vision of the pragmatic life course by definition makes of relation an intergenerational war in which maintenance of frail elders is perceived as taking from the progress of the healthy, holding back the professional development of the care giver, restricting the opportunities of others. It is this view that Mrs. Harding's children argued. Mr. Harding was disabled, a drag on their mother's life, and an imposition on her future. He no longer contributed and thus could be abandoned, they said, so that she could move forward with them.

Elder care, whether provided by relatives or by society at large, thus becomes not an entitlement of the long-serving social member, not a preservation of the valued other, but instead an act of burdensome charity toward members of an unproductive class (the severely ill, permanently disabled, ethnically and racially disenfranchised, for example), an issue of cost without return. The maintenance of seniors is therefore unrelated in this vision to the continuance of a valued relation but transformed instead into a debt owed by other individuals and an obligation of, if not family members, then the society at large. The idea of nonproductive support is something that is accepted, at best, only grudgingly by society at large.

But to the extent the individual is defined from the beginning as a person in relation, one whose value to the greater community lies not in future labor but in a net of historic ties, then his or her social importance will be perceived very differently. The earlier vision of Christian community is replaced by a vision of shared existential value, and the strengths that accrue to individuals and society as a whole come through the support of fragile members. In this, the act of caring is an affirmation, and society will assist those who choose this role. One might argue that Margaret Neilson's care of her grandmother defined her own human value while affirming, in a real way, the older woman's continuing importance to society. The grandmother becomes, in this case, not a burden or an obligation but a responsibility—not only for Ms. Neilson, but also to the greater society she represents. Care then becomes not a grudging gift—as it seems to be defined by Ms. Neilson's father—but a part of the broader social fabric to which the older woman has contributed throughout her life.

Policies of elder support are transformed, in this view, from a simple obligation to preserve the life of even "valueless" individuals, to the support of relations that bind individuals together as well as to an endorsement of the lessons one can learn in the process. What is returned to, in short, is a system of values based on a broader social perspective, a system that begins not with the isolated and functional individual but rather with the individual in community, standing in relation across time. It is, after all, only in community that the ideals of liberty, justice, equality, and love have meaning. Care givers may become the means by which we redefine ourselves within a community greater than the sum of its productive, individual parts. But for this to happen, the assumptions imbedded in the work of qualitative researchers and policymakers alike would have to change. Practically, an acceptance of the values these care givers affirm would mean a series of programs providing social services for and at the request of the care receiver. It certainly would mean support and perhaps funding of respite care and home-care workers who can assist the frail elder and the care giver in their home. Tax incentives for the care giver and the funding of programs that assure home care as more than altruism on the part of volunteers would affirm and reinforce a type of social vision that places responsibility for individuals in the communities where they live. To create a vast bureaucracy like Supplemental Social Security, whose purpose is to determine that home care by one for another is worth $44.44 a month, is to create the machinery that grinds individuals down rather than building up relations.

Initiatives that would shift even more of the burden of elder care onto the family and the private sector are being advocated in Canada and the United States. These are advanced in the name of family values and a belief in the efficiencies of the private sector as a means of adequately providing care for the majority of citizens. Historically, however, the shift from institutional to community care and from public to private responsibilities has not been accompanied by the types of support that would make that change not only cost efficient but also effective for care givers as well as care receivers. New programs are needed, because volunteer agencies like Meals on Wheels, support groups like the Alzheimer's Disease and Related Disorders

Association, and existing, official bureaucracies cannot and do not provide sufficient assistance or support to those who find themselves in the role of caring for a frail elderly relative.

What the coauthors of this book insist is that the tasks they are engaged in should not be so difficult. A little help from society at large would assure the continuity of support for the maintenance of their elderly at home in family care. What is needed, they say, are outreach programs that would make available a series of home-care services: respite for the care giver, housecleaning and cooking, out-patient nursing, therapy, and counseling for care receiver and care giver. Some might argue that such services assisting care givers for fragile relatives living at home would be both socially cost efficient (home care is less expensive than institutionalization) and affirming for those who choose to assist a frail other. In the same vein, the pay-in-exchange-for-housework argument advanced by women seeking validation of domestic labor could be applied to care givers in general. The argument is that, since as a society we define value through economic compensation, paying care givers would affirm the presently unrecognized efforts of those like Mrs. Pfeiffer, Ms. Neilson, Mr. Lypchuk, and others who choose to be with their frail elders. While it is a lesson of this book that caring for another involves a perspective that is not economic, financial support would both provide social recognition of the care giver's role and facilitate the choice of those whose decision to act for another results in financial hardship.

Such initiatives would benefit not only elderly care receivers and their younger care givers but the whole complex of disadvantaged individuals who require assistance in their lives. Parents of young but functionally disabled children, for example—like care givers of fragile seniors—today seek but rarely receive support and assistance in their tasks. There are also strong parallels between the problems of the fragile elderly and individuals with AIDS. In both, individuals with restricting disorders are being cared for by lovers, family members, and friends, who receive little official support, assistance, or recognition for those efforts. Similarly, the family, friends, and lovers of adults with varying types of restricting conditions—multiple sclerosis and cerebral palsy immediately come to mind—confront these same problems. In all these cases, society as a whole draws away from the care-giving individual, providing, as a rule, only sufficient support to assure the physical continuance of the ailing members of these groups.

New policies will result only from a change in society's view of the value of the individual in relation, and the lesson these care givers tell is that society at large has adopted a perspective that mitigates against care giving and the elderly. The limited vision of the Gilberts and the Humphrys is today ascendant, eclipsing the historical and relational perspective of families like the Williamses. We want to know Mr. Williams, but we sympathize with Mr. Gilbert. We admire, perhaps, Mrs. Pfeiffer's constancy but agree with those who would say that care giving carries too high an emotional price. We like Margaret Neilson but, like her father, think that we ourselves are too busy to do the same. We accept the plan proposed by Mrs. McLeod while nodding sympathetically upon hearing of her grandfather's outrage and her own subsequent pain. As people, most of us want to sustain a relationship and be sustained in relation, to be ontologically secure and aware as individuals. But we would prefer, perhaps, for this to occur painlessly and through the associations of professional work. Unfortunately, it rarely works that way.

What these care givers argue by example is that care for the fragile is affirmed first and foremost because those individuals are members of society. Second, they are and should be supported as people whose continued value to society lies in a complex of historically defined relations affecting not simply the "patient," but that person's whole historical and experiential world, one that includes the frail elder's significant others and us, society at large, as well. We are all judged and judge ourselves, these care givers say, not as individuals of the moment—today—but as people in relation over time. Thus, the issue of care and care giving is not one of simply maintaining Margaret Neilson's obese grandmother, the demented Mrs. Williams, or the fragile Mr. Lypchuk. It is, more importantly, one c ˆ affirming Margaret Neilson and her grandmother, the Williamse as a couple, the Leonards as a family, Bill Lypchuk and his father—all who are affected and involved. None of us can be considered alone, nor can these complexes of interpersonal history be seen outside a broader context of society and social values. These associations—frail elder and healthy relative—stand as part of our public body, as part of all of us and examples for a social vision and will.

Selected Bibliography

Beauvoir, Simon de. *The Coming of Age.* New York: G. P. Putnam's Sons, 1972.

Bettelheim, Bruno. *Freud and Man's Soul.* New York: Knopf, 1983.

Biegel, David E., and Arthur Blum, eds. *Aging and Caregiving: Theory, Research and Policy.* Newbury Park: Sage Publications, 1990.

Binney, Elizabeth A., and Carroll L. Estes. "The Retreat of the State and Its Transfer of Responsibility." *International Journal of the Health Sciences.* 18:1 (1988): 83–96.

Binstock, Robert H., and Stephen G. Post, eds. *Too Old for Health Care?* Baltimore: Johns Hopkins University Press, 1991.

Caroselli-Karinga, Marie. "Drug Abuse and the Elderly." *Journal of Psychosocial Nursing and Mental Health Services.* 23:6 (1985): 27.

Chenoweth, Barbara, and Beth Spencer. "Dementia: The Experience of Family Caregivers." *Gerontologist.* 26:3 (1986): 267–272.

Fisher, M. F. K. *Sister Age.* New York: Vintage, 1984.

Gabriel, Trip. "A Fight to the Death." *New York Times Magazine,* December 8, 1991, 47, 86.

Gaynor, Sandra. "When the Caregiver Becomes the Patient." *Geriatric Nursing.* (May–June 1989): 121.

Gilligan, Carol. *In a Different Voice.* Cambridge, MA: Harvard University Press, 1982.

Hanks, Roman S. and Barbara H. Settles. "Theoretical Questions and Ethical Issues in a Family Caregiving Relationship. In *Aging and Caregiving: Theory, Research and Policy,* edited by David E. Biegel and Arthur Blum. Newbury Park: Sage Publications, 1990.

House, James S., Karl R. Kandis, and Debra Umberson. "Social Relationship and Health." *Science*. 241 (July 1988): 542.

Ignatieff, Michael. *The Needs of Strangers*. New York: Penguin Books, 1984.

Kaye, Janet. "The Long Goodbye." *Los Angeles Times Magazine,* July 14, 1991, 18.

Koch, Tom. *Mirrored Lives: Aging Children and Elderly Parents*. Westport, CT: Praeger, 1990.

Laing, R. D. *The Divided Self.* New York: Pantheon, 1960.

———. *The Voice of Experience*. New York: Pantheon, 1982.

May, Rollo. *Psychology and the Human Dilemma*. New York: D. Van Nostrand, 1967.

May, Rollo. *The Discovery of Being: Writings in Existential Psychology*. New York: W. W. Norton, 1983.

Murray, Thomas H. "Meaning, Aging, and Public Policy." In Robert H. Binstock and Stephen G. Post, eds., *Too Old for Health Care?* 165–171.

Rosenmayr, Leopold, and Eva Köcheis. "Propositions for a Sociological Theory of Aging and the Family." *International Social Science Journal*. 15 (1983): 410–426. Also quoted in Ethel Shanas, "The Family as a Social Support System in Old Age."

Rowles, Graham. "Place and Personal Identity in Old Age: Observations from Appalachia." *Journal of Environmental Psychology*. 3 (1983): 305.

Sacks, Oliver. *Awakenings,* revised edition. London: Picador Books, 1982.

Shanas, Ethel. "The Family as a Social Support System in Old Age." *Gerontologist*. 19:2 (1979): 169–170.

Silverstone, Barbara, and Sarah Miller. "Isolation in the Aged: Individual Dynamics, Community and Family Involvement." *Journal of Geriatric Psychiatry*. 13 (1980): 39.

Stafford, Florence. "A Program for Families of the Mentally Impaired Elderly." *Gerontologist*. 26:6 (1980): 656–670.

Warner, Gene. "A Drawn-Out Farewell Finally Makes Sense." *Buffalo News,* June 17, 1990, E1.

Suggestions for Further Reading

THEMES

To sample the literature on care givers see, for example: Elizabeth A. Binney and Carroll L. Estes, "The Retreat of the State and Its Transfer of Responsibility" (*International Journal of the Health Sciences*. 18:1 [1988]:83–96). Sandra Gaynor, "When the Caregiver Becomes the Patient" (*Geriatric Nursing* [May–June 1989], 121); Barbara Chenoweth and Beth Spencer, "Dementia: The Experience of Family Caregivers" (*Gerontologist* 26:3 [1986]:267–272); Florence Stafford, "A Program for Families of the Mentally Impaired Elderly" (*Gerontologist* 26:6 [1980]:656–670).

For a list of practical books written for the care giver, see "Suggestions for Further Reading" in Tom Koch, *Mirrored Lives* (Westport, CT: Praeger, 1990, 213–217).

THE DRIFTER

Alzheimer's Disease: For more on family care see, as a sample: Donna Cohen and Carl Eisdorfer, *The Loss of Self: A Family Resource for the Care of Alzheimer's Disease and Related Disorders* (Albany, NY: Center for the Study of Aging, 1986); Art Danforth, *Living with Alzheimer's: Ruth's Story* (Falls Church, VA: Howarth Press, 1986); Barbara Chenoweth and Beth Spencer, "Dementia: The Experience of Family Caregivers," (*Gerontologist* 26:3 [1986]: 267–272); Nancy L. Mace and P. V. Rabins, *The 36-Hour Day: A Family Guide to Caring for Persons with Alzheimer's Disease, Related De-

menting Illnesses and Memory Loss in Later Life (Baltimore: Johns Hopkins University Press, 1981); Florence Stafford, "A Program for Families of the Mentally Impaired Elderly," (*Gerontologist* 26:6 [1980]: 656–670). Also quoted: Graham Rowles, "Place and Personal Identity in Old Age: Observations from Appalachia." (*Journal of Environmental Psychology*, 3 [1983]: 305).

THE TEENAGE BRIDE AND THE MIRACLE PILL

Parkinson's Disease: For information on home care see Nick Peterson, "Real-Life Training; Home Health Aides Learn How to Treat Parkinson's Disease" (*Independent Living* 5:4 [November–December 1990], 49–55). For more on issues of problems related to dementia, see R. Mayeux et al., "An Estimate of the Incidence of Dementia in Idiopathic Parkinson's Disease" (*Neurology* 40:10 [October 1990]: 153–155). For the story of L-dopa as a drug treatment, see Oliver Sacks, *Awakenings,* revised edition (London: Picador, 1982, 31–35). On currently available drug therapies, see C. D. Marsden, "Parkinson's Disease" (*The Lancet* 335, April 21, 1990, 948–953).

THE TORONTO BOY

Drug and Alcohol Abuse: See Gina Kolata, "Elderly Become Addicts to Drug-Induced Sleep" (*New York Times,* February 2, 1992, E4); W. C. Chenitz, S. Salisbury, and J. T. Stone, "Drug Misuse and Abuse in the Elderly" (*Mental Health Nursing* 11:1 [1990]: 1–16); "Alcohol & Drugs: Abuse & Misuse," A Special Issue (*Generations* Summer 1988). Also useful is F. Miller et al., "Unrecognized Drug Dependence and Withdrawal in the Elderly" (*Drug and Alcohol Dependence* 15:1 [May 1985]; Marie Caroselli-Karinga, "Drug Abuse and the Elderly" (*Journal of Psychosocial Nursing and Mental Health Services* 23:6 [1985]: 25–30. For a practical and preventative approach, see C. Isler, "Teaching the Elderly to Avoid Accidental Drug Abuse" (*RN* 40:11 (November 1977): 39–42).

THE ONLY CHILD

Codependence: For a sampling of the popular literature, see Lynette Lamb, "Is Everyone Codependent?" (*Utne Reader,* May–June 1990, 26–28); Elizabeth Kristol, "Declarations of Codependence" (*The American Spectator,* June 1990, 21–23); Lisa J. Moore, "Codependency" (*U.S. News and World Report,* September 11, 1989, 73); Melinda Blau, "No Life to Live: Codependents Take Over Other People and Forsake Themselves" (*American Health,* May 1990, 56–62).

HOST OR GUEST?

Cross-Cultural: Amy Tan describes similar mother-daughter relations and their developmental ramifications in her novel *The Joy Luck Club* (New York: Ivy Books, 1989). Her work follows Maxine Hong Kingston's *The Woman Warrior* (New York: Knopf, 1976) in this genre. Although both writers describe Chinese-American communities and April speaks about a Japanese-American experience, the resultant emotional insecurities are similar.

HOST OR GUEST? AND THE ANNIVERSARY GIRL

Supplemental Social Security: The SSI income program "penalizes family members for sharing living expenses with SSI recipients, which may be the only way such an elder can survive in the community. In addition, SSI benefits are extremely limited (substantially below poverty level) and only reach approximately half of those elders eligible for assistance," according to Elizabeth A. Binney and Carroll L. Estes "The Retreat of the State and Its Transfer of Responsibility" (*International Journal of the Health Sciences* 18: 1 [1988]: 91).

CHORUS

Gilberts: The Gilbert case was extremely well reported by various media at the time of the trial. Both that coverage and the trial transcript were reviewed in Roman S. Hanks and Barbara H. Settles, "Theoretical Questions and Ethical Issues in a Family Caregiving Relationship," in David E. Biegel and Arthur Blum, eds., *Aging and Caregiving* (Newbury Park: Sage Publications, 1990). The source of the quote used here was given by Hanks and Settles as W. Plummer and L. Marx, "An Act of Love or Selfishness?" (*People,* May 27, 1985, 100).

Hemlock Society: Derek and Ann Wickett Humphry's books, articles, and speeches about "dying with dignity" through assisted or voluntary suicide made them both public figures and their society an international movement. It was not until Trip Gabriel's article on Mrs. Humphry's own death that a dark side to her parents' supposedly idyllic assisted suicide—and its long-term effects on her—were revealed. For an earlier vision of the elder Wicketts' death see Ann Wickett, *Double Exit: When Aging Couples Commit Suicide Together* (Eugene: Hemlock, 1990). For more works by the Hemlock Society, see Derek Humphry and Ann Wickett, *Jean's Way: A Love Story* (NY: Harper Collins, 1986); Humphry and Wickett *The Right to Die: Understanding Euthanasia* (Eugene: Hemlock, 1990).

About the Author

TOM KOCH is a researcher, writer, journalist, and the author of books on elder care, news and electronic information, cycling and transportation. Among his earlier works is a companion to this book, *Mirrored Lives: Aging Children and Elderly Parents* (Praeger, 1990). *A Place in Time* is the second in a projected four-volume series.